# Conversations with Pirie

# Conversations with Pirie

## 30 Stories of People Who Reinvented Themselves

## PIRIE JONES GROSSMAN

gatekeeper press™
Columbus, Ohio

Conversations with Pirie

Published by Gatekeeper Press
2167 Stringtown Rd, Suite 109
Columbus, OH 43123-2989
www.GatekeeperPress.com

ISBN (paperback): 9781662917196

# Contents

৵৶

# INTRODUCTION

# What is reinvention?

ॐॐ

- *The action or process through which something is changed so much that it appears entirely new.*

- *To change your job and/or the way you look and behave so that you seem very different.*

- *To remake or redo completely.*

How do you reinvent yourself? What is necessary to take your life in a new direction? How do you stay on track, ignore the cynics, believe in yourself, and focus on your goal and vision against fear, doubt, and insecurity? Why reinvent at all? It's challenging and costly, it's defiant and debilitating, and it's the embodiment of the unknown.

Because often, it's the only way to fulfill a lifelong dream, gain a true sense of self-worth and confidence, and follow through with what has always felt intuitive, under your skin, or potentially an indication of your soul's purpose. But, more than likely, it's because what worked in the past no longer works for the future. Perhaps your inner voice speaks loudly and urgently: "I just can't do it anymore," or "I feel sick when I think of doing it for another five or ten years." Or maybe it's a voice that pleads softly and incessantly:

"I don't want to die without having tried this," or "I can't imagine who I will become if I don't change course."

We all have dreams and goals, but we don't move forward on them because our mindset gives us a million and one excuses, and one of the most common we tell ourselves is that it's too late. So if any of those thoughts above sound familiar, if they've been on your mind and in your heart, it's time to pause and remind yourself, it's never too late to start something new. Here's the truth—the only timeline you're up against is your own. So instead of bemoaning your age, race, gender, financial or marital status, or circumstance, begin by telling yourself YOU'RE RIGHT ON TIME.

If you need examples of those who came before you, here are a few to get you thinking that anything is possible.

- Martha Stewart started her "entertaining" business at 40 years old and eight years later published her first preview issue of Martha Stewart Living before becoming a household name. Did Martha take her cue from Julia Child, who worked in advertising and media before writing her first cookbook at 50 and quickly becoming an internationally-renowned celebrity chef?

- Vera Wang, a former journalist and figure skater switched careers at 40 to design skating costumes, then wedding dresses before she debuted her eponymous fashion line.

- Ray Kroc sold milkshakes devices before he purchased McDonald's at 52, transforming it into the world's biggest fast-food franchise.

- The Terminator? Arnold Schwarzenegger's done it more than once. From the bodybuilder to the actor and blockbuster titan to California's Governor at 56. BTW: he's still at it as the Golden State's "elderly statesman."

- The Zagats. In their 30's, these Yale Law School graduates, as husband and wife practiced corporate law, then decided to pursue their "hobby" by publishing a collection of restaurant reviews, which slowly blossomed its first decade, then burst into a fledging business that Google acquired in 2011.

- Spanx founder Sara Blakely sold fax machines for seven years before cutting the feet out of a pair of pantyhose and substituting them for her underwear. The result was a multi-million-dollar company and Blakely being crowned the first female self-made billionaire.

Did you know that age could not hold back Gladys Burrell, who ran her first marathon at 92, or Nola Ochs, who became the oldest person to receive a college diploma, or 84-year-old Theodor Mommsen, the oldest person to receive a Nobel Prize for Literature?

Now you do. And because you're aware of these liberators, these crazy-for-thinking-I-can-do-that believers, I am here to send you a message that no one can do what you've been dreaming and scheming of better than you. So, as many have said before me, why not you?

Here are some quotes that inspire me and can help you start creating the life you've always wanted, whether recreating or reinventing the second chapter of your life.

**"It's never too late to start something new." — Pirie Jones Grossman.**

You can transform your life at any age. From J.R.R. Tolkien, who at 62 published the first volume of his fantasy series, Lord of the Rings, to Grandma Moses, who didn't start painting until she was 79, thankfully being creative and innovative doesn't come with an age limit. So anytime is a great time to get started.

**"Leap and have faith that the net will appear."—Julia Cameron.**

If you take a chance and take action, you will not freefall! It's also possible that you might take flight! As Lao Tzu said, "The journey of a thousand miles begins with one step." The idea is when you want to try something new that you've never done, just start somewhere. Don't wait to have all the answers. Take a step and move in the direction your passion wants to go. You can ask for mentors and people who have had success in similar endeavors. People love to help. Usually, what stops us from taking that first step is us. It's our limiting beliefs or waiting for the perfect time to present itself. Most successful people will tell you when they attempted something new, they didn't know what the outcome would be but knew they had to try. When you let go of your doubts and transform them into trust, possibilities open up, and this is when the magic starts to happen. Trust in yourself, be courageous, have faith in the process, and know you'll be OK no matter what.

**"You can't go back and change the beginning, but you can start where you are and change the ending." —C.S. Lewis**

We can spend time living in the past and thinking about how we would have done things differently, which gets us stuck in the "what if" questions that keep us in guilt, shame, or feeling unworthy. This wastes energy. If we look back on the past, we can learn how to do things differently or better and use the past experiences as life's lessons. That has value. We can also address ways in which we recreate our past. And here is where I will mention forgiveness. Holding onto unforgiveness keeps us in the victim mode, where we remain in the same old story and narrative that holds us back from living a life of empowerment. It's time to let go and make room for something new. The forgiveness is for you; however, you might want to look into self-forgiveness as well. Sure, we all have stories of doing or saying things we are not proud of, but make amends to yourself and others, and let them go because they are not serving you now. Create a new story, be the character you are now. You have the power to recreate a new life and a new beginning, so start now. The world needs to hear your healing story so others can do the same in their lives.

**"Whether you think you can or can't, you're right." —Henry Ford**

So often in life, we're told what to do, who to marry, what profession to pursue, and we end up spending time wondering who we are and who we're meant to be. So, I ask you, what's your belief system? Do you know who you are? Do you know you're a powerful creator? Do you know you are responsible for creating the life you're living?

I have many clients come into my office, expressing the adverse circumstances that are occurring in their lives. After they finish expounding on the many tragedies, I simply ask, "Why did you create all these disappointments in your life?" At that moment, they look at me in confusion. It never occurred to them they had the power to change those circumstances. Again, I say, "What do you believe about yourself?" "What do you say to yourself?" Your words and attitude determine your success or failure. Attitude is contagious. What you say and the tone of your words determine your success. Ask yourself, "Am I fully committed to success?"

Henry Ford's quote suggests that people's beliefs about their abilities determine their chances of completing a task successfully or not. We refer to these beliefs as self-efficacy (the belief we have in our own ability to meet challenges and perform duties). This belief emerged in the 1970s as a theory in Albert Bandura's Social Learning Theory and Social Cognitive Theory. Studies of self-efficacy found consistently that using this theory results in positive outcomes and performance. So, before you initiate a new task, project, or career, check your attitude—what do you believe?

**"When you change the way you look at things, the things you look at change."—Wayne Dyer.**

We filter the world around us unconsciously. If we become aware of our filter, we can learn to challenge it. An example of this can be shown within a family. One family member will describe their childhood and share stories about their experiences—they will express their parents' and siblings' roles. For example, they might say they had a horrible childhood and felt they were bullied. Then, one of the siblings might say the opposite. They may describe a very loving childhood filled with many positive experiences. Then, another might share a time of being completely ignored. These are siblings from the same family!

How is this possible? It's important to note that no one's experience or view is "wrong." The same family may have experienced the same family members differently that formed perceptions in each family member.

When you change how you see the world, your life transforms into an amazing adventure when you search only for the good and hold positive and powerful intentions. Anything and everything in life are all up for interpretation. We create our own reality with our thoughts and beliefs. In the simplest of terms, you create your thoughts, your thoughts create your intentions, and your intentions create your reality.

**"You get in life what you have the courage to ask for." —Oprah Winfrey.**

What do you want in life? Go after those things. Do you believe you deserve a good life? That was a big one for me. I sometimes felt like an imposter. Did I earn the right to ask for what I wanted?

Did I need to be better educated? Was I good enough? These were all limiting beliefs I had to work through before I truly felt as though I deserved to live my dreams. Afterward, I prepared. I asked for support and created a team of people who could teach me what I needed to learn. And then I kept working towards my goal and never gave up! And you can't be afraid of rejection or not listen to feedback from those you trust. Also, use your voice! Speak up. When you ask for what you want or need, be clear, and expect others to help you. Be bold, strong, courageous.

**"The question isn't who is going to let me, it's who is going to stop me."—Ayn Rand.**

This quote implies I don't need anyone's permission to live my life. Or how I say it, "Don't put your life up for vote!" You only need your permission to live your life. Many will suggest, imply, and even try to coerce you to live your life their way. That's just a given. Everyone has an intention. What's yours? Are you willing to allow someone to tell you how to live your life? If someone is putting you down, telling you what to do, and speaks against what feels true to you, simply thank them for their opinion and change the topic of conversation. Remember, when people tell you how to live your life, they really share their paradigm of what the world is for them and what they believe is possible. Stay focused on all the reasons and possibilities that are out there for you.

**"Stop acting so small. You are the universe in ecstatic motion."—Rumi.**

Acting small is the equivalent of not allowing your Light to shine. It may be covered in layers of judgment, and low self-esteem, and low self-worth. When in reality, you have all the answers, capabilities, and skills within you. You can achieve your dreams, affect others' lives, and make a difference in the world when you believe in yourself. Act like the universe is excited that you are part of all the energy, beauty, and greatness in the world!

**"Your deepest beliefs drive what shows up in your life. So, what are you saying to yourself?"—Pirie Jones Grossman.**

Beliefs are the assumptions we hold to be true. They usually stem from real-life experiences. Our values and beliefs affect the quality of our lives, including our careers and relationships. Our beliefs shape our thinking, which then influences our behavior. Your beliefs also influence others' behaviors. What we say to ourselves also affects our beliefs and actions. I always tell my clients to speak to themselves like they would their best friend. Positive self-talk matters.

Research published in the Journal of Personality and Social Psychology found that people who spoke to themselves as another person would, using their own names or the pronoun, "you," performed better under stress than people who used the word "I." When people think of themselves as another person, "it allows them to give themselves objective, helpful feedback," says Ethan Kriss, associate professor of psychology at the University of Michigan.

With critical self-talk, identify why you are negative and focus on the positive. People who can master positive self-talk are thought to be more confident, motivated, and productive.

**"Your power to choose your direction of your life allows you to reinvent yourself, to change your future, and to powerfully influence the rest of creation."—Stephen Covey.**

You and you alone have the power to choose to reinvent yourself. However, in a world of constant change, you often must think about who you are now and where you're at in your life. Are you living the life you want? Are you going for your dreams? Or are you giving in to limiting beliefs? Maybe you're due for a reframe of those beliefs.

Here's how to do a reframe and create new beliefs.

- Recognize the limiting belief.

- Reject it.

- Reframe it into an empowering belief.

- Start seeing and believing the change one step at a time.

There are a lot of things that can seem impossible in your life. The truth is, they aren't impossible—you just think they are. Limiting beliefs aren't true. They begin as a thought. As you continue to affirm these thoughts, they become beliefs. These beliefs sit deep within our subconscious mind and keep us from seeing and believing in any kind of possibility. We are prone to believe what we want to believe, but it's just as easy to believe in a positive outcome as it is a negative one. Which do you prefer? When you start on a journey of reinvention, clear out any limiting beliefs and then practice positive self-talk.

It can be incredibly empowering to start a new chapter. Alternatively, it can serve as a reminder that you can be an example to yourself and others. However, the glory in reinvention is the ride—the feeling of rocking your own boat, and catching the ear and eye of others who might want to take you down and choosing to move ahead, and prove to yourself that this is the journey you've been waiting for. To defy yourself and those non-believers for a higher-happier self who is unable to say no to the dream of becoming someone new, you'll ultimately believe in the statement that "this is what I've always wanted to do," and accept yourself.

In this book, you'll read about those who took the plunge, made the leap, and stepped into the unknowingness. These stories confirm their "why," and more importantly, the "how."

But, first, here is my "why." In February, just as COVID began its grip on the world, I started working with the publisher of Authority Magazine. We agreed I would choose my own topic and write questions surrounding that subject. I immediately knew I wanted to address the idea of "second chapters." When the subject was submitted to the publisher's diverse and extensive list of media contacts, the response was overwhelming. The topic, undeniably popular because many of us had begun thinking about our second chapters while we adapted to the lockdown, became the source of the stories I received.

In March, I contracted COVID. There was nothing fun about my experience with the virus that took me down rapidly and without remorse. One Saturday morning, I felt especially icky, yet I decided to begin reading through the stories I'd received. From nine AM to just past seven PM, I read over 120 stories. When I came through my bedroom door into the living room for a dinner my boyfriend prepared, he looked at me and said, "What happened to you?"

In those ten hours, my energy and mood had shifted dramatically.

"I just finished reading over a hundred stories and they were so inspirational that I think it transformed my whole being!"

I knew the mind-body-spirit connection was real because I'd studied it voraciously while getting my master's in Spiritual Psychology at the University of Santa Monica, however, I'd never experienced it so completely just by reading the words of others, by feeling their spirit, courage, and strength on a page. Not only had my mood changed, my body felt better, my appetite resumed, and I slept soundly that night. If reading inspirational stories had done this to me, I knew it was possible it could do the same for others.

On Monday, I called the publisher and told him my "second chapters" medicine worked! I asked him what he thought about doing a book. His answered affirmatively.

Now onto the "how." Although we might have a plan in our back pocket of "why" we want to start a second, third, or perhaps fourth chapter in our lives, we really struggle more with the thought of "how," how to start, how to move forward, how not to give up. The people in these pages explain their "why" and "how" in their stories. You'll discover what it took for them to succeed. Yes, for some it's creativity, or intelligence or business-savvy, but they all share straight-up a heady cocktail of hope, grit, and resilience.

The magic to feel "more you" than ever is waiting. So accept it, wear it, own it, do it, because the only thing between you and your "yes" is gratefully offering it to yourself and the world. When you're ready to reinvent yourself, you'll be powered by the exquisite and powerful you.

The day is here. The time is now. Welcome to your second chapter!

# CHAPTER 1

# Pirie Jones Grossman

ॐ∞ॐ

*It's never too late to start something new.*

**Share with us a bit about your upbringing.**

I was raised in South Texas by my loving father, alongside my younger brother and sister. I was also raised by a schizophrenic mother, who put a gun to the back of my head when I was five years old. She said she had to kill me because my father loved me more than her. After that life-altering incident, my father committed her to a mental institution for three years.

My entire home life, from elementary school throughout high school, was about keeping secrets. When my mother returned, my siblings and I endured physical and emotional abuse while watching her struggle with alcoholism and drug abuse. My father tried to pretend it wasn't happening and soon became a prolific workaholic, traveling weekly for business trips and leaving the three of us with a nanny to fend off our mother. Over the years, he successfully removed himself from the daily rhythms of our lives, preferring to wear rose-colored glasses to displace the guilt he felt having had committed her. Unfortunately, he also put the burden of "taking care of Mom" on us.

But he was also my best friend. He brought joy, laughter, and play into our home. He was an excellent provider and very supportive of me and anything I chose to do. Because of that, I became part daddy's girl, part protege. He was responsible for teaching me about business and entrepreneurship. When I was about six years old, he helped me create my first business when we ordered a holiday card sales kit from the back of a magazine, and I went door to door selling them. It was the beginning of my adventure in sales and meeting new people in my neighborhood. At that time, my mother's absence held the possibility for a normal life, and my dad did his best to protect me from the memory of my near-dear experience. But the fear never left me, and I continued to see my mother as a person who threatened my very existence.

## What is your life lesson quote? Can you share its relevance in your life?

*"Your power to choose the direction of your life allows you to reinvent yourself, to change your future, and to powerfully influence the rest of creation."*—Stephen Covey

I've always loved the vision behind this quote.

## How would your best friend describe you?

I asked her, and she said, "Beautiful, fearless, empathic, honest, intuitive, and a light that shines brightly reflecting love, hope, faith, and curiosity. Oh, and that I was a damn good mama!"

## Tell us about your career before your second chapter.

After I graduated from Oral Roberts University and after my first divorce, I moved to Hollywood, California. I had met my college sweetheart when I was only 16. We went to ORU together and then became youth pastors. However, he really wanted to be an entertainer and be on stage. I always wanted to be an actress and live a life of glamourous fun. One issue: he wanted me as his wife to stay home and raise children. He didn't care much about my dreams.

I went with my then-husband to Los Angeles for a two-week trip to pursue his dream. While he recorded his album, I had an opportunity to meet a casting director. She set me up on my first television commercial audition for Bud Light. After many callbacks, I booked it! Regrettably, my husband wasn't supportive of my burgeoning new career. He returned to Dallas, Texas, and I moved to LA, and within the year, we were divorced. I was just 27.

Thankfully, my first commercial ran for three years, and after many hours of studying acting, I discovered I was a terrible actress. However, if I played myself, the girl next door type, and used my gift of gab, it helped me book many commercials, infomercials, and small TV parts. But my real success came when I became a host for E! Entertainment Television and Entertainment Tonight. I traveled the world interviewing actors, producers, and directors, visiting many movie sets, and had the time of my life doing it for nearly ten years.

I loved interviewing people and hearing their stories. I still enjoy it, which is why I created the *Second Chapters* interview series. Storytelling is so powerful because we learn from one another. We can inspire, teach and share our stories to help others grow and heal. That is still my primary calling and life's mission.

**Your second chapter's transition was remarkable. What was the trigger that made you decide you needed to make a change in your life?**

It started when I met and married my third husband, Steve, in Los Angeles. He was a very successful movie producer (think *Pretty Woman* and *Dirty Dancing*), and I was a successful TV personality on E! and other networks. (I also had a marketing company called,

High Heels and Loafers, where we found and created beauty products to sell on QVC and infomercials.)

We fell in love at first sight! It was a whirlwind romance. We were seen as one of the industry's power couples.

Now I want to interject a little-known fact before we go any further. I never wanted kids. Ever! I could never imagine myself as a mother. I never knew one that I could emulate. I was comfortable and satisfied being a career girl and didn't experience an ounce of FOMO. My life was exciting, fulfilling, and bursting with travel and zero responsibility to and for anyone else.

But weeks into our relationship, I learned that Steve had a four-year-old daughter who lived with him part-time. Now, what? No one I ever dated had kids!

Steve adored his daughter and wanted us to meet. But, to put it bluntly, I was scared and had no idea how to do "kids." So, Steve arranged our meeting, and I remember nervously asking him, "What do I do?" He smiled and said, "Don't worry, she'll show you." The minute she and I set eyes on each other; we fell in love. She grabbed my hand, took me to her bedroom, and showed me all her favorite toys and books. I then laid down next to her, and I read her story after story until we both fell asleep.

The three of us had a love affair, so as one would expect, the conversation soon flowed to our having kids together.

We tried naturally, and nothing happened. Then we entered the IVF world and endured many procedures to the point that I was in and out of hospitals. Again, nothing happened. Our next step was to employ surrogates, and again neither of them could get pregnant from the embryos we created between us.

However, I kept at it, determined, we could make a child, yet all I was accomplishing was getting sicker and sicker. Finally, Steve wanted me to stop. I tried talking him into adoption, but he laughed at the thought of raising "someone else's genes," as he put it. The more I tried, the more he pulled back from me. Our love affair vanished . . . quickly, and our marriage began to disintegrate.

After my last hospital stint and multiple blood transfusions, I was so weak that Steve declared he was done. He then said he would travel with his daughter to Sun Valley, Idaho, where we had a second home to think about what to do. I couldn't travel and remain in our Bel Air home by myself, filled with shame that I couldn't give us a child.

When he returned from Idaho, he walked into our home and immediately asked for a divorce. I begged him to give us a chance to heal. I even told him I would give up my dream of having a child . . . just to not leave me. But, he said no, and announced that he no longer loved me and thought I should call my parents and head to Houston as soon as possible. My head swirled as my heart broke. I couldn't believe this was my life.

Within moments of his turning his back on me, I fell on the sofa and just cried. All of the fertility drugs coursed throughout my body like a heatwave. I was on several medications and drugged up to the hilt. But not enough to dull the piercing pain in my heart.

How could I start my life over at 39 years old? I had retired to be a full-time wife, which he had asked me to do. And because I knew he didn't love me; I felt my life didn't matter. My world crumbled around me, and I had to stop this excruciating pain. But, how?

I looked at the table in front of the sofa, and I received the answer. If I swallow all the pills in every bottle, I could just go to sleep. Then the pain would be gone, and so would I. That was my best answer. So, I did just that. I slowly swallowed over two hundred pills and laid down, said a prayer . . . "Now I lay me down to sleep, I pray the Lord my soul to keep. And if I die before I awake, I pray the Lord my soul to take."

I woke up vomiting while my husband held me in our bed. After that, I don't remember much more other than lights and yelling. Then, I was taken to the hospital for a drug overdose and a suicide attempt.

A few days later, I woke up. I didn't remember why I was there until a lovely social worker kindly asked me if I remembered that I tried to end my life. I was shocked! How could that be? Where was my husband?

Within a week, I returned to Texas to stay with my parents. There, I began to receive help for the layers of abuse I had endured from others and the recent tragedy I had imposed upon myself.

I remembered how much I was willing to give away to someone else! How could I have done that? I felt so much shame and guilt. But a light bulb went on, and I thought how lucky I was to survive . . . once again. And that my life was worth something. And that God had a better plan for me, and it wasn't my time to leave the planet. I had more things to do.

## How did you reinvent yourself in your second chapter?

I decided to move to Sun Valley, Idaho, to start my healing process and find the healthy woman I knew was within me but, I didn't know where to start. I didn't care that I was thrice-divorced because I had survived!

I also realized I needed to find out who I really was and stop hiding behind my past. I was loved and adored by being the fun, perky girl on television, and I had many friends who admired me because I had a successful husband and lived in a big house in Bel Air. But I had no idea who I was without a husband, a job, or my tribe of girlfriends.

And I sure as hell didn't love myself or think that I was worthy of being lovable. I felt like a fraud. So, I had to start over.

I only had a few acquaintances in Sun Valley, and most of those relationships were friends of Steve and me. Some felt they had to pick a side, and they did. Guess who got left behind? But it didn't matter because I only wanted to heal. I had carried my childhood wounds across state lines for the second time. It was time to deal with my shame, guilt and address what's known as the Mother Wound.

I decided to read spiritual books, listen to people's stories of how they healed, and begin the deep inner work of healing, which resulted in many dark nights of the soul. I connected with nature by taking long hikes and learning how to ski. I discovered how to be alone and like it. I attended church again because I had forgotten my faith in God. I was careful who I became friends with because I wanted people who weren't toxic because I was releasing so much toxicity within me.

Each day, I got stronger and stronger. I stopped performing for people to be liked or loved. I was just myself, and it was enough. I found spiritual teachers who taught me excellent tools and techniques. I remembered what was important in life again.

Then after some time, I met a wonderful man filled with light and an infectious child-like wonder for the world. We fell in love and had two beautiful children together—naturally! It became apparent there was no reason for me to continue carrying the limiting belief that I was incapable of bearing children—I could finally release the inescapable feeling of hopelessness when it came to motherhood.

I gave birth to my son at 44 years old and my daughter at 46.

As time passed, so did my ex-husband. But before he died, we had an opportunity to forgive one another. I'd never been so grateful.


**How are things going with this new initiative? (How are things now? What are you focusing on?)**

Everything is wonderful! I've lived in Sun Valley for 25 years now. My children are grown, and I learned that I'm a great mother! Remember when I said earlier that I didn't think I'd be a good one? But, I realized that I would know how to love myself and the children I might have if I healed my Mother Wound. When that happened, and I embraced my worth and didn't have to be anything but authentic, I could be lovable and able to love others unconditionally.

My two children are the recipients of my healing. I call them my miracle children, and I love taking care of them. I finally recognized what unconditional loving looks and feels like because of them. They've given me that gift, and I have learned to give it right back.

I also desperately needed to learn forgiveness. I held onto horrible feelings towards my mother and knew that I needed to forgive her if I wanted to forgive myself. So, I went back to school in my 50s to learn how to do that. I enrolled at the University of Santa Monica and received a Master's in Spiritual Psychology. During my two-year program, I learned how to forgive her and gained knowledge in my necessary journey of self-forgiveness.

I acquired many tools and techniques from USM that helped me heal. I now teach others how to heal using the techniques that helped me. As a life empowerment coach, author, speaker, and teacher, my life's work is guiding women to empower their lives and start making their dreams come true. My mantra is, "It's never too late to start something new." My specialty is helping women create the second chapter in their lives and clear their limiting beliefs, obstacles, and childhood wounds. It is rewarding to work and witness the healing.

## Is there someone you are grateful to who helped you along the way?

Drs. Ron and Mary Hulnick, the founders of USM were instrumental in my healing, and approach, knowledge, and acceptance to and for self-forgiveness. In addition, my classmates were lifelines to a curriculum that we all equally enjoyed, but came with the pain of our respective journeys. I cherish those bonds. I spent one week a month in Los Angeles in school, and each time I returned home to Sun Valley, I felt renewed by the Hulnick's teachings, and my classmates' willingness to move forward and through their deepest fears.

I was also renewed by my group of girlfriends' unconditional acceptance of my decision to go to school. I was and am grateful to those women who inspired me then, and continue to inspire me daily with their insight, laughter, and literally, *joie de vivre.*

My kids. I remember sitting them down before I started school and asking them what they thought. I reminded them that I'd be out of town for a week every month for two years; that I might miss some of their ski races or school events. They acknowledged the schedule, and completely agreed that Mom going to school was different than "the other moms," but they were excited to see one of my dreams realized. I will always remember that day and their confidence in me.

### Have you ever struggled with believing in yourself? If so, how did you overcome that limiting belief?

Yes, I did! I had countless limiting beliefs! I think my biggest one was that I wasn't lovable. And that one came early on for me. My mother's sickness made her do and say things that always confirmed to me that she didn't want me. She tried to get rid of me because she felt I was taking my dad's love away from her. She wanted attention and love because she didn't receive it from her parents. It was a vicious and cruel cycle, and those wounds hurt deeply. That's why if we don't heal our younger selves, we can't be healed as adults.

When I was old enough to know about my mother's mental illness, then I felt guilty. How could she help herself? She's sick. I needed to be the one to take the higher road because I didn't have any kind of mental illness. Do you see the dangerous cycle there too? It was the perfect limiting belief that I didn't deserve to be treated well by my mother because she was sick. So, I became the perfect caretaker for my parents, with my needs coming in last. I was repeatedly told I was the lucky one. My reaction and its behavior told me I didn't deserve to ask for anything more.

The limiting belief that I wasn't lovable unless someone else said so is the underlying reason why I was married and divorced four times. I believed that the more successful the husband, the more lovable I would feel. Because if he loved me, then I must be lovable. That's why I needed to learn how to value and feel confident with who I was and who I could become. It's simple—we all deserve love if for nothing other than being born.

Every one of us has the Divine within. We reflect love back to one another, but we must have it within us first before reflecting on others.

## Do you have a support system that keeps you strong?

Oh, my yes! First of all, God is my guiding grace. I learned about God when I started going to church with neighbors who helped my dad take care of me when my mother was institutionalized. I was a believer immediately. It would be harder not to believe in God or have faith than to believe there wasn't a higher energy or spiritual being in my young eyes. I learned how to pray when my face was in the dirt with my mother's hand holding a gun to my head. My life has been saved many times from illness and events when I should have been dead. I don't understand everything in the spiritual world; however, I believe because of my experiences.

My support system is bolstered by my exceptional girl tribe, who keep me laughing, connected and loving. They also tell me the truth! And, although I don't always like their feedback, I know they love and want the best for me.

My kids also provide support in the form of pure love, which I can't deny fills me by just being in their presence.

I'm also fortunate to have a fantastic life partner who loves and supports me no matter what the day brings. He's patient and listens lovingly—what a gift.

Lastly, my spiritual teachers consistently provide the wisdom and knowledge to keep me on my path. They remind me of my calling in life. And I know they're available to me at a moment's notice. They help me when I need to untangle a problem or re-examine what I need to focus on to live the life I want.

**What are five things you wish someone had told you before you started leading your business, and why?**

Challenges don't last forever. There is an ending to them all. So don't stay stuck in the emotions they might bring to you. Feelings come and go—be patient and know, "This too shall pass."

You have all the answers you want within you. So don't look to the outside for your biggest questions. Although you get to ask for advice or feedback from others, trust yourself. Ask that still and small voice within you for the answers. Then give yourself silence and space and time to listen and hear the answer.

You are good enough! You can do anything you want. So don't put yourself up for vote . . . ever! You have the talent and ability to make your dreams come true. You're just as capable of making your dreams come true as anyone else.

You are entirely responsible for what you create in your life. I know this is a tough one to believe. But it's true. You're not in control of the things that happen to you necessarily, but that's never the issue; it's how you handle the issue. You are the co-creator with the energy you choose to use to create. Your thoughts, words, actions are all based on your decisions. No one can control you except you. You give yourself the power to create the life you want. So, what is it going to be? Victim or empowerment? Your choice!

You can change how you respond to your past. You can heal it—and you can choose to forgive or not. It's never too late to forgive yourself or someone else. I lived most of my life believing I wasn't worthy of love because of my mother's actions. But as she got older and as I did, we became different people. I chose to forgive her for me. I wanted to change that narrative, and I did. You can, too, no matter what happened to you.

**You are a person of significant influence. If you could inspire a movement that would bring the best outcome to the greatest number of people, what would that be?**

I would inspire a movement of women waking up and knowing and believing their power. They don't have to play in a man's world. It's a woman's universe! We live with the power of femininity. The Divine is nurturing, loving, intuitive, peaceful, and strong. Those qualities are wanted and needed globally. I would teach women that we are not in competition with each other. Think how strong we could be if we united?

We want to heal the world and create a beautiful environment where our children can grow and develop even more beauty, prosperity, and longevity. We can live in peace and be in integrity together no matter our race, gender, or religion. Love and compassion are the common denominators between us, and they are born from the Divine Feminine.

**Dreams come true. If you could invite anyone in the world to dinner, who would that be?**

First, my goal is to have dinner with everyone in this book! However; since I can't have dinner with Maya Angelou (although I have had lunch, and we became friends after that first meal in her home), I'd happily dine with our first National Youth Poet Laureate, Amanda Gorman. I am astounded by this awakened, upcoming leader whose presence and confidence are the definition of optimism, unity, and strength. I'd love to speak with her about where she thinks our nation is headed. I'd like to share what I've learned in my 64 years with her, and ask what I could be doing right now that would help her generation. I would love to have the opportunity to guide her through any personal obstacles she might be encountering so she can be a leader without any limiting beliefs. She is the epitome of our rising generation.

I am consistently in awe of New Zealand's Jacinda Ardern. As the youngest female prime minister in the world, she is an example to women and girls globally that the future is female. Her devotion to improving women's rights and her passion for climate change is exceptional and will redefine modern leadership. Her open-mindedness and honesty blend perfectly with her empathy and respect for all of New Zealand's communities and those beyond its borders. I am a big fan!

## Where can we follow your work?

piriejonesgrossman.com
On all social media channels: piriejonesgrossman IG/FB
LinkedIn: piriegrossman

# CHAPTER 2

# Sassy Gran

ॐ ॐ

*I wish someone told me that failing isn't a failure, that it's a learning experience. It took me many years to look back and realize that I had gained incredible knowledge and value from pulling myself back up from my setbacks. If I knew then, I might have been easier on myself.*

Doris, also known as Sassy Gran, is a famous 95-year-old social media celebrity. Her videos online have been seen over 250,000,000 times. She is the world's grandmother, giving advice and sharing wisdom with her fans around the world.

**Share with us a bit about your upbringing.**

I was born in Colorado in 1925. My family moved west to buy land and become ranchers. I know it's hard to believe looking at me now with my love of designer jewelry and false eyelashes, but I basically grew up shoveling horse crap and plowing fields.

**What is your life lesson quote? Can you share its relevance in your life?**

"You don't get to the Promised Land without going through the Wilderness. You don't get there without crossing over hills and mountains, but if you keep on keeping on, you can't help but reach it."—Martin Luther King Jr.

I say keep on keeping on often in my videos. It's pretty simple. Never give up; life constantly changes, we continuously evolve. If you keep moving forward, you'll grow in good times, and you'll make it out of the bad times. I believe that's why I'm so active and healthy. I just keep on keeping on.

**How would your best friend describe you?**

At 95 years old, most of my lifelong friends have passed on. However, my best friend throughout my life used to describe me as a bumblebee. He would say that you didn't want to make me angry for fear of my sting but that I was the catalyst to make things bloom and blossom.

In 1955 being an openly gay man wasn't easy, but I encouraged my best friend to come out of the closet and be true to who he was anyhow. We fought bigotry and homophobia when there was virtually zero support from the world around us. Life was hard, and coming out didn't make it easier on him, but he became an incredible force because he lived his truth. We fought for civil rights side by side for decades. Sadly, the AIDS epidemic of the 1980s took him from me. But, because of him, I'm still a champion for the LGBTQ community, and I often speak of it in my videos.

**You have been blessed with success. What are three qualities you possess that helped you achieve your goals?**

Longevity. This is something that I truly have no control over, but with this many years under my belt, you're bound to see history and people repeat their actions. You learn to see it coming and make preparations to either fight or get out of the way.

Determination. Whatever the circumstance, I will find a way to a better outcome. I left my cheating and abusive husband in the 50s. I took my kids and slept in the car. I worked three jobs while the kids were at school until I saved enough for our own place. Many, many years later, at age 93, I broke my back in multiple locations. We know this is a death sentence for seniors. But, I was determined not to die in bed and fought every single day to get up and walk again. It was excruciating, exhausting, and overwhelming sometimes, but I did it. Today at 95, I still work out in my gym every day, dance, and do yoga.

Empathy. Listening to the needs of others and finding resourceful ways to empower people to reach their full potential. If we don't honestly care, we aren't listening to the nuances of body language, eye movements, and behaviors. Sometimes words alone aren't the whole story.

**Tell us about your career experience before your second chapter.**

When I left my husband, the biggest obstacle was trying to make sure my children were safe, so I could work. There weren't many single working mothers back then, and to be honest, it was frowned upon. I didn't have the support system that I needed to succeed. So, when I finally established my own living situation, I decided that there was a need for affordable child care. I started by babysitting children in my home and grew it into a larger daycare center aimed at working mothers. I had a program for mothers that were on welfare or struggling financially. I provided free childcare for them because I knew that the thing they needed most was peace of mind, so they could put their efforts into bettering their situation for themselves and their children.

## How did you reinvent yourself in your second chapter?

I reinvented myself quite by accident. I think it was a combination of several things;

Fashion, technology, and a pandemic.

As a young woman, I always adored fashion. I would collect magazines and dream of wearing the haute couture designs of Jackie O, movie stars, and French runway models.

We lost photo albums in a storage fire, and my grandson began filming me every time we were together. He would prank me, or he would ask me about my past, or just sit and gossip. But it was all filmed.

The pandemic arrived, and people were stuck home and looking for escapism. Technology helped a lot of people survive by connecting them to the outside world. My grandson uploaded his videos of me to the internet, and overnight I had become a social media sensation.

## Your second chapter's transition was remarkable. What was the trigger that made you decide you needed to make a change in your life?

It started before Los Angeles. I was living with another family member in a small town. There was very little to do, and I was incredibly lonely. I spent more and more time in my room, in my bed, existing but not living. I was literally waiting to die. I thought, "Is this how I'm going to go out? This is what my life has ended up to be?" I was 90 years old, and there wasn't much hope.

One day I called my grandson and said, "Please come and get me out of here. I love my family, but I have so much more life to live." Within a week, I was living in Los Angeles with a wholly renewed lease on life. The first thing I did was join a dance class.

## What did you do to discover you had a new skill set you hadn't maximized?

I've been afraid of the camera my whole life. I've never been comfortable in front of it. But then, my grandson talking to me in such a one-on-one manner made me forget he was recording. But, once I saw the videos, and I heard the comments around the world that I was inspiring people to live life to the fullest, it changed my outlook. Each time he asks me a question, I know somewhere someone is listening and hopefully learning that seniors have validity and are still important.

## How are things going now?

Well, I'm answering these questions for your interview, so that's incredible. My videos have almost 300,000,000 views across the internet. The ability to reach so many people, young and old, in so many countries is astounding. I'm about to launch a book series called Sassy Gran Presents. I'm collecting stories from disabled children and incorporating them into books that will be inclusive to everyone. My great-grandson is blind and autistic. Children are honest and curious when they see him, but parents are too polite and don't allow them to ask questions for fear of offending. I'd like to break that barrier and encourage them to learn more about their differences and similarities.

## Is there someone you are grateful to who helped you along the way?

Obviously, that would be my grandson. He is responsible for all of this. Without him recording the videos and posting them, I wouldn't have any of this. I can't express how grateful I am that at 95, my entire world has been changed and fulfilled. How does this happen for anyone?

**Share an exciting moment that happened since committing to your second chapter.**

I suppose that being recognized by people each time I go out. I've had young women grab onto me and start crying. They've told me that I bring back memories of a lost loved one for them and that watching my videos gives them comfort. To know that I might bring a little love or comfort to someone that I've never met is the most fascinating thing in the world to me.

**Have you ever struggled with believing in yourself? If so, how did you overcome that limiting belief?**

This might sound terribly narcissistic, but no. On the contrary, I believe that if another person can do something, why can't I? With the proper training, practice, dedication, focus, hard work, and fine-tuning, we can achieve anything we want.

**Typically, I encourage my clients to ask for support from those who believe in their vision before they embark on a new chapter. How did you create your support system?**

Interestingly enough, I didn't have any support from my family before moving to Los Angeles. How do your children support a 90-year-old woman moving cross country, away from them, the grandkids, and the great-grandkids? They don't. They were outraged and completely unsupportive. I'm sure they thought they would never see me again, and that possibility still holds true. But I dedicated my entire life to all of them. In the end, I was mostly alone and sad. So, I had to do what was right for me. Putting yourself first is one of the hardest things for people to do.

**Starting a new chapter requires leaving your comfort zone behind. How did you do that?**

I think I touched on this before, but being on camera wasn't comfortable. I also don't like my accent and my grammar. Hearing myself speak has given me chills of embarrassment at times. But then I read the comments that are so loving and supportive that I realized my approachability comes from my personality. A woman wearing designer clothing and jewelry and lots of makeup can sometimes come across as snobby or stuck up. I realized that my down-to-earth and genuine personality inside the designer gift box reaches more people; they see and hear the real me; that really helped me get comfortable with things I didn't like before.

**What are five things you wish someone had told you before you started your endeavor?**

I wish someone told me that I didn't have to follow the path that society built. Getting married, having children, becoming a homemaker. People need to ignore the preconceived ideals they believe their parents or others think are best for them. Instead, do what is suitable for you no matter what.

I wish someone told me about darker issues in life we don't realize until they are too late, codependency, cycles of abuse, and addiction. We don't talk about these things early enough in life, and they can affect and prevent everyone from living a full and productive life.

I wish someone told me the importance of being active and working out on the mental and not just the physical part. I didn't care about being physically fit; many people don't. But the benefits of reduction in stress and elevating my mood were things I didn't know until I started. Now it's something that I can't live without.

I wish someone told me that failing isn't a failure, that it's a learning experience. It took me many years to look back and realize that I had gained incredible knowledge and value from pulling myself back up from my setbacks. If I knew then, I might have been easier on myself.

## You are a person of significant influence. If you could inspire a movement that would bring the best outcome to the greatest number of people, what would that be?

I don't think it's possible; the genie is out of the bottle, but I would inspire kindness and transparency on social media. I feel the facade of social media and the ability to hide behind created personas have really affected how people treat each other. The things people say and do to each other on the internet used to stay on the internet, but it's bleeding into real life and changing how people communicate with one another, and not always for the best.

## How would you like to be remembered?

That I wasn't afraid to live my life, and I wasn't afraid to die. I want young people to embrace life at every stage and realize aging isn't a punishment.

## Where can we follow your work?

Social: Instagram @sassy_gran_doris
Facebook / YouTube / TikTok

# CHAPTER 3

# Monti Carlo

*Keep learning, and don't stop your hustle. While I was still waitressing and staging in kitchens, I got cast to host a digital show about baby food for Jessica Alba's Honest Company. When the director talked about finding a chef to make the baby food, I offered to develop the recipes, and they said yes. That's when I taught myself how to create and write recipes. During the shoot, I watched the camera guys and dissected the script. After that, I decided to start making digital content. Unfortunately, I didn't have the money to hire a writer, a camera person, or an editor. So, I taught myself how to write, shoot, and edit. Eventually, that led me to teach a class on creating food content for James Beard. Every step is an opportunity to get better and expand your brand's footprint. Take it!*

After leaving a dysfunctional marriage and a disheartening radio career behind, Monti Carlo found herself facing homelessness. When Gordon Ramsay chose her to compete on MasterChef, her second act began. Monti placed in the Top 5 and is now an acclaimed Puerto Rican Chef and TV Host, with shows on Food Network, Cooking Channel, Tastemade, PBS, and FYI.

**Share with us a bit about your upbringing.**

First, thank you for making room for a Puerto Rican chef's voice! I was born on the island to a teenaged mother, and my grandparents raised me. We lived in a remote beach town on a defunct dairy farm just a block from the ocean. My grandmother cooked simple, delicious, traditional Puerto Rican meals with ingredients straight from the farm or the local fishermen. Some of my first memories are of watching her at the stove.

Our farmhouse burned to the ground when I was five years old, and my brother and I went to live with my mother in San Juan. She was in a relationship with a very wealthy businessman, and we lived in a fancy condo overlooking the ocean. We ate at restaurants that served elaborate, complex dishes, but it was still Puerto Rico's flavors on my lips.

When I was six years old, my mother separated from her boyfriend, and we moved to Texas. My mother could only find work as a house cleaner, and so times were tight. My twin brother and I were latchkey kids. I learned to speak English by watching PBS, Scooby-Doo, and Donahue. I missed Puerto Rico desperately. Every time my mother made a traditional island dish, it transported me back to my home. That is when my love affair with Puerto Rican food began.

**What is your life lesson quote? Can you share its relevance in your life?**

"Leap, and the net will appear." —John Burroughs.

That quote has always given me the courage to stop my "What if I fail?" self-talk and go for it. I followed those words in 2000 to jump head-first into a career in radio and comedy. I was in my mid-20's and full of self-doubt. But I took a chance, dropped the money for broadcasting school, and began what ended up being a very lucrative career.

In 2010 I walked away from the life I had spent a decade building. "Leap, and the net will appear." That quote gave me the strength to leave radio, get a divorce, and sell everything I owned to move to California with my two-year-old son. But, unfortunately, getting hired as a single mom is easier said than done. Six months after landing in Los Angeles, we were facing homelessness.

Then I got the opportunity to audition for MasterChef. I was scared to death of leaving my son to shoot the show. I had a crippling fear of failing spectacularly and making a fool of myself on national TV. But, "Leap, and the net will appear." Taking that leap of faith gave birth to my second act and transformed my life into everything I had always wanted.

### How would your best friend describe you?

I asked my best friend, and she said, "Generous, kind, and thoughtful." In her own words:

"Monti is the person who remembers your birthday, and knowing you are stuck at work surprises you with a homemade cake and your favorite wine. She is the friend that automatically offers to drive you to your first colonoscopy and will wait all the hours to take you home! Monti is also the friend who makes you homemade pasta just because you were hungry! Her smile is infectious, her eyes sparkle when you mention anything food, and she is always the first person I want to tell anything good or bad to."

### You have been blessed with success. What are three qualities you possess that helped you achieve your goals?

Passion. Determination. And the uncrushable belief that I can achieve anything I set my mind to.

**Tell us about your career experience before your second chapter.**

For me to do that, I have to give you some backstory. When I was 24 years old, after years of working in restaurants, I signed up for broadcasting school. It was a six-week course. On Day 1, my instructor asked what my dream was, and I said I wanted to host a Food Network show just like Emeril. On my way to my third day of school, my car got t-boned by a dump truck. I woke up from a coma to find that I had 19 broken ribs and a punctured lung. I checked myself out of the hospital as soon as I could stand and finished the last three weeks of school, picking broken glass from my scalp and popping Aleve like M&M's.

In the 12 years that followed, I forgot about Food Network and became a radio host. I started a career in stand-up comedy. In the process, I moved across state lines seven times. I fell in love, got married, and had a son. I built a beautiful life for myself.

Things got turned upside down, as they sometimes do, and I got divorced. I quit comedy and radio. I spent my savings nursing my son back to health from a bout with MRSA. My best friend got murdered in cold blood, and I couldn't afford to go to his funeral. I found myself in the darkest depression of my life. I was an unemployed, broke, single mom, and I was scared to death.

Somewhere in the fog that followed, I remembered my dream of hosting a show on Food Network. I thought, "It's too late. I'm too old." And then the true blessing of hitting rock bottom revealed itself: I had nothing left to lose.

**How did you reinvent yourself in your second chapter?**

When I got the opportunity to audition for Gordon Ramsay on MasterChef, I was 36 years old with no job prospects, no money, and nothing to my name left to sell. I found myself in the ludicrous position where trying to win a world-renown cooking competition was the only way I was going to keep my kid and me off the street. I had no formal culinary training and no way to afford it, so I did what I had to do and taught myself.

I spent three months cooking non-stop in a tiny 400 square foot studio apartment. I'd take care of my two-year-old son during the day and read cookbooks at night while he slept. I was on a $10 a day food budget. I couldn't afford the ingredients to practice advanced techniques, so I taught myself knife skills with dollar store veggies, which became soup the next day.

I learned how to make dressings and sauces. I could afford flour and eggs, so I taught myself how to make pasta and quick breads and every which way you could make an egg. I didn't sleep for weeks and weeks on end.

I wasn't the best cook in the MasterChef kitchen that year, by far. But I was determined to stay for as long as possible to collect the day rate producers gave us ($50 a day) and use it to pay my rent.

I made it to the Top 5. I didn't win the cookbook deal or the $250,000 in prize money that I so desperately needed. But I did get my foot in the door. And when you're stubborn AF, sometimes that's all it takes. So, I decided to pursue my dream of becoming a Food TV personality full steam.

**Your second chapter's transition was remarkable. What was the trigger that made you decide you needed to make a change in your life?**

Hitting rock bottom forced me to take the plunge. After researching homeless shelters for me and my two-year-old, I knew I had to do whatever it took to find a way out. Competing in the MasterChef kitchen was the awakening I needed. I found the meaning of life on a cutting board—dream of a dish, gather the ingredients, prepare them, and make it real.

**What did you do to discover you had a new skill set you hadn't maximized?**

The short answer is I hustled. After leaving MasterChef, I knew I had to pursue my dream of hosting Food TV. I devoured cookbooks and experimented in my home kitchen non-stop. I worked in restaurant kitchens two days a week for free so that I could learn more. To help make ends meet, I waitressed double shifts five days a week. I was on my feet so much; I had to go up two shoe sizes to make room for the swelling. When people asked me what my real job was, I would say, "I'm going to be a Food Network star."

I was obsessed with that show. I watched every episode of every season of Food Network Star. I filled two notebooks with the judges' advice and ideas for what I would have done in every challenge. I defined what it was that I wanted to say in the food world. I started a blog with Puerto Rican recipes.

Two years after MasterChef, I got to host a special on FYI called "Make My Food Famous," where home cooks competed to get their dishes on their favorite restaurant's menu. I kept hustling. I started catering what I dubbed Cali-Rican cuisine: dishes that showed off Puerto Rico's flavors developed with California technique. I started working as a line cook.

Three years after MasterChef, I landed the opportunity to host a digital series about baby food for Jessica Alba's Honest Company. I asked the director if he needed help and landed my first scriptwriting and recipe development gig. First, I taught myself how to shoot and edit and started creating content. Then, I started running a kitchen.

Four years after MasterChef, I got a call from Todd Weiser, the Senior Vice President of Programming and Development for Food Network. He wanted me to audition to host a show. I was in the middle of a waitressing shift. I felt so faint I had to sit on the floor. I had prepared for four years straight. Finally, I was ready, and I nailed it. Before my show aired, Todd wanted to introduce me to the Food Network audience by having me on various shows.

I ended up on Food Network Star. Not as a contestant as I had dreamed, but as a judge sitting next to Giada De Laurentiis, Bobby Flay, and Robert Irvine.

My first Food Network show debuted on Monday, April 10th, 2017. It only took me 17 years to make my dream come true. Since that day, I've shot shows for multiple platforms, including PBS, Cooking Channel, Tastemade, and Studio Ramsay.

## Is there someone you are grateful to who helped you along the way?

Without a doubt, it's Gordon Ramsay. Nine years ago, I walked into a dusty warehouse in Los Angeles to cook for Gordon. I did not know it then, but it was a day that would change the course of my whole life.

I had a minimal understanding of who Gordon was—a famous chef that liked to yell. I had never seen the show. I had no idea it played in 192 countries. All I knew is that getting into the MasterChef kitchen was the only way to keep my son and me out of a shelter because they gave you a $50-day rate. The only way in was to get one of just eighteen aprons, slim chances considering my lack of experience and the skill level of the ninety-nine other hopefuls in that dirty warehouse.

I had no idea my elbows could tremble when I was scared enough. But when I finally got the chance to audition for Gordon, holy-ish, was I scared enough. I couldn't afford a new outfit, so I auditioned in my old maternity clothes. I covered the holes in my shirt with an apron, the hole in my right shoe with duct tape. I felt less-than.

One of the producers led me to the double doors that Gordon was sitting behind. She smiled gently at me and said, "You can do this," as the doors opened. And then all the air rushed out of my lungs, and I started to cry. Because I didn't think I could. I was wrong.

Gordon tried my dish, called it delicious, and said there was something to me. He gave me one of his 18 aprons and, with it, the chance to compete in the MasterChef Kitchen. I guarantee you've never seen someone so happy to put on an apron.

Even though I had made it past the first obstacle, I was still depressed and full of self-doubt. Gordon pulled me up by the bootstraps. He could care less what I was sad about; he wanted me to cook for my life. When I didn't think I could do something, Gordon asked me to think of my son. He threw challenge after challenge my way and pushed me further than I ever thought I could go.

I made lunch for 101 soldiers in a field so muddy it swallowed my shoes whole. I worked the line at a Michelin-starred restaurant as Gordon frothed at the mouth, yelling out so many orders. I killed my first animal. It wasn't anything crazy like a bunny; it was a jumbo prawn. But he looked like he had just walked off the set of "Little Mermaid," his big eyes pleading with me not to do it. I cried as I made a risotto with his flesh and a broth with his bones.

Gordon forced me to look at what had been right in front of me the whole time: life goes on. The bad things that happen to you are not the things that define you. You define yourself. He taught me the essential recipe for success: Fall seven times. Get up eight. It's been almost ten years, and I still can't watch the video of him handing me that apron without getting choked up. He saved my son and me. He taught me to believe in myself. The cookbook, commercials, TV shows, the press, none of that would have happened without Gordon.

## Share an exciting moment that happened since committing to your second chapter.

I'll never forget when I had to film a commercial for KitchenAid in New Orleans. I walked off the plane to find that a tropical storm was rolling into town. The director wanted to start shooting that hour to beat the bad weather and the floods that would follow.

The shoot was outside in the French Quarter. We filmed well into the night, with dozens of lights on that acted like magnets for thousands of mosquitos. Every time I opened my mouth to say a line, a mosquito would fly in! They covered me in bug spray every ten minutes and had a production assistant fanning me with posterboard to keep the bugs off me. It was hilarious!

## Have you ever struggled with believing in yourself? If so, how did you overcome that limiting belief?

There were many times I doubted myself—especially on my way home after an 18-hour day, with feet so swollen it hurt to press on the gas pedal. I could only afford a one-bedroom. I slept on the couch so my son could have his own room. I was on government assistance. It was a challenging time. I thought that maybe all I would ever be was a forty-year-old waitress that had been on a reality show once.

I kept going for my son's sake. I put Post-it notes all over our tiny apartment with my goals written on them. They were a constant reminder for me to continue reaching. I invested in the tools that I needed. I didn't turn a single opportunity down. Little by little, my brand continued to grow.

## Typically, I encourage my clients to ask for support from those who believe in their vision before they embark on a new chapter. How did you create your support system?

My little sister Marji and my twin brother Joel were my support system. They encouraged me when I doubted myself. They comforted me when I didn't think I could keep going. My brother moved in with me for a bit after my divorce to watch over my son and me. My sister took care of my son so I could compete on

MasterChef. After the show, when I couldn't make ends meet, my brother loaned me money to pay my bills. He built websites for me so I could market myself and my recipes. My sister is a stylist, and she helped me with my wardrobe. I wouldn't be here without their love, their grace, and their generosity.

### Starting a new chapter requires leaving your comfort zone behind. How did you do that?

I think the most I've ever pushed myself out of my comfort zone was my first appearance on Home Shopping Network. I had never sold anything on TV, much less live TV. I was presenting the iconic KitchenAid stand mixer on its 100th anniversary. It was a "Today's Special," a segment that starts in the evening and goes on for 28 hours straight. That meant being peppy, remembering KitchenAid's history and facts about the stand mixer for a marathon amount of time with no sleep.

I didn't think about staying awake for 28 hours. Instead, I thought about the show in increments. I told myself, "Do your best for the next 45 minutes. We'll cross the next bridge when we get to it." Twelve hours in, I started losing my voice, and one of the hosts dropped six cough drops in a cup of hot water, mixed it until they melted, and had me chug it. It worked. I wrapped the 28 hours with thousands of sales. I have mad respect for the HSN team. They are the hardest-working people I have ever met. No doubt.

### What are five things you wish someone had told you before you started leading your business, and why?

Expect more from yourself than anyone else does. I wake up at three or four in the morning seven days a week and work until six or seven at night. I push myself harder than anyone else ever would. That alone has helped my brand *grow* faster than I ever expected.

Lean into your strengths while you work out your weaknesses.

I'll never forget my first shoot for Food Network. I had to do a cooking demo for a struggling restaurant owner, which meant cooking and teaching while simultaneously playing to the camera. I had never done anything like it, and I was incredibly nervous. To calm down, I started joking around with the restaurant owner while I cooked. We laughed, and the cameras disappeared. When I finished, everyone was quiet, and I wondered what I had done wrong. Then, Todd walked up to me with a massive smile on his face. He said that very few people nail their demos in one take and that he was impressed.

It was then that I realized that ten years in radio and comedy, where you go live, engage with an audience, and get zero do-overs, gave me the chops I needed to make me stand out as a Food TV host. The skill set I had perfected in my old career gave me the foundation to launch myself into the world of food TV. I learned to lean into my strengths.

Keep learning, and don't stop your hustle. While I was still waitressing and staging in kitchens, I got cast to host a digital show about baby food for Jessica Alba's Honest Company. When the director talked about finding a chef to make the baby food, I offered to develop the recipes, and they said yes. That's when I taught myself how to create and write recipes.

During the shoot, I watched the camera guys and dissected the script. After that, I decided to start making digital content. Unfortunately, I didn't have the money to hire a writer, a camera person, or an editor. So, I taught myself how to write, shoot, and edit. Eventually, that led me to teach a class on creating food content for James Beard. Every step is an opportunity to get better and expand your brand's footprint. Take it!

Have a mentor. Learn as much as you can from people that have been there, done that. There are so many women in the food world that I look up to, like Barbara Fairchild, the former editor-in-chief of Bon Appetit, Dianne Jacob, the author of Will Write for Food, and Giovanna Huyke, the Julia Child of Puerto Rican food.

They have given me invaluable advice, and I would not have gotten as far as I have without it.

**You are a person of significant influence. If you could inspire a movement that would bring the best outcome to the greatest number of people, what would that be?**

I would bring dinner back. Everything connects to the dinner table: the health of your family, your community, and that of the planet. Yet, so many of us skip the opportunity to break bread together. We ignore this moment to catch up, get nourished, and strengthen our relationships. Maybe it's because we think we can't cook, that it's too expensive, or that we don't have the time.

I want to show people how to make better decisions about what they put on their dinner tables to reduce their carbon footprint. I want to teach them how to curb food waste. I want to inspire them to cook with easy, budget-friendly recipes. I want them to experience being mindful and present while they're sitting with loved ones at a dinner table.

If I can accomplish these goals, our world will get a little greener. Our communities will get a little closer. We'll spend time genuinely talking to each other again. Instead of focusing on the things that divide us, we can celebrate the things we all have in common, like a love of food, friendship, and laughter.

**How would you like to be remembered?**

I'd like to be remembered as a great mother, a fighter, and one who gives back.

**Where can we follow your work?**

Website: themonticarlo.com / islandgirlcooks.com
Social:　　@themonticarlo

# CHAPTER 4

# Cynthia Besteman

৯৵ ৵

*"Don't compromise just because you feel you don't know everything. I tend to second guess if someone in authority says something should change or can't be done. I compromised on a few product designs at the beginning I knew weren't right. After one of my friends called my labels "grandma-ish," I then had to spend double the money to redo them. I knew she was right. And I'd known it all along. I thought because I was new, that others knew more than I did."*

Cynthia Besteman landed in New York City determined to find her way as an actress. Unfortunately, after working on Broadway for ten years, she received a breast cancer diagnosis in 2011, and her successful career came to a skidding halt. While undergoing cancer treatment, one of her first actions was to toss out all beauty products with harmful chemicals. She noticed that the "natural" beauty products she wore contained parabens known to work as endocrine disruptors. She used her knowledge and passion for naturally-derived skincare ingredients to formulate her consciously-produced product line under her brand name, Violets Are Blue. She's grateful to cancer for bringing this into her life.

**Share with us a bit about your upbringing.**

I am the youngest of three children, born in Seattle. Our family moved to New Jersey for six years, where I fell in love with Broadway. My mom wanted me to be a professional figure skater, but I broke my leg in my first lesson, so there went that dream! My family then moved back to Seattle, where I finished high school. I attended the University of Oregon and the University of Washington for college but left once I graduated to participate in an acting conservatory in New York City. I worked as a Broadway actress for ten years before tiring of the lifestyle. Then I went into real estate, where I quickly became the top broker in my office.

**What is your favorite life lesson quote? Can you share its relevance in your life?**

"Worry is like a rocking chair; it will give you something to do but won't get you anywhere." I tend to be a catastrophic ruminator. I think a cancer diagnosis can do that to a person. But, I also think it's a defense mechanism, so I am prepared for the worst. I am realizing, however, that living in that space is not healthy. When I start to feel anxious and go to my default setting, I picture myself in the rocking chair, standing up and walking forward!

**You have been blessed with success. What are three qualities you possess that helped you achieve your goals?**

Resilience is the first. I get knocked down, but I get up again. I think my diagnosis is an excellent example of that, as I wanted to make sure my illness would mean something important in my life. I didn't want to go back to my life before; I wanted a better "normal" rather than a "new normal." So, I researched things that I could do, like Reiki, acupuncture, herbalism. Something that would help me get back up from being hit with a cancer diagnosis.

Humor—this is key. You need the humor to stay sane when starting a business. You need it to not take the issues you confront too seriously and laugh at the places you find yourself in; otherwise, I'd be crying a lot.

Vulnerability. This is not the usual answer for someone starting a business, but I think it works in my favor. I am an open book; I share what I know with other business owners, founders, and product developers. I believe in being an open book, and if I get burned, well, that says more about the person "using" me than it does about my vulnerability. I often wore my heart on my sleeve in business meetings, and you immediately see the human element come into play. Suddenly it's not about business anymore but a company wanting to help someone like me build a brand that will help people. This happened both with my manufacturer and fulfillment center. If I hadn't shared my story with them, I would have been considered too small for them to work with. However, because I shared, they made exceptions to take me on.

### Tell us about your career experience before your second chapter.

I knew from a very young age that I wanted to be an actress. That was the only career on my mind my whole educational life. I wanted to be a stage actress, specifically. I majored in theatre in college and moved to NYC to attend Circle in the Square Theater School. From there, I worked with an amazing theatre company and other projects both on stage and screen. To support my stage life, I worked as a receptionist, at a ballroom dance studio (which was a blast) and at an art gallery for up-and-coming artists. I started suffering from anxiety on stage. It wasn't talked about at that time, so I was confused about what was happening to me.

I started dreading going on stage. Feeling burnt out and poor and not having the same joy as I had on stage, I decided to go into real estate as I thought I could make a lot of money and that I did! I'd never made a salary like that and loved the money aspect but quickly felt unfulfilled; I felt tied to the job and never had a break. It was exhausting. I think that is part of why I got sick; my body did what my mind couldn't do. It created cancer for me to stop.

**How did you reinvent yourself in your second chapter?**

My reinvention happened by accident. When I was diagnosed, I took a leave of absence from my firm. My husband took over everything as we were business partners. I started investigating Reiki, acupuncture, meditation, and anything that would connect my head and body. I had felt so disconnected. I was cleaning my house of things I thought may have played a role in causing my cancer. This included my skincare.

I googled how to make organic ingredients, and oddly enough or a divine intervention, a class was starting the next night ten blocks from my apartment. I signed up, and that night changed everything. I finally felt my head and body connected as I was focused on making something that could help me with my current skin issues, but more importantly, I was taking control of my health. I then started to dabble in creating my skincare line.

My oncologist and the women in my treatment group noticed how healthy my skin stayed throughout my journey. When I told my doctor what I was doing, she connected me with the department head to see if I could bring products for their patients. They wanted healthier skin options but were more focused on curing us, not making our skin look nice!

I came home and told my husband what I wanted to do, and he told me to go for it! I worked for two years formulating and testing. In 2013 the Beloved line was born, followed by Violets Are Blue's full launch. It was slow and steady for sure, but we got there.

**Your second chapter's transition was remarkable. What was the trigger that made you decide you needed to make a change in your life?**

I think it was chatting with the people at my hospital and hearing how excited they were about clean skincare. I realized there was a need for it and how it could help women physically and mentally. If they are given beautiful, healthy products, I hope they'll have a similar response of reconnecting with their mind and body and the feeling of taking control of their lives.

Also, my super, supportive husband didn't blink when I told him what I wanted to do. If he wasn't on board, there was no way for me to make it work. He believed in me, sometimes more than I believed in myself!

## What did you do to discover you had a new skill set you hadn't maximized?

I think why I took to this so well is because it fired up my creative side again. It combined the best of both worlds, business and arts. I felt the way I did at the beginning of my acting career—excited, driven, hopeful but without the anxiety and fear. It took me a while, though, to get into the true mindset of being an entrepreneur. I remember in the beginning; I didn't handle setbacks very well. I would get emotional and say that maybe it wasn't meant to be, and perhaps the universe was telling me to forget it. My mom then told me that this is what happens in business, and if I didn't like it or didn't think I could handle it, then I should get out. But, if I put on my big girl pants and act like a boss, I can deal with the issue. She said there is nothing wrong with not wanting to be a business owner; I just had to decide if I was one or not. That changed everything! I keep my big girl pants near me at all times and remember her words every time I run into a snag.

## How are things going now?

The business is going well. We doubled our sales last year during the pandemic, in part because people wanted self-care products when they were stuck at home, but also because the word is spreading about us. We have won several awards in the last two years, and I am excited about the new products we are launching this year. Nothing gives me greater joy than getting an email from one of my customers saying how much they love our products.

I respond to every email I get, and many of them are newly diagnosed women or women over 40 who are looking for cleaner choices that work for their skin.

### Is there someone you are grateful to who helped you along the way?

Can I say two people? My husband David is the best. He is my rock and who I lean on, cry to, and celebrate with. And day after day, I make him sample products. Some days have been difficult, and I've wanted to quit, and he has never said, "yeah, maybe you should," but instead convinced me I am doing hard work that is well worth the effort. He has sacrificed so much, and he is a neat freak, so he has dealt with more than your average person.

My mom is also right there with him in terms of support. I call on her when I feel like I am getting off track or just need someone to tell me to buck up and not stress the small stuff. She was the one who sent me the rocking chair quote. She knows me and how I respond to things, and she knows just what to say to snap me out of my fear and anxiety.

### Share an exciting moment that happened since committing to your second chapter.

When I was a child, I dreamed about becoming a famous actress and being in the magazines I read. Of course, the chances of that happening were slim, and dropping out of acting, I thought my face would never be in my favorite magazine. But I did get into a couple of major, national publications! Looking at the full page spread with my picture, my quotes, and the 4-inch heels, I realized my dream in my head was true, just not necessarily the way I envisioned it. I now believe in my visions and know it may look a little different, but not to give up on my dreams!

**Have you ever struggled with believing in yourself? If so, how did you overcome that limiting belief?**

It should be more like; is there a time I don't struggle! I deal with imposter syndrome on most days. Every time I am asked to speak at an event, I think, seriously, do they think I know what I am doing? I had this happen when I was asked to talk to a group of female skincare founders. I was terrified! What if they ask me a question I don't know the answer to? What if they don't like my products? What if they think I'm using my cancer diagnosis as a way to sell products?

I shared my vulnerability and fears with these women and what happened, in turn, was an incredible conversation about how we all felt this way. We were all puffing up trying to compete when we were all feeling the same way deep down. We had a wonderful, emotional evening which turned into a sisterhood. Our facades came down, and we are now there for each other when we feel insecure. It helps me to remember this in times where I feel like I may not belong.

**Typically, I encourage my clients to ask for support from those who believe in their vision before they embark on a new chapter. How did you create your support system?**

My family rallied around me. I remember specifically my brother said when he heard I was diagnosed with cancer, "Well. Let's circle the wagons." That has stuck with me. I want to know I am surrounded by people who will circle the wagons for me. I have girlfriends who I acted with who are my closest group of friends to date, and we have all been through disease, divorce, job loss, love loss together, and I know I would not be where I am today without them.

These women show up for each other, and my family is very tight-knit, and between these two groups, I am good. I have also created an incredible group of women friends from the green beauty space, and we have each other on speed dial. I speak to some of them daily. In the green beauty space, we are in some ways competitors, but in many ways not. No one has just one brand in their bathroom; they have several products from different brands. We all get this, so the belief is, if one does well, we all do. We are all growing and celebrating together.

### Starting a new chapter requires leaving your comfort zone behind. How did you do that?

Unlike my acting career, in which I always felt weird selling my talent, it is easier for me to sell my products and, although it would hurt to hear someone doesn't like them, it's not as painful as someone not liking *you*. Selling products is more of my comfort zone. In a way, doing speaking engagements as myself rather than being on stage as a performer is scary for me. I spoke at a corporate event in Laguna Beach, California, a few years ago, and for some reason, I was nervous about forgetting my lines. I rehearsed and rehearsed my speech until I could do it in my sleep. Sure enough, I completely forgot my lines during the presentation, which I never did as an actress, and after the flop sweat and panic hit, I realized I knew the story because it was my story!

I took a deep breath and spoke from my heart about how I started my business and why the products were so important. Looking back, I laugh at how nervous I was and how I stressed over learning my own life.

### What are five things you wish someone had told you before you started leading your business, and why?

Nothing about launching a product will go smoothly. This is huge for me as every product launch has never gone as planned. In retrospect, I am always grateful for the monkey wrenches as they made the product better, and knowing that ahead of time would've saved a lot of stress! I did a run of 10K deodorants that weren't mixed properly and ended up mushy. Tens of thousands of dollars were wasted with my old manufacturer and product development team pointing their fingers in different directions. I had to walk away and start over, which almost tanked my business. In hindsight, the changes I made in manufacturers and formulas were well worth it. It is now our top-selling product.

Don't compromise just because you feel you don't know everything. I tend to second guess if someone in authority says something should change or can't be done. I compromised on a few product designs at the beginning I knew weren't right. After one of my friends called my labels "grandma-ish," I then had to spend double the money to redo them. I knew she was right. And I'd known it all along. I thought because I was new, that they knew more than I did.

Don't be afraid to say, "I don't know." I'm continually working on this, and I think, in the beginning, I overcompensated. I was so green that I lost out on learning things because I was too proud to say I didn't understand or didn't know. Take time to enjoy the wins! As my business grows, so do its needs; it's like feeding a teenager; I am constantly looking ahead and determining what we have to do. So, I need to take time for the wins, sit for a bit, and look at what I have accomplished. The journey is the fun part, not the result.

## You are a person of significant influence. If you could inspire a movement that would bring the best outcome to the greatest amount of people, what would that be?

One word, sustainability. Sustainability affects every human and animal on the planet. As I learn more about plastic waste and pollution, I am horrified about what we have done as humans. We are working to produce fully sustainable packaging by sourcing and knowing exactly where and how our ingredients are harvested, who harvests them, and how they are manufactured. We are also looking into our carbon footprint and how we can educate others. In my own home, we are expanding our zero waste options.

**Dreams come true. If you could invite anyone in the world to dinner, who would that be?**

Hands down, without a thought, Marcus Lemonis. My husband jokingly asks, "If Marcus told you to do such and such with your business, would you?" and before he can finish, I say, "Yes!" I am amazed at how he runs his, for lack of a better word, empire! The thing is, he does it all without being cocky. He shows that people who are cut from a particular type of cloth can be successful. We can be warm, care about those we work with, make a difference and still make money. People, processes, and products are always at the forefront of what I do.

**Where can we follow your work?**

Website: violetsareblueskincare.com
Social: Instagram / Facebook @violetsareblueskincare

# CHAPTER 5

# Michelle Tunno Buelow

ళ∞⊸

*Find your own measuring stick for success. Success is not just about the money. For our brand, success is measured in meal donations. I didn't feel like our company was big enough to deserve a seat at the table early on. Even as we doubled year over year, our company never seemed to be growing fast enough or hitting the big numbers that I watched other brands hit. Over time, I've learned there will always be a faster-growing, more profitable, larger company than yours when you measure your success on sales alone. But when your success is linked to something beyond the numbers, your passion, drive, and confidence become explosive.*

Michelle Tunno Buelow is the founder and CEO of Bella Tunno, a modern, innovative, purpose-driven baby accessory brand with a mission to end childhood hunger. For every product sold, Bella Tunno donates at least one meal to a hungry child. To date, Bella Tunno has donated more than 5.4 million meals. Michelle lives in Charlotte, North Carolina, with her husband and two teenage daughters and serves on many philanthropic boards.

## Share with us a bit about your upbringing.

I grew up in a tiny, dot-on-a-map town in Western Pennsylvania. I was raised in a nuclear family, just my mom, dad, brother, and me. My mom was a teacher, my dad, a government employee, and my brother, my best friend. We grew up playing games at the dinner table and taking family vacations in a paneled station wagon. My parents were very religious and strict, like one hour of television a week and one sweet snack a week strict. We spent most Wednesday nights, Saturdays, and all-day Sunday at church. We did everything as a family and my brother, Matt, was my person. I was a soccer player and gymnast growing up.

I loved school and loved learning. I attended college at Pennsylvania State University. Growing up in such a small town, I felt like successful people were doctors and lawyers. So, that's what I thought I'd be. I entered college pre-med, then changed to pre-law, then after about three other changes, graduated with Business and Psychology degrees. I always knew I wanted to get out of the small town, so all my life, I took every single opportunity to travel, explore, and adventure. I did internships at Walt Disney World, studied abroad in Australia, and traveled to Europe for three months the summer after graduation.

After that, I moved to Charlotte, NC, to start my first job. Then, when I was just 27 years old, my brother passed away due to an accidental overdose after a 14-year battle with addiction. That was when my entire life shattered.

## What is your life lesson quote? Can you share its relevance in your life?

"The two most important days in your life are the day you are born and the day you find out why." —Mark Twain.

Everyone wants to find their purpose—the true meaning behind why they are put on this earth. But many people wait for it to be wrapped up and delivered to their porch. Sometimes purpose comes in more like a hurricane than a soft breeze, and it's so far from what we expected or envisioned that it's hard to accept. I now know that my purpose is to run a company and use my platform and profits to change people's stories. It's a company where I can help as many people as possible not experience the pain my family experienced after losing my brother. But I fought hard to push my purpose away because I didn't want this to be my story. I didn't want to accept the loss or deal with the grief, or even admit that I was scared to move forward without my brother. The purpose isn't always shiny. It's not always pleasant, and it's certainly not always as expected, but that doesn't make it any less powerful. So, often it's our pain that unveils our purpose, and then it becomes our passion, and from that, we can find our power.

### You have been blessed with success. What are three qualities you possess that helped you achieve your goals?

I'm comfortable in the uncomfortable. I have always put myself in growth situations. I grab opportunities, and I hang on tight. I don't like comfort zones. I feel the most alive when something is brand new, and I have no idea how it will unfold. Being comfortable in the uncomfortable is where I thrive.

In December of 2008, I got an email from the Target Innovation Team that said, "We are interested in your brand and would love for you to come present to us." Other than that, it had very little detail. I had never been in touch with Target before, and my brand was only 2.5 years old. I immediately called the number on the bottom of the email, and as luck would not have it, the contact was already out for holiday break. I emailed back and said I would love to know more. Then I checked my email every hour during the holiday break.

On a Monday in early January of 2009, I received an email asking me to come to Minneapolis that same week to present. I had no idea what to show or how mass retail worked, but I knew

I was going. I bought an airline ticket that same day and hopped on a plane with every sample I had, and just showed up. After I displayed my line, they peppered me with questions all containing acronyms I'd never heard before, but based on their tone, the answer to all their questions was supposed to be yes. So, I said yes and hoped I'd figure it all out later. I committed to a line in Target with no mass production leads, no idea what case packs were, and no clue how I would deliver. But somehow, I did it, and we still work with Target today.

I'm resilient. I fall often, but I find a way to get back up every time. I guess you could say, I bounce! And each time, I come out a little stronger and stand a little taller. The key is to learn from the mistakes and appreciate the scars. I'll never forget my first trade show in New York City. I had been invited to join a showroom, and they were going to display my brand under their larger brand umbrella. New York City was the big time for this small-town girl from Pennsylvania, and I was honored they selected me. I was thrilled to be represented on such a big stage. In fact, I was so proud that I invited my mom and dad to join me on the trip. My mom was still in a massive depressive state after losing my brother, and I wanted to show her what I was doing in his honor. I knew she'd be proud.

Deep down, I hoped it would also snap her out of her depression. So, I flew them up to the show, and we all arrived early on a Monday morning to see my booth and start selling. But there was only one problem: I couldn't find my booth.

We walked the showroom area for over 30 minutes and still couldn't locate the Bella Tunno products. Finally, I found the showroom owner, whom I'd only spoken with on the phone, and introduced myself. When she heard my name and brand, her face fell. She had completely forgotten about me! She didn't leave space for my brand and didn't bring my products into the show. She left me standing there for an hour, with my parents right behind me, while she tried to think of a solution. There are no words to express the disappointment and embarrassment I was feeling. I brought my parents to New York to show them what I'd created in hopes that they would beam with pride. Instead, I stood there doing everything I could to hold back tears.

The showroom owner came back with a handful of my products that she found in her car and a flower pot for me to display them in. Yes, that's right . . . A FLOWER POT! She put everything on a 2' x 2' tray table—like a television tray straight out of the 1970s. I begged my parents to leave because my eyes were burning, and I knew the tears would start flowing if they kept standing there looking at me with pity. I stood behind my flower pot for three days straight, and only two people stopped to hear my story. Who could blame them? I mean, who wants to talk to the company's founder with a few products sitting in a flower pot on top of a television stand?

I came back from New York thinking I had no business launching Bella Tunno. I wanted to quit. I wanted to put it all behind me and go back to the fast-paced life I loved. The one where I felt like I mattered. But I didn't because I knew I had to change people's stories in my brother's name. I learned so much from that experience about humility, forgiveness, and the importance of planning ahead. But perhaps the most valuable takeaway was learning just how resilient I was.

I'm scrappy. My ways aren't polished, and they are certainly not by the book, but I get things done. My approach is unconventional, and it's homegrown, but it's who I am.

Several years ago, Baby GAP asked us to create a diaper bag. At the time, we didn't do diaper bags. I referred them to a few companies that made terrific bags, but they said they loved our mission and wanted the bag to come from us. We only did cotton burp cloths and changing pads at the time, so this was a considerable stretch, but they insisted. I had one week to deliver the bag from North Carolina to California.

I called every home seamstress I knew to see if they could

construct a bag from a drawing. They all said no. I called every small factory within driving distance to ask the same question. The answer was still no. Not being one to take no for an answer, I drove to a fabric store and bought upholstery weight fabric, then to the hardware store for a staple gun. I tried constructing over 10 different styles of bags, and finally, with one day to spare, I stapled a diaper bag together with great form, excellent functionality, and a sleek look. I overnighted it, and the minute I dropped it at UPS, I realized the absurdity of sending a stapled diaper bag. I honestly never expected to hear from Baby GAP and assumed I just gave them a good laugh and lost $81 on overnight shipping.

Believe it or not, they called, and they loved it—as long as it could be made without the staples, of course! I was thrilled to hear the news but told them I didn't have a way to get it manufactured. So, they introduced me to their bag factory in China, held my hand through the entire process, and together, we launched one of the most successful diaper bags Baby GAP had ever sold.

**Tell us about your career experience before your second chapter.**

My first "big girl" job out of college was as a Change Management and Human Performance Consultant for Accenture. Coming from a town the size of a dot on a map, I badly wanted to see the world. I only applied for jobs that would allow me to travel the country. This role was what I considered a dream job: it was fast-paced and pushed me beyond anything I thought I could do, both emotionally and mentally. Working 80-hour weeks was standard practice. I traveled every week and went above and beyond in every project I touched. Climbing the corporate ladder and making as much money as possible was the goal. I tried to earn a gold star everywhere I went. Once, on a project in DC, I slept under my desk because I wanted to finish ahead of time and get promoted. I went on to run a brand strategy department at a marketing firm at the age of 25. It was a great gig, and it required international travel.

## How did you reinvent yourself in your second chapter?

I didn't choose to start my second chapter. My second chapter chose me. So, the only choice I had in the matter was how I would deal with it and find a way to move forward.

While I was busy climbing the corporate ladder, two rungs at a time, chasing accolades and promotions, my brother and best friend were in a downward spiral of drug addiction. He had been struggling for 14 years in and out of rehab programs. Just as my life was lining up to be the exact life I envisioned, his was literally crumbling. Then, on August 5, 2003, in the middle of the night, I got the call I always feared but prayed I'd never get. My brother was dead. It was an accidental overdose.

At that moment, everything changed. All of a sudden, my world stopped, and nothing else mattered. The projects, the pay raises, and the gold stars no longer meant anything. I quit the job I loved and went into a deep depression. I stayed down for about a year. I kept wondering if I could ever be happy again if life would ever feel like it mattered again.

About a year after my brother died, I had a very surreal moment of clarity. It was like my heart and mind both woke up simultaneously, and I remember making a promise that I would dedicate my life to helping as many people as possible to avoid the pain I felt.

I didn't know exactly what that meant at the time, but looking back on it, I realize that moment of clarity was when the concept of Bella Tunno was born. I wanted to start a fund in my late brother's name that could do two things: one, leave a legacy for people to remember all the good about him. He was more than an addict, and I wanted the world to associate his name with all of the good. Two, protect as many families as I could from going through the pain I felt.

With that, I started the Matt Tunno Make a Difference Fund and simultaneously launched Bella Tunno.

**Your second chapter's transition was remarkable. What was the trigger that made you decide you needed to make a change in your life?**

Pain. The pain was the thing. Realizing that although I was alive, I was not really living. Launching Bella Tunno seemed huge to others, but it seemed like the only option to me. I needed to heal, and I needed to honor my brother. It was the only option for my survival.

**What did you do to discover you had a new skill set you hadn't maximized?**

I learned to fail forward. I had no idea that I possessed true leadership qualities. I didn't realize I had a good design eye. I never thought of myself as a salesperson. Turns out I'm pretty good at all three of those things. I also realized I'm a terrible accountant and possibly even worse at customer service. When I started Bella Tunno with a $6,000 investment (of my own money), I had to do everything myself. I designed the products, sewed them, marketed them, sold them, invoiced them, shipped them, etc. In my past roles, I had one job with a shortlist of focused responsibilities. Now I was one person running about seven departments of a company by myself. So, I tried, and I failed. I fell, and I stumbled, but I learned.

Perhaps the most important lesson was to gracefully accept my mistakes and not make the same mistake twice. I didn't mind failing because it always meant I was growing and learning—I just wanted to make sure my failures were new. We have a motto at Bella Tunno, "learn and turn." We celebrate failure because we extract the lesson and apply it to the next opportunity. That's how I've learned to uncover my new skill sets, and when something is just clearly not in my wheelhouse, I've learned it's a sound investment to hire someone who can take it off my plate.

I heard Barbara Cochran speak once, and her advice stuck with me. She said to divide a piece of paper right down the center and on the left, write the things you love to do, and on the right, list the things you dread doing. Then, give yourself six months to get everything on the dreaded side off your plate. That advice has genuinely been a game-changer for me.

## How are things going now?

To most people, success might look like products on Target, Nordstrom, and Buy Buy Baby shelves, or 3,000 boutique accounts that choose us, along with multiple international distribution relationships. But at Bella Tunno, we measure our success by how much we give.

We focused all our charitable work around drug and alcohol rehabilitation, education, and addiction prevention in the first five years. Trying to save other families was my passion. In a project called Extreme Mission Make-Over, we pulled 70 individuals and 18 companies together to add five double-occupancy rooms and a bathroom to a local rescue mission. This allowed 40 more clients to participate in the program annually. We hosted a one-night charity event called Posh with Purpose that raised more than $30,000, which allowed 30 women to go through a 120-day rehabilitation program. We provided Christmas, complete with presents and a meal, to all 90 clients at the local rescue mission. We sponsored rehab for a year for at least four male clients and gave scholarships to unwed teen moms, as they are at extremely high risk for addiction. It was good work. It was personal and healing work.

But in 2014, I came across some research stating that one in six children in America faces hunger daily. That was more than 13 million children right here in the US at the time (now it's one in four due to the pandemic). I also read an article that linked food insecurity in childhood to addiction as an adult. This was where all the dots connected. The statistics about child hunger haunted me, and the link between child hunger and addiction fed my personal purpose.

In 2014, we became a one-for-one social impact brand, when we decided to donate at least one meal to a child in need for every product sold. To this day, we've kept our Buy One, Feed One promise, even in 2020, throughout the COVID-19 pandemic. Along with our partners and customers, we all share a vision of ending child hunger in America. Together, we have donated more than 5.4 million meals, and every month we celebrate success (we call it throwing confetti) based on how many meals we donate.

## Is there someone you are grateful to who helped you along the way?

My husband has always believed in Bella Tunno and in me . . . some days, more than I did. He never gave up on my dream, even when I wanted to. I remember three years into the business, we were growing at an uncanny pace. We didn't have any employees or systems to scale the business, yet we had a deal with GAP and were in talks with Target. I was still working out of our bonus room with a three-year-old and an infant. We couldn't keep up with anything, and I didn't even feel like we had time to hire someone to help. We had no childcare, and there were times when I truly felt like I couldn't breathe. We would stay up packing and charging orders until 3 AM, and most nights, I'd have tears streaming down my face while we did it. I'd never worked so hard in my life, and I felt like we would never catch up. I was sacrificing everything for the business and felt like it was taking everything from me.

I wanted to quit. But Todd would say, "Go to bed, I'll finish," and stay up all night. Then he'd roll right into his "real" job at 8 AM. He never wavered in his commitment to the brand—never got angry or showed me he was tired. He was working a full-time job outside of Bella Tunno and never once complained. Behind the scenes, he was interviewing distribution centers, submitting me for awards, and landing PR opportunities. I have too many "Todd to the rescue" stories to count. He's the heavy lifter behind Bella Tunno.

**Share an exciting moment that happened since you committed to your second chapter.**

I found myself. I found the beauty in not wishing your life was something other than what it is. I realized that this is my one precious life, and although I wouldn't have authored my story this way, it's my story and mine alone. I learned that tragedy is a teacher, and it's better to learn from it than run from it. Although I'd give almost anything to have my brother back, I'm happy to say I've finally found joy again. I think it comes from knowing I've made the most of the life I've been given, and in doing so, I'm helping others every single day.

**Have you ever struggled with believing in yourself? If so, how did you overcome that limiting belief?**

I battled imposter syndrome the first 10 years of running Bella Tunno. Who was I to be a CEO? At 27 years old, I had six years of work experience and had never managed a team. I remember the first time I won a national award with 10 other amazing, fast-growing women-owned companies. I traveled to California to receive it. I was terrified to show up, scared they would realize they made a mistake. I was in the elevator heading down to get the award, and another winner was in the elevator with me. She had a presence, and outwardly she looked perfect. I introduced myself and congratulated her. She leaned over, pulled some lint off my dress, and said, "Oh honey, didn't you bring a lint brush?" Her only intention was to make me feel "less than," and she won. I felt like I shrunk and shriveled, and it was all I could do to follow her to the 1500-person room where the award was being given. I felt so inadequate. I felt seen in all the wrong ways—judged without being known.

Overall, I think women are tremendous supporters of other women, but not every woman gets it. Maybe it was her own insecurity speaking. But that day, after a quick cry in the bathroom,

I put myself back together and walked up on the stage with my head held high (and lint on my dress!) and felt sorry for her. Sorry for a woman who didn't think there was room on that stage for all of us. Ever since I've gone out of my way to be supportive and make space for other women to succeed.

**Typically, I encourage my clients to ask for support from those who believe in their vision before they embark on a new chapter. How did you create your support system?**

I'm not sure I did that intentionally. I think starting Bella Tunno was more of a "ready, fire, aim" story than a "ready, aim, fire" one. I didn't have a business plan, and I definitely didn't feel ready. But, at the same time, there was a fire burning in me to do something in my brother's name and help change other people's stories.

Although I didn't know it at the time, the corporate world was the support system I needed to start Bella Tunno. International travel taught me to be independent and fearless. The consulting work gave me insights into many different companies and their cultures, missions, visions, values, and operations.

I started building a virtual 'business backpack' and filled it with all of the positive things I'd experienced while learning from any negative experiences or missteps. I learned how the best companies treat their people and how they are hyper-focused on their goals. I had three corporate jobs before I started Bella Tunno, and each one taught me so many valuable lessons.

**Starting a new chapter requires leaving your comfort zone behind. How did you do that?**

Early on, I was my own biggest obstacle. I had a firm belief that when you give back, make charitable donations and help others, it should be in private, not something you let others see or know about. So, it felt disingenuous to share all the philanthropic work we were doing—almost like announcing how much money you give before putting it on the offering plate.

I also hadn't come to a place where I wholly owned my own story. I didn't want to share my brother's struggles. I didn't want that to be my family's story. As much as I wanted to change other people's stories, I hadn't let go of the shame associated with my own. I just wanted to make great baby products and donate part of the profits behind closed doors. That mentality was actually inhibiting our giving potential, and, in a way, I was cheating my customers too. By not letting them know about the donations, I was limiting our company's growth potential and our customer's ability to realize they were part of a solution. As time started to heal me, the passion for doing more just kept growing, and I had to get out of my own way to really start helping in a meaningful way.

### What are five things you wish someone had told you before you started leading your business, and why?

Align your purpose and your product. Bella Tunno was launched with a mission of breaking destructive cycles and changing lives, and we've never once wavered from that. However, our giving was all directed toward drug and alcohol rehabilitation efforts in the first seven years. This was my passion and personal story, but there was a massive disconnect from our target audience. Our customers were new parents who just brought a brand-new life into this crazy world. The last thing they wanted to think about was that sweet little bundle potentially becoming an addict. While it felt good for me personally, it was a complete miss for the brand. So, when I came across the link between food insecurity in childhood and addiction in adulthood, we immediately redirected the mission and created a fully aligned brand story. We were selling feeding products for children and donating meals to children in need for every product sold. This alignment became a story that made sense to our customers and made them want to share the story themselves. That newfound alignment between our products and our purpose was more profound, and it united our team. We are all mothers and aunts and mentors to the children in our lives, and we all relate to wanting children's core needs to be met. Our entire team volunteers once a month at a local school. We set up a food pantry through our food bank partner and hand out more than a week's worth of healthy meals to each family. It's our favorite day of the month because we get to meet the people we are serving. We talk and share with them and see where our donations are going, which means so much more than simply writing a check. Everyone shows up—not because they have to or get paid to. It's our shared purpose. It's fulfilling, and it gives us meaning.

Now that our purpose aligns with our product, our customers are proud to use our brand and excited to join our mission. I remember in 2014 when we launched our Buy One, Give One initiative at Market in Atlanta. We wanted an impactful way to show how many meals each customer was donating through their order, so we bought enormous bags of mini pom-poms. After each order was written, we tallied the donated meal count and handed that same number of pom poms to the customer. Then we would have them add the pom-poms to a giant glass container that we kept on our table all week long. I still remember the first order from that market. It was for 204 products. We literally counted out 204 pom-poms on the table and had the customer add them to the jar. She started crying and kept saying, "I did that? I gave all those meals?" She sure did! That same customer sent three more people our way just within that market week. And now our customers talk about the meals they donate all the time. People are good, and they love being part of a solution. We have just been named the eighth fastest-growing company in Charlotte for 2020, and I truly believe our mission alignment is the driving force for our growth.

Fiercely commit to your values. Set your brand values and use them to guide your decision-making. No matter how big or small the decision, use them as your North Star and if a potential decision does not align with your values, walk away. Our company values are: SOCIAL IMPACT. The commitment that we will use our company to make people's lives better. CONFETTI THROWING. The celebratory art of uplifting and recognizing goodness. CREATIVE FREEDOM. The unconventional permission to dismiss the status quo. COLLECTIVE POWER. The shared belief that we can do more together.

UNAPOLOGETIC CURIOSITY. The need to constantly question the norm to rise above it. When I look back at mistakes I've made in hiring, selecting company partners, or new product launches, I can tie each one back to a sacrifice of company values.

Fail forward. The entrepreneur's journey is not for the weak. You will fail. Over and over and over again. The only fundamental mistake in failing is if you choose not to learn from it. Failure is growth. It means you are pushing beyond what feels comfortable, and you are trying something new or something more significant. It's critical for expansion and crucial for change. It's also painful if you look at it as a negative. So, don't. Celebrate failure and share those mistakes, as well as what you learned from them, with others on your team. At Bella Tunno, we have what we call "Failure Fridays." We kick off our meeting by sharing our biggest failure of the week and teaching the rest of the team what we learned from it. It's fantastic to all come together and support each other like that. It invites vulnerability and encourages creativity. Framing failure as a positive gives people permission to try new things, think bigger, and feel more ownership. Failure is not a dirty word, so don't treat it like one.

Find your own measuring stick for success. Success is not just about the money. For our brand, success is measured in meal donations. I didn't feel like our company was big enough to deserve a seat at the table early on. Even as we doubled year over year, our company never seemed to be growing fast enough or hitting the big numbers that I watched other brands hit. Over time, I've learned there will always be a faster-growing, more profitable, larger company than yours—when you measure your success on sales alone. But when your success is linked to something beyond the numbers, your passion, drive, and confidence become explosive. Meal donations drive everything we do at Bella Tunno because that's how we measure success. It's meals donated, not dollars earned. Of course, the money has to be there, and the two things are directly related, but measuring success in meals is so much more impactful. The most important lesson I've learned since starting this company is: When your purpose is shallow, the victories are empty. And when your purpose is deep, the victories are meaningful.

Own your story. Our stories are what make us uniquely who we are. I spent so much time trying to hide from what made me the person I am. It had so much negative power over me. It wasn't until I accepted it as my story that it had positive energy. Our stories are the most powerful form of human connection we can have with one another. They're what make us uniquely qualified to do big things, and they make us raw and vulnerable enough to know we need each other to make it happen. When I started sharing my story on bigger stages, I'd have people lined up afterward to share theirs in return. So many people had similar experiences, and I realized there was freedom in knowing they were not alone.

During one panel I spoke on, a woman in the third row cried the entire time. Turns out, she had just lost her son a month before to an accidental overdose. This was her first week back at work and her first time in public since his passing. Her pain was so raw, she had no idea how to function without him. She came up and hugged me and shared her story. We cried together. She said she felt seen. Some of the undeserved but unshakable shame and guilt she felt was lifted in that conversation. We were both part of a club no one would ever choose to join, but we both found a clearer path forward in that shared connection. She wanted to start helping others and donating her time and resources to families that still had a chance to change their stories.

Owning your story can be painful, but connecting to that pain could be what helps you find your passion and your purpose. I consider that a gift.

### Dreams come true. If you could invite anyone in the world to dinner, who would that be?

That would definitely be Guy Raz, the host of NPR's *How I Built This* podcast. To say I'm a major fan of the podcast feels like an understatement. Guy is such a great interviewer, and I love listening to other innovators, creators, and entrepreneurs talk about how they built their companies from the ground up. I get really excited when a new episode comes out, and I can't wait to listen. I especially love the Resilience series. Hearing how other people, particularly those who are successfully running well-known companies, are getting through these crazy, uncertain times keeps me hopeful and inspired. And since resilience is kind of my thing, those conversations feel so relatable to me.

We've sent several emails to the HIBT team, sharing our story in hopes of being brought on as a guest, but we haven't gotten a response yet. So, if you have some connections or happen to know anyone who works on the show, we're totally open to an introduction. Ha ha!

Seriously though, it's not lost on me that his guests are heavy hitters in the business world, and many of them are the incredible minds behind the world's best-known companies. But to have a seat at that table, and to be given a chance to share the Bella Tunno story with Guy Raz, would be an absolute dream come true for me.

### Where can we follow your work?

Website: bellatunno.com

# CHAPTER 6

# Rick Elmore

ે૭⊷ન્ઉી

*You can't control everything, so control what you can. In business, as in life, there are more factors at work than you could ever account for. Sometimes things turn out the way you expect, but just as often, something unpredictable happens, and your plans go out the window. I've learned to accept this variability and view it as a challenge. I work hard to control what I can while remaining flexible enough to alter course if the need presents itself. There are limitations in every system, and entrepreneurship requires you to recognize them to plan ahead.*

Rick Elmore is a former college and professional football player who is now a successful entrepreneur and sales and marketing expert. As Founder and CEO of Simply Noted, Rick developed a proprietary technology that puts real pen and ink to paper to scale handwritten communication, helping businesses of all industries stand out from their competition and build meaningful relationships with clients, customers, and employees. Founded in 2018, Simply Noted has grown into a thriving company with clients of various sizes across the country, including hospitality, real estate, insurance, nonprofit, franchise, B2B, and others.

## Share with us a bit about your upbringing.

When I was younger, I grew up in Simi Valley, California, and spent most of my time outside playing sports, riding my bike, skateboarding, or camping at the beach. I do not think there was a single day I was not doing something active or outside in my life. I remembered from a young age having a great competitive spirit and liking challenging things. If it was easy, it didn't interest me, or I quickly lost interest.

As a kid, I knew I wanted to do something significant with my life. I had aspirations to be a professional athlete from a young age. In my mind, no matter what, I was going to make it happen. I dedicated most of my middle and high school days to working out and learning everything about football to increase the chances of making my dream a reality. I genuinely loved every minute of it.

## What is your life lesson quote?

I have a few favorite quotes. First, "How you do some things is how you do all things"—My first manager at Stryker, Aaron Hurlburt, and its meaning hit me hard. I never wanted to be known as a guy who cut corners. Second, "Loyalty is royalty"—This was taught to me by Jason Mitchell, who runs the most successful real estate brokerage in the United States. I met him in my early days as an entrepreneur, and he treated me the same then as he does now three years later. Lastly, "What you do speaks so loudly I cannot hear what you are saying"—This was in my college team's meeting room, and I saw it every day for five years. I thought it was a great reminder that excuses do not matter; only results do.

## You have been blessed with success. What are three qualities you possess that helped you achieve your goals?

Dedication—picking something you love and sticking to it. Perseverance—sticking to something when it gets tricky. And passion—without it, people will not buy into your vision.

**Tell us about your career experience before your second chapter.**

Before my business career, I was a college and professional athlete. I was convinced I was going to play until I was 30. After making it all the way to the NFL, my professional football career ended at age 25, and I was unsure what to do. So, I started speaking with mentors and those who have gone through similar transitions. My mentors told me to get into sales because my background was perfect for it.

My first professional business job was with Stryker, where I spent two years learning the ins and outs of selling. Then, I was presented with an opportunity to build a dollar territory for a company called Straumann, which excited me.

**How did you reinvent yourself in your second chapter?**

I kept searching for what that next chapter was going to be. After work, I went to networking meetings, and in 2017, I pursued my MBA (where the idea for my company, Simply Noted, began). I continued to stay in touch with colleagues and friends and joined new clubs, etc. Connecting with people and building relationships is critical in everyone's journey.

**Your second chapter's transition was remarkable. What was the trigger that made you decide you needed to make a change in your life?**

Most businesses are born out of solving problems. While I was in sales, I experienced that it was hard to get in front of my clients. In 2017 when I was pursuing my MBA in a marketing class, my professor explained marketing success rates. Everything was marginal; from email to direct mail, it was single-digit success rates. The professor then ended the lecture and, half-heartedly joking, said that handwritten envelopes had a 99% open rate. I thought that this obvious statistic meant I would have more success by reaching clients with handwritten notes but who had the time to sit down and do that.

I had 400 clients when I was in medical sales, and one year, it took me over two weeks to write and mail my holiday cards. So, to make this process more efficient, we developed a robotic technology that holds a pen and produces genuine pen-written notes. I used it, and I sent out 500 letters to clients, and the response rate was astounding. It was good and worked so well that I literally went all-in and started pursuing this technology to help other companies.

### What did you do to discover you had a new skill set you hadn't maximized?

I would say discovering the power of software, and handwritten notes led me to my second chapter. I was unaware of the technologies out there that could automate our lives' "busy work." Once I started learning about this, it allowed me to scale my productivity by 10x. When I was in sales, I always looked for anything that would give me a competitive edge. One day I found the integration tool Zapier, and it changed my life. If you work within a CRM (Customer Relationship Management) or do anything in marketing, Zapier should be your best friend.

### How are things going now?

Over the past three years, we have averaged 300% growth and have outgrown our office space three times. We are about to move into approximately 6,000 square feet of office space, which is terrific since year one started in a home office.

### Is there someone you are grateful to who helped you along the way?

I am grateful for my wife and family; anyone who is an entrepreneur knows how hard starting a business is and how that affects those around you. Without her and the support I have from my family, this would not be possible.

## Share an exciting moment that happened since committing to your second chapter.

I would say the opportunity to work with Fortune 100 companies has been the most exciting experience for me. Last November, I was asked to present to a company's executive team whose annual revenue is over $1B. This was an amazing opportunity and experience if it weren't for being an entrepreneur or owner of a business that I would never have been able to be part of. This opportunity opened the door and paved the way to great new relationships!

## Have you ever struggled with believing in yourself? If so, how did you overcome that limiting belief?

It is easy to get caught up in how difficult the journey will be in the early days. I like to think of it as hiking a mountain; you are one step closer to the summit's peak with every step. There have been days where it would have made sense to give up, but I am too stubborn to reach the goals that I set for myself. When those difficult times arise, I get to work. Hard work creates opportunity. If I ever fail, it won't be because I didn't work hard enough.

## Typically, I encourage my client to ask for support from those who believe in their vision before they embark on a new chapter. How did you create your support system?

One of the major purposes of life is to build relationships and impact those around you positively. After I got done with playing professional football, this became more apparent to me than ever. In my five years after sports, I tried to surround myself with friends and colleagues who positively influenced my life. This is one of the most important things we can all do because you will have a group you can lean on when you need them most when times get hard.

## Starting a new chapter requires leaving your comfort zone behind. How did you do that?

I am naturally an introvert. It wasn't until I started my career in sales and entrepreneurship that I really started to get outside my comfort zone. I was never the person to walk around the room and shake everyone's hand and start a conversation until it was my job to do that. After a couple of years, I learned I actually loved meeting and talking to new people. It is inevitable if you want to grow professionally and personally that you get outside your comfort zone. If you don't, it is almost impossible to reach your full potential.

## What are five things you wish someone had told you before you started leading your business, and why?

You can't control everything, so control what you can. In business, as in life, there are more factors at work than you could ever account for. Sometimes things turn out the way you expect, but just as often, something unpredictable happens, and your plans go out the window. I've learned to accept this variability and view it as a challenge. I work hard to control what I can while remaining flexible enough to alter course if the need presents itself. There are limitations in every system, and entrepreneurship requires you to recognize them to plan ahead.

Don't turn down opportunities lightly. I like to think about opportunities I've had that seemed small but blossomed into a large account with a boatload of ongoing work. There's a chance I might have considered turning one or two of them down, either because I was too busy, the customer seemed hard to work with, or the size of the job wasn't worth my time. If I had, I would never have known how much future work I was actually turning away.

You never know where your next sizeable opportunity might come from, and you never know where new business ideas might be hiding. That's why I think long and hard before turning someone away. I might think I know what I'm rejecting, but I really have no idea what it might turn into.

Always follow up. In the same way that you never know which opportunities could grow into something bigger, you never know when someone might say "yes." I tend to treat a "no" as a "not right now." My service might not be relevant to a prospect at the moment, but a month, six months, or a year from now, their situation could change. So, I follow up with prospects regularly and often, keeping the conversation going. I find this keeps me at the front of their minds, and when things change, and they often do, I'm there, ready to help.

Don't expect perfection. Winston Churchill famously said that "Perfection is the enemy of progress." I've learned to take that lesson to heart. You can't expect perfection from yourself or other people. If you do, you'll waste valuable time trying to hit an unrealistic benchmark and miss out on opportunities. If I'm writing a proposal, I shoot for good . . . maybe great. But once I have something I'm happy with, I just move forward, trusting that the work my team has done will be enough. Remember what we learned earlier. There's more at work than you could ever account for. Even if you achieve "perfection," it might not be correct or enough. So do your best and then let it go.

Think of challenges as gifts. Challenges are growth opportunities. They can be painful at the moment, but you and your business can wind up stronger, more resilient, and better positioned to take advantage of future entrepreneurship opportunities if you persevere. In this way, obstacles and difficulties are a gift. They force you to rethink assumptions that could be holding you back and create new ways of looking at your situation. Plus, framing challenges as gifts removes negative connotations that can shut you down, preventing action.

**You are a person of significant influence. If you could inspire a movement that would bring the best outcome to the greatest number of people, what would that be?**

You can do anything you set your mind to. I think this is completely true and can be so inspiring if you sit back and really think about it. I usually like to try and reverse engineer my goals by looking at the end goal and mapping out a plan of attack to get there.

**Dreams come true. If you could invite anyone in the world to dinner, who would that be?**

Gary Vaynerchuk (@GaryV) has so much influence; I would love to experience that energy in person. I love positive energy!

**Where can we follow your work?**

Website: simplynoted.com.

Social:    Facebook - SimplyNoted1 / Linkedin.com/company/
            simplynoted/

# CHAPTER 7

# Lisa Gair

❧ ❧

*Determined to keep our home and our sanity, I needed to find a way to help keep our heads above water. So, I trialed a small variety of The Yummy Yank products, initially, at our local farmers' market with about a dozen different types of bakes, all authentically American. I designed a logo, had some banners and business cards printed, and sold my products monthly. Slowly, people began to order outside of the market, and business began to take off.*

Sixty-three-year-old Lisa Gair is an American who has lived in the United Kingdom for the past 24 years. At the age of 48, and as a result of personal and business life changes, she decided to take her passion for food, particularly baking, to a commercial level. She is the founder of The Yummy Yank, a business that bakes authentic, American desserts—baking in the North of England but selling worldwide.

## Share with us a bit about your upbringing.

My early childhood was spent in a tiny town called Arnold, outside of Annapolis, Maryland, where my father owned the drugstore, my mom worked alongside him, and my older sister went to the local high school — and we literally lived above the store. People of all socio-economic backgrounds and colors lived together in this one town where social integration was happening. Arnold consisted of my dad's drugstore, three gas stations, a post office, a volunteer fire hall (where all things social happened), and a six-room schoolhouse I attended.

When I was 11, we moved to a suburb of Baltimore because the site of my father's drugstore was being developed for a supermarket. My father took a job with Rite Aid while thinking about rebuilding in Arnold, but delays in building and discount chains opening, caused him to rethink, and we remained in Baltimore.

When I was 16, my dad had his first major heart attack, which he was lucky to survive. Thankfully, he had given up his three-pack-a-day habit five years earlier, and that saved his life.

As a "daddy's girl," this had a massive impact on me, realizing that someone so important could be taken away from me. As a result, I cut classes and partied hard. After high school, I took time off to live and work on a kibbutz, learning Hebrew in an Ulpan program. When I came back from Israel, I went to college, studying art education and art therapy. Looking back on my first 20 or so years, I gave my parents a run for their money. I had a very happy childhood with many fond memories, good friends that I still have today, and the best family that I could hope for. There were successes and certainly lows, but they have all helped form the person I am now.

## What is your life lesson quote? Can you share its relevance in your life?

"You can't go back and change the beginning, but you can start where you are and change the ending" — C. S. Lewis.

My journey has had various successes and failures, and all need to be learned from and even celebrated. A failure isn't the end of the story; if anything, it's the new beginning. I also like to say "take a hot bath" — in my opinion, and one frequently shared with my family, it will fix anything!

## You have been blessed with success. What are three qualities you possess that helped you achieve your goals?

Life experience. Going through a very bitter divorce with three young children, and my only experiences being a mother and a wife. I needed to redefine my life and realized the only person looking after me was me.

The gift of the gab. My mother, could sell ice to Eskimos, and I seem to have inherited this trait. It serves me well. I build sincere relationships with everybody that I meet in my personal and business life. These are genuine, and people know that I am very approachable, no matter the situation.

Belief in myself. As a person who never moved further than five miles away from her childhood home, I picked my life up at the age of 39 and moved to a foreign country. Although the language is the same, the culture can be very different, and I was determined to rebuild my life. Since making that huge move, I now know that I am capable of doing anything.

## Tell us about your career experience before your second chapter.

When I first arrived in the UK, I worked in my now husband's business, promoting the company's professional audio products worldwide at trade exhibitions. This would lead to "follow-ups" to build on those contacts and relationships made. Many years of this enabled the company (and me) to build strong bonds across the globe in an area of business I had no previous knowledge of. I learned quickly, I believed in the company, and my communication skills got put to good use. Regrettably, the business was subject to insuperable competition from East Asia and also taken over by investors who had no desire to compete on the quality position that the company had endeavored to pursue.

Having lent the company money on several occasions and using our home as security, the principal shareholders worked very hard at destroying all that had been achieved. Shortly after we parted ways, the company went into liquidation. This was a painful lesson on my journey.

## How did you reinvent yourself in your second chapter?

Determined to keep our home and our sanity, I needed to find a way to help keep our heads above water. I trialed a small variety of The Yummy Yank products, initially, at our local farmers' market with about a dozen different types of bakes, all authentically American. I designed a logo, had some banners and business cards printed, and sold my products monthly. Slowly, people began to order outside of the market, and business began to take off.

As this particular farmers' market was slowing down, I decided to take on another farmers' market the following day because I was tired of giving my husband leftover stock for his work colleagues! Upon doing the second farmers' market, I was asked to take a stall at a market with a three-year waiting list because the market manager had never received such positive feedback about a producer before. The markets grew, sales grew, and I now had a viable and successful small business.

## Your second chapter's transition was remarkable. What was the trigger that made you decide you needed to make a change in your life?

I was still baking everything in my home kitchen, with the local authority hygiene regulator's approval. By this time, my product range had grown. Working within the constraints of a home kitchen and available time, I had to make a decision. Being a person who, at the time, did not like to delegate and believing that no one could do it like me, I went back and forth on the idea of finding a contract baker. I was already making a decent living, but my growth would come to a standstill if I continued in my own kitchen. I physically could not do anymore.

I spoke with people in the food industry. I found a company that I was comfortable with and confident about taking The Yummy Yank to the next level after various meetings and discussions. The company that I now work with is primarily a confectionery manufacturer, not a bakery. We worked together to create a complete, professional kitchen/bakery in available space within their facility. They signed a confidentiality agreement which was so important to me as you cannot protect recipes. They are a BRC "AA" rated business which is a globally recognized food production standard.

We shared the same ethos about quality, sustainability, and ethical sourcing. Everything is baked to my standards and specifications with training carried out by me without compromising the product's quality or the ingredients. What comes out of the facility is exactly as I would have produced it. Moving to this facility has enabled my business to satisfy any demands arising from my expansion into multiple major food festivals across the UK, retail, wholesale, and a sizeable online presence.

## What did you do to discover you had a new skill set you hadn't maximized?

I formalized my recipes, never having believed that baking was a science. Having previously measured ingredients with my eyes, I now had to ensure every recipe was precisely detailed to the gram so they could be picked up by any of the trained people at the facility and baked according to my exact specifications. By going through this process, I was able to get to grips with delegating something that had been solely my effort in the past. As a result, I now work very closely with my team, and together we are developing a new product launch in retail outlets across the country.

Initially, I found this process challenging as it was foreign to how I had done things in the past. However, if I was going to be able to take my business to the next level, it was a "needs must." I needed to listen to suggestions from other people regarding costs, scalable manufacturing, and legal requirements regarding food products. This was all a learning curve as I had not previously needed to deal with shelf-life testing and testing for microorganisms. Working together with a team that I trust enabled me to listen and learn.

## How are things going now?

They are going really well! Since working with a contract baker, our business has not been constrained in any way, allowing growth beyond my wildest dreams. When COVID-19 first struck and the lockdown was enforced, an "influencer" put one of my products on her Instagram story. I suddenly saw a surge in sales which made me believe I had been hacked!

Once I realized what had happened, I was terrified about how we would fulfill these orders. If I had still been doing the baking myself, it would never have been possible. Extra shifts were put into place and, despite having to slightly increase our turnaround time, every order was fulfilled in a timely fashion.

We are also in the process of developing a new product to launch throughout the UK and, hopefully, beyond. This has been in development for nearly two years, with advice from technical about water content and various issues that I would not have been aware of before now. Using equipment that would not have been available to me before, we tweaked and tweaked the recipe some more until we finally reached the desired end result. These are exhilarating times.

## Is there someone you are grateful to who helped you along the way?

I can't name just one person that has helped me, as there have been so many, but I can certainly pick out two. My husband and my factory manager.

My husband is my biggest advocate and truly believes that I can do anything that I set out to achieve. He is my accountant, my hard labor, my driver, my business coach, and the one who tries to keep me reined in, with "tries" being the operative word. As a financial director in the corporate world in a previous lifetime, he has embraced the name "Mr. Yummy" as given to him affectionately by our customers and staff.

I could not do without my factory manager. When we first met, he was entirely against the idea of setting up a bakery within their facility. However, after sitting with the owner, accountants, technical and himself for more than eight hours, tasting what I had brought from my products, talking about my vision, hearing about what they do, I slowly watched his mind being changed. From being reasonably negative regarding the whole idea, I could not ask for a better person to be on my side now. He is instrumental in the growth of my business, and I am forever grateful.

## Share an exciting moment that happened since committing to your second chapter.

All businesses seek to promote themselves to as broad an audience as possible. So I was pleased to be asked to feature in Sainsbury's Magazine (then the UK's most prominent food publication) as a woman in business. This feature covered two pages and included a link to a signature recipe online. A well-known photographer spent an entire day with me reenacting a day in the life of The Yummy Yank. A couple of years later, the feature ran again in another of their publications, specifically baking. It was a testament to how far I had come.

**Have you ever struggled with believing in yourself? If so, how did you overcome that limiting belief?**

Yes. After my first marriage failed, I felt that I was a failure at life for some time. I was made to believe, and as a result, did believe, that I was not capable of achieving anything worthwhile.

When working with my now-husband, the belief began to come back that I could relate to people from all countries and cultures and completely understand a new world of technical manufacturing. When The Yummy Yank launched, and its popularity grew, becoming a brand, people still looked at me as if I am the only one behind it. They stand and look in wonder, like a child in a candy store. When people say that my desserts are the best they have ever tasted, even Americans in America, you can't help but believe that what you do is pretty special. I now realize that I am capable of taking on anything.

**Typically, I encourage my clients to ask for support from those who believe in their vision before they embark on a new chapter. How did you create your support system?**

My momentous change was moving to our facility with contract bakers. From first meeting the people involved, I knew that we could work together to build a future, calling on their manufacturing expertise combined with my own baking skills and unique recipes. Making this move involved a relatively large financial commitment that we could not take on ourselves at the time. They invested in and paid for The Yummy Yank equipment, with me choosing what was needed. This was on the condition of 50% being repaid over time against production quantities.

Due to this support, The Yummy Yank sales were unlimited, and the agreed 50% repayment was achieved within six months. Our production partners were very willing to happily carry the remaining 50% as their investment into the future. While you cannot be absolutely sure of this on day one, working together and calling on their specialist skills and knowledge has been how I have been able to grow my business and develop new products. Collaboration of this sort has been the only way to achieve this. With a major new product launch imminent, again we are looking for another support system in a different capacity to the first time, as this is an even more giant leap than the first one. Production expertise, finance, and manufacturing space are all new challenges that are about to be undertaken.

### Starting a new chapter requires leaving your comfort zone behind. How did you do that?

I had reached a point in my business where the potential for any more growth was not possible. As I have said previously, I could not physically produce any more products than was already being achieved.

For several years, I was going back and forth, trying to decide whether or not to take on a contract baker. One of the issues was that I was too small for a larger contract and, to find a smaller contractor, there was every possibility that they could steal my recipes. This did not sit well with me. I had another major dilemma; was I willing to take a significant financial risk at this stage of my life? One reaches a point where they are comfortable financially and know that the future is provided for; I questioned if I wanted to jeopardize that stability.

After much hemming and hawing and discussions with my husband, I knew that The Yummy Yank had the potential to be so much more. I then decided that I had to find the right company to work with and help the business grow.

When I called upon the people I now work with, I did not expect them to take me on, as my business was not what they did. However, when the owner contacted me, within 30 minutes of my email, I honestly expected him to give suggestions as to where to go for support. I did not foresee, for one second, that he would be willing to take on my venture.

**What are five things you wish someone had told you before you started leading your business, and why?**

That I would be working harder than I ever have before in my life! From the beginning, being on my feet baking 14 hours a day to being on my feet at festivals and exhibitions 14 hours a day has now changed to a constant mental challenge to create new products, tweak recipes, adapt equipment, learn, and teach new skills.

Stick to your guns, and you can still be a nice person. I'm constantly reminded that I need to think of my team as employees, not as friends. It was, and still is, a challenge to let my team know if I'm disappointed in how a product is produced or presented. I would not treat anyone differently from how I expect to be treated, so there is a fine line in getting my point across, but still doing it in a way that my team understands and respects. I think it's essential that my team feels valued and that I always have their backs. This can be done with humor and a smile, and, yes, even friendship. As a result, I have a team that listens to what I say. I listen to what they say, and we have mutual respect for each other and what we create.

Be adaptable and prepared for change. I think we can all say that in this current climate. Never would I have believed that COVID-19 would hit every industry so hard and suddenly. This could have been a devastating time for my business but, thankfully, as we are a food production company, we weren't forced to shut the doors when lockdown began over a year ago. As a business that had traveled the nation participating in various food festivals and exhibitions, we faced the terrifying concept that our company would halt, as all such events were canceled. We had to adapt our business and focus on our online potential, honing our social media and marketing skills. We did it, and it proved to be one of our best years to date. As horrifying as this time has been, we rose to the challenge and learned how to change our business plans quickly in unprecedented times.

The value of delegation. This has been my most difficult

challenge. I've always been one to think that no one can do it as good as me! It was hard for me to get to grips with other people sharing the responsibility of my business. To me, it was like giving up a part of something you created. When my customer base first learned of my plans to expand by moving my production to a contract baker, I had one particular customer who declared that he would be able to tell the difference. As a person who had tried every one of my products, he carried out his own taste test. When he came back admitting that the products were unchanged and just as delicious as always, I realized that the power of a good team is invaluable and necessary.

You're never too old to live your dream. Don't let anyone tell you that once you're beyond 50, your life is over, especially if you are a woman. In fact, in my opinion, it's just the beginning. Before I began The Yummy Yank, I can honestly say that I didn't know what I wanted to do when I grew up! But, I guess I grew up because I'm living my dream and loving every minute of it. Belief and knowledge come with living and observing life, and I am proof that anyone, at any age, can achieve whatever they want.

**You are a person of significant influence. If you could inspire a movement that would bring the best outcome to the greatest number of people, what would that be?**

Teach the world. I'd love to ensure that every person across the globe receives education and is taught a skill to enable them to have self-belief, self-worth, and self-sufficiency. I believe that, in the 21st century, no human should go hungry or be suppressed by culture, race, gender, or religion. There isn't anything in any one of us that isn't as valuable as the next person. We all may have different skill sets, but they are skill sets, nonetheless, and all should be allowed to be developed. This comes with education.

I'd also love to start a movement around age awareness and stop the editing of women of age. Because a woman reaches a certain age does not mean that her zest, creativity, passion, beauty, knowledge, and contribution to business and society ceases. I want to bring awareness, especially to the media, to embrace age, particularly in women, as something that should be celebrated, not disguised.

## Dreams come true. If you could invite anyone in the world to dinner, who would that be?

Oprah Winfrey. Oprah is the epitome of success. She overcame so many barriers that could have prevented her from succeeding on many levels. Failure, however, was not an option. Despite poverty and abuse, she had a good education, worked hard to get into media, and achieved, achieved, and achieved. Nothing could hold her back.

I first became aware of Oprah when she came to Baltimore to work at Channel 13 WJZ TV in the 1970s as a reporter. There were a couple of stories that she covered where I briefly met her. She then was a co-host on a local TV talk show with a well-known local TV anchorman. While she was co-hosting this show, I was a guest in the audience with my oldest daughter, about 6–7 months old. The show was on parenting, the struggles, the challenges, the highs, and the lows. Finally, the closing credits rolled with my daughter on Oprah's lap. Even then, with Oprah being virtually unknown to the nation, you just knew that she had something special. She was intelligent, witty, warm, and genuine.

To sit at a meal with Oprah would be awe-inspiring. I would love to hear what gave her the impetus to overcome her obstacles. I would like to discuss how she wants to live out the second half of her life. As a woman of a similar age, I would like to hear her views on women and their relationship with the media. I also would want to know how she manages to stay so grounded and how she handles being one of the most successful businesswomen in the world. We share so many passions—education for all, women's rights, equality. Her philanthropy never ceases to amaze. Dinner would not be enough; there is so much I'd want to ask her. She'd be invited for the weekend!

## Where can we follow your work?

Website: theyummyyank.co.uk

Social:    Facebook - The Yummy Yank / Instagram and Twitter @theyummyyank

# CHAPTER 8

# Kristy Harvey

❧

*It only takes one "yes." In writing and so many other fields, rejection abounds. Lots of agents didn't want to represent me, but one did. Plenty of editors didn't love my manuscript, but one did. It only takes one "yes" to set you on your path!*

A Phi Beta Kappa, summa cum laude graduate of the University of North Carolina at Chapel Hill's School of Journalism, Kristy Woodson Harvey is the USA TODAY bestselling author of eight novels, including *Feels Like Falling*, *The Peachtree Bluff* series, and *Under the Southern Sky*. Her writing has appeared in numerous online and print publications, including *Southern Living*, *Traditional Home*, *USA TODAY*, and *Domino*. The winner of the Lucy Bramlette Patterson Award for Excellence in Creative Writing and a finalist for the Southern Book Prize, Kristy is the co-creator and co-host of the weekly web show and podcast *Friends & Fiction*, and blogs daily with her mom Beth Woodson on *Design Chic*.

## Share with us a bit about your upbringing.

Growing up, I was always an avid reader and often found myself making up little stories in notebooks and journals. But I also loved sports and was very social and lucky to have parents who were always happy to have a house full of my friends.

In my later high school years, I thought I wanted to be a doctor and planned on majoring in biology in college, but when I got an internship at my local newspaper—and my own weekly column—I knew I wanted to explore more writing.

## What is your life lesson quote? Can you share its relevance in your life?

One of my favorites is: "Fortune favors the brave."—Terence

So many of us—myself included—are afraid to put ourselves out there, to fail, to try something new. So, whenever I'm on the fence about starting a new project that feels scary, I repeat those words to myself.

## How would your best friend describe you?

I didn't know so I asked her! This is what she said: "Always put together, ambitious, loyal and bubbly." I am definitely not always put together, but I'll take it! But I know for sure I'm very loyal and ambitious!

## You have been blessed with success. What are three qualities you possess that helped you achieve your goals?

I am doggedly determined, excellent at pivoting and focusing on my goals without holding onto them too tightly. But, sometimes, you have to take a step back to find what's meant for you.

## Tell us about your career experience before your second chapter.

I graduated from graduate school during the recession in 2008. My plan had been to teach or lecture at a college or community college, but I couldn't even find jobs in my area to apply for. Then, while searching, someone asked me to interview for a sales job in the financial services industry. I couldn't imagine. Math was the only thing I wasn't passionate about. But I went through a long and rigorous series of interviews and realized that perhaps this was fit for me after all. I absolutely loved what I was doing, and I learned so much about business and finance in the process that has been utterly pivotal for me in reinventing my life.

### How did you reinvent yourself in your second chapter?

I think when you're a writer, you simply are a writer. There was nothing I could do about it. Even still, I had always said I liked telling real people's stories and never imagined writing a book. So, when I wasn't working on the weekends, I started taking on a few freelance pieces here and there just to keep myself in the game. I also knew I had a book idea, but it took me months to sit down and start writing. I felt like it was a colossal waste of time. But the story just wouldn't let me go.

### Your second chapter's transition was remarkable. What was the trigger that made you decide you needed to make a change in your life?

I had just finished a manuscript I was really proud of, and I signed with a literary agent very quickly, which I knew was uncommon. At the same time, I won the writing contest that ultimately landed me a contract at Penguin Random House for my first book deal. I believed then that this would become a natural career path for me.

### What did you do to discover you had a new skill set you hadn't maximized?

I had been trained in journalism, but writing fiction is an entirely different animal. And, honestly, I didn't think I could do it. I started off by reading books about craft, but I finally realized that I couldn't create something I was happy with under the constraints of all those "rules." Sometimes, I think when we're starting something new, our ego is so terrified that it convinces us we don't know what we're doing. But that deep inner knowing is often there if we can just tap into it.

## How are things going now?

Amazingly! My first novel came out in 2015, and now my seventh novel, *Under the Southern Sky*, releases April 20, 2021, from Simon & Schuster, and I'm under contract for numbers eight and nine, releasing October 2021 and Spring 2022. I never imagined that I would be a *USA TODAY* bestselling author and have this amazing career doing what I love. I'm grateful every day!

## Is there someone you are grateful to who helped you along the way?

So many. My parents were always really supportive of whatever dreams I had, but, really, I think so much credit goes to my husband, Will. It's scary to take a leap into the unknown, to let go of a steady income and a book of business you've worked really hard to build to chase a dream. I remember telling him one time that statistically, I had a better chance of being struck by lightning than getting a book deal. And he said, "They have to publish someone. It might as well be you." His confidence never wavered, even when mine did.

## Share an exciting moment that happened since committing to your second chapter.

My life has changed in many ways. Before the pandemic, I did almost 100 live speaking events annually throughout the country, and I have met the most fascinating, incredible people everywhere

I have been. I feel like my world has gotten so much bigger in the best possible way. But the night before *Dear Carolina*, my debut novel, released, I was so nervous about it coming out into the world. Unable to sleep, I got up and checked my email. I had a note from an early reviewer saying that reading the book had given her the courage to tell her children that she had had a baby as a teenager that she had given up for adoption. She said she felt free like she could finally start living. And I remember thinking that if the book tanked and everyone hated it, and my career ended, that one person's life being changed was more than enough.

### Have you ever struggled with believing in yourself? If so, how did you overcome that limiting belief?

Oh my gosh, yes! Even now, with every book, I always struggle with periods where I doubt my abilities or how good the book is, or a million other things. I have a big box under my bed where I keep beautiful letters from readers, and when I'm having one of those moments, I pull them out and read a few!

### Typically, I encourage my clients to ask for support from those who believe in their vision before they embark on a new chapter. How did you create your support system?

So, this is one area where you could say I failed pretty mightily. I was terrified of failure in this new endeavor. I didn't tell anyone but my husband and parents that I was writing. Over the years, I have made fantastic author friends and, during the pandemic, co-founded a weekly web show and podcast called *Friends & Fiction* with fellow authors Mary Kay Andrews, Kristin Harmel, Patti Callahan Henry, and Mary Alice Monroe. It has taken off in a way we never could have fathomed, and, even better, I have gained the most steadfast, true-blue support system that I could ever have imagined.

## Starting a new chapter requires leaving your comfort zone behind. How did you do that?

It might sound dramatic, but sending that manuscript into the world for the first time is beyond terrifying for a writer. I worked on this book alone for a year, and it didn't seem real. It didn't have to be real. But once I sent it out to literary agents, people were going to read it. People were going to criticize. I might have factual proof that my dream was never going to come true. But, well, sending your work out into the world is obviously necessary, so I had to let it go.

## What are five things you wish someone had told you before you started leading your endeavor?

It only takes one yes. In writing and so many other fields, rejection abounds. Lots of agents didn't want to represent me, but one did. Plenty of editors didn't love my manuscript, but one did. It only takes one yes to set you on your path!

Sometimes, what you don't know is your best asset. When it came to publishing publicity, I had no concept of how "things were done." But I had a successful blog and website, so I knew at least a little about marketing. I asked my publisher for hundreds of advance copies of my books and then asked everyone I could think of with any sort of platform to help me spread the word. I asked my design blogger friends, contacted hundreds of book influencers, and reached out to local newspapers and magazines in towns I would visit on tour. Later, when I mentioned this to other authors, they were astonished. Evidently, people sending out their own books wasn't very common. That's what we had staff publicists for. But, my way went a long way toward giving me a successful debut novel, so I don't regret a moment! I don't physically send the books out myself anymore, but I still do a ton of my own outreach. (And thanking!)

Find your "why." I think it's kind of cliché now, but figuring out why I do the things I do has been a game-changer. The busier I get, the more I have to make hard decisions about what to take on and what to let go of. Knowing why I'm doing what I'm doing always gives me a barometer by which to measure the choices I'm making.

You can't do everything alone. But, of course, in the beginning, sometimes you have to! Sure, I had a team at my publishing house, but I was so green and definitely not a top priority. And I couldn't afford to hire publicists or managers or marketing directors or even an assistant. So, it was me and only me. I still struggle with this, but I have learned that I can't do absolutely everything and do it all well.

Don't forget to look back every now and then to see how far you've come. Every now and then, I feel overwhelmed by how much further I have to go to achieve my ultimate career goals. But looking back at where I started, at things that seemed impossible six years ago that are now commonplace, helps me to remember how far I've come.

**You are a person of significant influence. If you could inspire a movement that would bring the best outcome to the greatest number of people, what would that be?**

Wow. What a question. A laundry list of ways to answer this question is flooding my mind because we have so much work to do. But I have always believed that reading connects us with people we'll never be and gives us insight into people we don't know in a way that nothing else can. In addition, readers are more empathetic, and reading is the single fastest way to lower stress levels. So, for me, global literacy is still one of the most important causes, not only from an educational standpoint but also from the lens of societal change.

## How would you like to be remembered?

I hope that I've created work that makes people happy, that takes them out of the problematic parts of their lives, and gives them respite. That is more than enough for me.

## Where can we follow your work?

Website: kristywoodsonharvey.com / mydesignchic.com

Social: Instagram.com/kristywharvey / Twitter.com/
kristywharvey
Facebook.com/kristywoodsonharvey / Facebook.
com/groups/friendsandfiction

# CHAPTER 9

# Carole Hopson

ॐ ॐ

*Reinventing yourself is not easy. First, it is navigating and learning how to adapt, learn and grow. But that's not all; it's applying those lessons learned to each new endeavor. Starting over makes you vulnerable. I am not afraid to start over and to say that I am new. That means you ask for help and seek mentors and assistance. Second, it's the courage to do something even though change is unsettling. I want to be good. Change is a step-by-step process. Someone who says I want to be President, own my own company, play on an NBA team or lead a movement will need to take many steps to achieve a lofty goal. So, what may appear as an eclectic path at first glance is not really that odd. Instead, a person who is doing something very different is formulating their way. It appears different; because it is. I was a swimmer; you don't get to the other side of the pool in one stroke. It takes many targeted strokes. I want to be in front of the change, not wagging behind it.*

Carole Hopson flies the Boeing 737 for United Airlines as a First Officer, based in Newark, NJ. After a remarkable career as a journalist and an executive at the National Football League, Foot Locker, USA, and L'Oréal Cosmetics, she followed her dream to become an airline pilot. Leaving those corporate jobs at the peak of her accomplishments, Carole went to flight school full time. Family is her first love; flying is her second. She, her husband, Michael, and their two teenage sons reside in Jersey City, NJ. However, her passions don't stop with family and flying — writing is devotion. Her first novel, *A Pair of Wings*, published by Tursulowe Press, is a breathtaking historical fiction that chronicles the life of pioneer aviator Bessie Coleman.

Carole's goals include her book's launch and seeing it become a movie. Both ventures fuel her passion to enroll 100 Black women in flight schooland create a 100 Pairs of Wings pathway.

## You have been blessed with success. What are three qualities you possess that helped you achieve your goals?

I love this question. It is hard to boil blessings down to three; when you are spiritually connected to your higher power, one feels that blessings are in every small wonder and embedded in each big victory. If you force me to name three, I will pick resilience, tenacity, and optimism. These three gifts are linked. It is hard to have one without the other. If one is resilient, there has probably been a mess of trials and challenges. Those difficulties, as the old folks say, will produce "a testimony." Testimony means to bear witness, which is another way of saying that one has learned a lesson and a willingness to tell the story behind that lesson. Attempting a thing, despite the challenge, becomes tenacity. If one is not a supreme optimist, then giving up seems like an option when conflict or trouble stirs. But I rarely want to give up. Optimism is like pixie dust, and added to learning and tenacity, one will try again, dusting off a scrape and powdering oneself instead, with that magic pixie dust. Embracing another go at things with learning and belief then demonstrates resilience.

**Tell us about your career experience before your second chapter.**

My husband of 25 years was a friend from my undergraduate days. Michael has become my best friend, mentor, and love of my life. He says it's okay to feel uncomfortable when taking calculated risks. My "cracker crumbs in the bed" analogy is a metaphor for never settling in too deeply. Getting comfortable is a sign that it's time for a new challenge. Having said that, I always wanted to fly, but it was a circuitous path because it was not a clear one. As a girl, I desperately wanted to pursue this path. But I was a Black female who wore eyeglasses. I had never seen anyone who looked like me on the flight deck. So, I had to figure out how to take a risk and make a significant change. Change happens incrementally, a step at a time. Every big goal is made up of small steps, and humbling oneself to ask for help in each phase is the only way through the maze. Even now, if I want to change jobs from First Officer to Captain, I plan on interviewing every Captain I know. I want to learn from their mistakes and their successes. The power of the interrogatory is a reporter's primary skill, and I carried it with me from my first job into this one.

**How did you reinvent yourself in your second chapter?**

Reinventing yourself is not easy. First, it is navigating and learning how to adapt, learn and grow. But that's not all; it's applying those lessons learned to each new endeavor. Starting over makes you vulnerable. I am not afraid to start over and to say that I am new. That means you ask for help and seek mentors and assistance. Second, it's the courage to do something even though change is unsettling. I want to be good. Change is a step-by-step process. Someone who says I want to be President, own my own company, play on an NBA team, or lead a movement will need to take many steps to achieve a lofty goal. So, what may appear as an eclectic path at first glance is not really that odd. Instead, a person who is doing something very different is formulating their way. It appears different; because it is. I was a swimmer; you don't get to the other side of the pool in one stroke. It takes many targeted strokes. I want to be in front of the change, not wagging behind it.

**Your second chapter's transition was remarkable. What was the trigger that made you decide you needed to make a change in your life?**

I was at a crossroads—I had the good fortune of being a Vice President/Director of an entire training group. Then, I took a job as Director of Human Resources for Logistics for a cosmetics company. I could have ridden out my career in positions like these. They were high-paying roles, and I was beloved by headhunters. But I realized that what was up ahead of me was more of the same. For the next 20 years, I would be doing something I liked but not doing what I loved. That was enough to make me say that I was more afraid to continue in the direction that I was headed than take a left turn and run after what I really wanted to do.

I always tell people to take a discovery flight . . . not I want to be a jet pilot. Go see if you can live in a little plane that weighs less than a minivan because you will be there for several years before you graduate to jet pilot.

Dreams and dreamers—the difference between a dream and a goal is that a goal is a dream with a date. Then once you start, you get momentum, and then once the momentum is in your favor, there is no stopping you!

Let's say you throw out a wish: "I want to make one million dollars," but the first bonus is only $5000. So, you get frustrated, impatient, and then quit. A dream is like this—amorphous. But once you start putting a definition to it, you create steps to achieve your goal. If you see the $5000 this year as a stepping stone and reinvest it in your business, your career, your education, then $20,000 next year and $100,000 the next . . . then $500,000 will follow, and the one million dollars is not so distant. A goal is a dream with a date on it, and every big plan has many little steps. It's incremental.

## What did you do to discover you had a new skill set you hadn't maximized? And how did you find that, and how did you overcome the barriers to manifest those powers?

Some disciplines become strengths—a second language, solid math, writing, and interrogatory power. These are all useful and transferable skills in demand in a world where new relationships are formed every time we start a new trip. There is the technical part of the job, which is embedded in our standard operating procedures. This is indisputable. But there is also the notion of what we call Crew Resource Management (CRM). It's a fancy way of saying that we pilots must get along with one another while on the flight deck—we don't discuss politics, religion, or sex at 36,000 feet. You see, most people get nervous when they start a new job. They get a new haircut, a new pair of shoes, and a new suit to make the best impression, perhaps even practicing introductory conversations on their way to work. But each time we go to work, it's a brand-new crew; imagine Groundhog Day every time. But it's not trite because there is a lot at stake.

Being a police reporter demands communication skills; while these were honed in a corporate environment, a bonus was not having thin skin while communicating. I gained from being a police reporter, living in a corporate environment, and leading inside of volunteer organizations. As pilots, we communicate with our fellow pilots, flight attendants, passengers, ground crew, etc. We have to listen, clarify and get things right. We can't be so thin-skinned when criticized that we don't gain from the lessons. Learning is the experience, and distilling those lessons becomes a requirement.

## How are things going now?

The 100 Pairs of Wings project is an initiative aimed at recruiting and training 100 Black female pilots. We have gotten a head start on the project with a donation from General Atomics. We seek to raise five million dollars. If each woman pays for her own private pilot certificate, this is the first step in a seven- or eight-stage process; this ensures "skin in the game." After that, we will be able to assist and make flying a reality.

## Is there someone you are grateful to who helped you along the way?

Captain Albert Glenn. Although I never stopped flying, as a stay-at-home mom, I had to build flight hours before applying for an airline job. Captain Albert Glenn, ret. FedEx invited me to build time on the plane that he owned. He told me to come down to Memphis. Before we left the parking space, he had me put out my hand, and into it, he put three keys—one to his pickup truck, one to his home, and one for his airplane. "I am headed to India for 17 days; you can bunk at the house and fly with some of your students. Go be the mentor that you want to become." I flew with three young black women, and that experience taught me that to be great, you have to lend a hand to someone else.

Captain Jenny Beatty. When I finally decided to pursue flying, I went on a fact-finding mission. I was an executive at Foot Locker who slipped away to check out this world of pilots at a Women in Aviation Convention. There, I met a woman at one of the networking events. She befriended me, and on the last day of the three-day convention, she gave me a gift. She presented me with an elegant coffee mug. There was a picture of Bessie Coleman on the front, the same one on my book cover. On the rear were two paragraphs that talked about her life. I was stunned. I had never heard of Coleman before. With a master's degree from an Ivy League university, I, a college graduate, considered myself well-read. Yet, I had never heard of Bessie Coleman. So, I decided to write a book to tell the world who this extraordinary woman was. And the woman who gave me the mug, Captain Jenny Beatty, became one of my best friends.

First Officer Randall Rochon. There is a lot of work that goes into a major airline interview. Randall helped to prepare me with technical questions and an HR-style mock interview. Randall was an excellent guide; he is a respected and trusted colleague.

First Officer Andrea Weeks. Andrea is a love. For eight years, she continued calling, writing, and telling me that I should apply to the regional airlines. I interviewed and got the job. Andrea sent me care packages every other weekduring the nine weeks of training—aromatherapy, fruit, candles, tea, a coffee mug. This one said, "She believed she could do it, so she did!" Then Andrea interviewed and was hired by United. When it was time, and I had built the requisite flight hours, she encouraged me to join her at United, and she wrote me a letter of recommendation attesting to my dogged persistence.

Captain Ray Evans. Maybe one of the best instructors I have ever had. He is all in. Professional, always studying, and renowned not just at United but also in our industry as THE subject matter expert on the Boeing 737. He is excellence personified at United Airlines and in our industry. I have learned many lessons from him.

## Share an exciting moment that happened since committing to your second chapter.

My children have an example of a working mother who dedicated time to them yet pursued a career. When my eldest son was in pre-school and the children were asked what their parents did for a living, Joshua said that his father was a banker and his Mommy was a "pirate."

I showed up for pick up, and I had some explaining to do.

Arghhhhh! We all still laugh about that to this day. I learned that my children were less interested in our occupations and more interested in our time together. Being a mom has been one of the greatest joys of my life.

### Have you ever struggled with believing in yourself? If so, how did you overcome that limiting belief?

I rarely struggle with believing in myself. But because I am different from the average airline pilot, in both race and gender, I have often had to prove myself again and again. But competence and excellence are their own remedy.

### Typically, I encourage my clients to ask for support from those who believe in their vision before they embark on a new chapter. How did you create your support system?

Years of investment—both in professional organizations where I volunteered and worked feverishly and as a mom, with my community of moms. I was a stay-at-home mom for 14 years. Just days before I started my job as a pilot at United Express, my eldest son had broken his leg. It was a severe break, and he used a wheelchair. Schooling had to be done at home by teachers whom the district would send to our home. My husband's full-time job took him away for long hours, and the family friend who was supposed to be a part-time caregiver had to be moved into a full-time role. It was expensive and challenging on many fronts. On the day I left for training, rain poured for hours.

I will never forget the tenacity of my eldest son. He was outside in the rain, playing wheelchair basketball. Telling this story will enrage some moms. How could she leave? She's heartless. At 50, I had a decision to make. We had wanted my husband to retire, but financially, we just didn't feel secure enough. It was a difficult choice, but one that I discussed with my husband and children.

They all agreed that it was now or never for me. I came home from Houston to New Jersey every chance that I could. I prepared meals before leaving and froze them; I would go back to class on FedEx to spend the day with my family and then crawl into class by the 8:00 AM start. It was a challenge, but it was what I wanted. I have a friend who says that every treasure is surrounded by dragons—in this case, family, passion for flying, time, and energy were the treasures. Each required protection, and I did my best.

The simulator sessions were grueling, as it was a vertical learning curve going from slow piston aircraft to .8 Mach speed jets. Still, I relied on that support network I had built and nurtured both as a professional pilot and a parent. My mentors were just a phone call away. Cpt. Ray Evans stopped by with a roller bag and tested a classmate and me. "My work here is done," he announced as we passed his test. He wheeled away from us, but honestly, he was only a phone call away. We had sufficiently answered his questions about every button and switch on the overhead panel. Phew!

**Starting a new chapter requires leaving your comfort zone behind. How did you do that?**

When I left L'Oréal Cosmetics, I was making six figures a year. My first flight instructor job paid $17 per hour. But I had never been happier professionally in my whole life. Money is not happiness. Satisfaction and self-worth are my measures of both success and self-respect.

**What are five things you wish someone had told you before you started leading your endeavor, and why?**

Planning and decision-making. Start here.

Organization. Critical for long-term success.

Communication. You can never over-communicate critical things.

Time. Keep moving. You can make many things, but you can never make more time.

Money. Try to start with some. It will go fast. Decide and spend well. Save and fundraise as soon as you are able. When you get backers, keep them. It's not just their money that counts; it's their belief in your mission that lasts.


## You are a person of significant influence. If you could inspire a movement that would bring the best outcome to the greatest number of people, what would that be?

I feel so strongly about so many important causes. Homelessness, shelter pets, clean drinking water, recycling, and fair and equitable education tug at my heart. But I believe in focus. Where you invest your maximum energy, there will be maximum return. I think that 100 Pairs of Wings is a movement that people can identify with, get behind, support, and grow.


## Dreams come true. If you could invite anyone in the world to dinner, who would that be?

Wow. Let me start my list! David Rogier, the founder and CEO of MasterClass. LeBron James and his *I Promise School* initiative fits with what I want to do. Sir Richard Branson. He is an icon in the aerospace and STEM (science, technology, engineering, and math) world.

Isabelle Wilkerson. She has single-handedly chronicled the Great Migration. Oprah. Her dedication to education, women's issues, great movies, and books makes me swoon. Ron Howard and Ava Duvernay, both remarkable storytellers. Jurnee Smollett. An actress who would make Bessie proud. Michelle Obama. I would like a blurb on my book from her and a matching blurb from her husband, Barack. David McCullough. He wrote a book entitled, *The Wright Brothers* and took all of us along on their pursuit.

## Where can we follow your work?

Website: carolehopson.com
Social:    YouTube channel

# CHAPTER 10

# Rachel Binder

ॐ ॐ

*Change the menu. The perfume industry has been marching on the same road for about 100 years. It is time to change how we look at perfumery, include practices outside of the current colonial construct, and explore new kinds of smells. The same is true in life. Sometimes you just need to switch things up and look from a different angle.*

Rachel Binder is the "nose" and brand owner of Pomare's Stolen Perfume based in Venice, California. In addition, she is a Certified Sommelier with the Court of Master Sommeliers and a wine educator at Future Food Institute and Matthew Kenney Culinary. Rachel is a winner of the Art and Olfaction "Aftel" Award for handmade perfumery for her work on the perfume *Rasa*. She also is the recipient of the New Luxury Awards Brand of the Year for sustainability in natural perfume.

## Share with us a bit about your upbringing.

I moved a lot growing up and wound up in a small town in Northern Maine at around 12. We lived in the country surrounded by potato farms and pine trees—there were no malls, no internet, no fancy clothes, but there was a tremendous work ethic. We got off three weeks every fall from school to work the potato harvest. People were so proud to work the land that their parents or grandparents had worked. I lived not far from the Great Northern Maine Woods, which is a kind of wilderness that many can never experience.

The seasons were mighty. When we were snowed in, my sister would sit down with my father, open the almanac, and dream of all of the places she would travel. I still have the aromatic imprint of the clothes, incense, and jewelry my sister brought back from India. Saffron, silk vine, sandalwood, and dhoop sticks seemed to speak of the entire world I had yet to experience. Even this year on lockdown, I often felt like I was channeling my sister as I used the time to dream of far-away places.

### What is your favorite life lesson quote? Can you share its relevance in your life?

"Leap and the net will appear." —Julia Cameron, *The Artist's Way*.

You cannot wait for permission from the world to take that risk, to pursue your dreams or goals. That may never come. At some point, you have to jump off that cliff into the unknown, take that scary risk and go for it with every fiber of your being. The universe has wonderful ways of showing up to support you when you do.

To release and bottle my 2019 vintage perfumes, I had to take time away from my then day job, take out a loan and put absolutely everything on the line. It was nothing short of terrifying, but I felt that determination down to my toes and knew it had to be done. One of the best decisions I ever made.

## How would your best friend describe you?

She says that I'm effusive, brave, and fiercely creative. And she loves that I would take three trains with her to buy the best chocolate in town.

## You have been blessed with success. What are three qualities you possess that helped you achieve your goals?

For so much of my life, I never really fit in. I always saw the world from a different perspective, which can be difficult, especially when you speak your truth. But, on the other hand, it's kind of its own superpower because I don't live with the idea that I have to be anything like anyone else but myself.

Secondly, I have been studying the senses through many mediums for my entire adult life before ever becoming a perfumer. I studied aromatics in the theatre, storytelling (in several mediums), and through years of yoga and meditation, grew my palate through blind wine tastings and culinary exploration. So, I credit not just my nose but the variety of non-traditional ways that I approached my work as a perfumer and brand owner. It can be scary to make perfume in a different way than most everyone else. But the response has been so overwhelmingly supportive. Especially the niche perfume community on Instagram, who have been so wonderful.

Lastly, I am crazy determined. I may have taken the long road—especially considering the journeys I took in the first chapter. But, I never gave up on learning new things or myself, and that's what led me here.

## Tell us about your career experience before your second chapter.

Having spent most of my life in the arts also means I've had many day jobs! All of them were valuable, even if I didn't know it at the time. I worked in retail, restaurants, the environmental sector, and the wine world. From each of those jobs, I learned something integral to launching my own business. Working as a sommelier was vital to my developing my brand. It was so wonderful being able to shift a person's taste perspective with a suitable pairing recommendation. I think people really want to taste and smell new and different things—it can turn an average Monday night into a special memory. This is just as true of a new scent as it is for a wine varietal you have never tried.

**Your second chapter's transition was remarkable. What was the trigger that made you decide you needed to make a change in your life?**

About ten years ago, I was waiting tables and twisted my ankle. I knew I wasn't on the right path in my life, so I went home and reevaluated. That is when I dreamt of the idea that would become Pomare's Stolen Perfume. Several years later, the real impetus that would come and put a fire under me was being pregnant and unmarried. It gave me absolute clarity and urgency.

However, the most exciting trigger came in April 2020. I worked in wine sales and felt like my values were no longer aligned with the company I worked for. So, when I was laid off on April 3 due to COVID-19, I felt a deep sense of relief because it would give me time to really focus on my perfume business. I considered it "my shot."

I didn't have to wait long for an affirmation of this new direction. On April 14, my Artisan perfumer nomination was announced for Art and Olfaction Awards (for my work on *Rasa* when I created the first natural whole fruit passionfruit accord out of local fruit from the farmer's market). This gave me a certain amount of international attention that has been vital in running my business, even on a lockdown. Then, when I won for handmade perfumery in September, I became one of a handful of people ever honored on the international stage for handmade craftsmanship in the olfactory arts. I'm still just so humbled and honored.

**What did you do to discover you had a new skill set you hadn't maximized?**

Initially, I didn't even consider that I had an extra skill set; I just knew that I couldn't find the smell I wanted in a perfume. I already didn't wear synthetics due to chemical sensitivity, so there were fewer options on the market for me. So, I just went down the rabbit hole and started reaching out to the people I knew that were most conscious about their ingredients: bartenders, winemakers, distillers, native plant experts, organic farmers, and chefs. I had started my own redwood extractions years earlier. Still, it took tons of research and trial and error to determine the wellness and safety components of using a totally new ingredient like redwood in perfume.

To sum up, it was really researching, blind faith, and a knowing determination that whole ingredient perfume was not only possible but could be a significant player in how people connect to the earth and shift their energy. My willingness to create outside the dominant paradigm in perfume is what led me to even knowing I had this skill set. It was something that I wouldn't let go of. It was an insatiable curiosity.

**How are things going now?**

I am so grateful every day that I get to create art that gets sent worldwide; it is such a blessing! This year I created the first vintage of my peach-based perfume, Beulah (made from the best peaches of the summer, "Cali Red" from Frog Hollow Farm), where I made the entire peach accord from those peaches using some winemaking techniques. There are few things in this world as gorgeous as a ripe peach at the height of summer! Although, my daughter loves to "steal" my peaches and passionfruit, I always have to order extra when I get it for the perfume.

I have also really loved getting to know people around the world in the oud community! Oud is a perfume ingredient made from aloeswood and is one of the most expensive ingredients on the planet. Working with real oud is nothing short of magic. One moment it is fruit, then a flower, yet another moment it is chocolate tobacco, and another barnyard. But, when combined with natural ingredients, it takes on a life of its own. Working with natural oud is true alchemy and both challenging and joyful.

My *Rasa* perfume got listed in many Best of 2020 Lists from Indy100 (The Independent) to a renowned perfume reviewer, "Therapeutic Fragrances." However, being listed next to luminaries, Ensar Oud and Agar Aura (distilling legends in the oud world) was humbling.

## Is there someone you are grateful to who helped you along the way?

Many people have helped me along the way. I have neighbors who have been in my quarantine bubble helping move and set up my new studio. I have very supportive friends who have helped me with everything from marketing to logo design to offering judge-free listening zones.

My mother raised me with a core idea that is central to my work as a perfumer and business owner: "There is nothing more perfect than nature." Because of her, I studied Rachel Carson (*Silent Spring*), grew up on whole ingredient food, and without the presence of many petrochemicals. As a kid, her response to almost everything was, "Why buy that from a store when you can just make it yourself?" She also would pass on many of the ancestral and family stories that would come to inspire my work. She was the first person who thought that starting a natural perfume brand was a great idea, and she has stood by it ever since.

## Share an exciting moment that happened since committing to your second chapter.

The Art and Olfaction Awards were in September, so they took place over Zoom. My friend and fellow perfumer, Layla of Fūm

Fragrances, wanted to make it extra special for me. She cooked me a spectacular meal, including a saffron cake paired with my nominated perfume and a handmade gold leaf pear in honor of the award itself. Other friends from the wine world sent me a bottle of Leclerc Briant Champagne to honor the occasion.

I made leis for Layla and her partner Kenny and a floral lei for myself (as is traditional in Raiatea, my grandfather's island in Tahiti). I knew that winning was a long shot because so many spectacular niche perfumers from all over the world enter, so I wanted to make the day unique no matter what. So, when the Aftel Award for handmade perfumery came up, my heart was in my chest. The Aftel Award is named for Mandy Aftel, a legendary natural perfumer I was lucky enough to study under. At that moment, my friend pretended to "go to the bathroom" and went into a different room where she started on the live broadcast. She gave me the most gracious introduction I could have ever dreamed of (made even more special because she is also incredibly talented and had been there for me since the day we met) and was able to hand the "Golden Pear" award to me in person. It was just the most magical day, made even more special by the fact that I could share it with a friend.

### Have you ever struggled with believing in yourself? If so, how did you overcome that limiting belief?

I absolutely had many limiting beliefs about myself! For a time, I even drew people towards me that would reflect this perceived lack. At every turn, I would find another major fear or insecurity that would drain my energy and focus from a project. Ultimately, I had to step away from the people who did not reflect my possibilities. I stopped allowing unsolicited advice into my life, and I had to lose some friends in the process. Some traits I had perceived as a weakness turned out to be a strength for running a business.

Several entrepreneurs that I worked for through the years would fall short of my idea of how perfect you had to be to achieve that position. They were juggling a house of cards in some cases, but their vision, daring, and determination always persevered.

I have come from generations of folks who did not have two cents to rub together. My grandmother Beulah (who I have a perfume named after) had to raise a houseful of children virtually on her own. But she always magically pulled through. When I feel that I may not pull it together, I think of her and how she hustled to get food on the table for my mother and uncles, and aunt. When I am most afraid that I am not enough, I place my feet on the ground, close my eyes and try to pull the spirit of the ancestors that came before me. I remember that I am the granddaughter of Beulah, and I remember that those who came before me are still here, whispering their wisdom.

**Typically, I encourage my clients to ask for support from those who believe in their vision before they embark on a new chapter. How did you create your support system?**

The most significant first step was learning to trust my own counsel. Other people may not yet share your vision, so trusting your own viewpoint is everything. From managing self-care to how I spent my downtime, I had to find ways to be my own first line of support. This included stepping away from those who did not reinforce positivity. Next, I had to decide that I was utterly committed to my vision, and when I did, more and more supportive and amazing people came into my life and helped hold up my dream of Pomare's Stolen Perfume.

**Starting a new chapter requires leaving your comfort zone behind. How did you do that?**

The old comfort zone had simply stopped being comfortable. To get there, I had to commit myself in somewhat uncomfortable ways to make things move forward. For example, in my first year in wine sales, I ran a pop-up perfumery on the weekends over the holidays. I was exhausted but entirely determined.

## What are five things you wish someone had told you before you started leading your business, and why?

Trust yourself. There are alleged "experts" and opinions out there that could derail you if you let them. Your vision has to be strong enough so that it is unshakable.

Think Champagne. Bigger is not always better, but excellence is everything. Champagne makers have a limited quality yield every year, and they produce the exact number of bottles they can do exquisitely. This is the perfect model for high-quality ingredient natural perfume and for life. So do what you can with the utmost grace and excellence.

"Everything is energy," says Champagne maker Herve Jestin. As an artist, this phrase always meant so much to me, but as a business owner, I think of it often when it is time to shift my energy from what I can't control to what I can do for my brand's progress.

Never forget your busser. You must be able to do every job within your company with competence to hire the strongest team. Anyone who has worked in a restaurant will tell you that bussers are some of the hardest workers who don't get enough thanks. So, make sure you are always willing to do that hard work with a smile—it creates an important tone.

Change the menu. The perfume industry has been marching on the same road for about 100 years. It is time to change how we look at perfumery, include practices outside of the current colonial construct, and explore new kinds of smells. The same is true in life. Sometimes you just need to switch things up and look from a different angle.

**You are a person of significant influence. If you could inspire a movement that would bring the best outcome to the greatest amount of people, what would that be?**

The movement would be toward whole ingredient natural perfume that reflects the quality of soil, seasons, and energetic imprint of the land. Many "naturals" are made predominantly of natural synthetics, which lack the same feeling tone as complete ingredients. In reflection of the emergent field of quantum biology and biophysics, there is an "x" factor in how certain aspects of nature work in concert with one another (a scientific difference between incorporating ingredients that contain the spark of life and creating without it).

For so long, we have viewed the world through the lens of everything being isolated from one another. One doctor for your heart, one for your head, as though things weren't connected. Dr. T. Colin Campbell talks about it beautifully in his book, *WHOLE: Rethinking the Science of Nutrition,* and I find it relevant when it comes to perfume. We are so used to everything being isolated and separate we have forgotten the magic that happens when whole universes of ingredients come together. Synthetic jasmine has a small number of molecules, whereas a natural can have thousands. We are only just now beginning to understand our sense of smell! We do know that study after study supports the therapeutic benefits of real jasmine. So, putting on a truly natural perfume can offer therapeutic aspects of those plants. Suddenly, wearing perfume can shift your day, your energy and connect you to the earth itself.

When scientist Luca Turin introduced his "Vibrational Theory of Olfaction," which argues that we experience scent more similarly to sound, it made sense that something containing more high vibrating materials would offer something unique to the wearer. In biodynamic farming (which has yielded some of the most beautiful grapes globally), even the tides and the moon are connected to when it is optimal to reap and sow. The most spectacular wines were made from excellent farming practices and reflect the soil and seasons. As a result, they age well and evolve with time. So why shouldn't natural ingredient perfume offer the same thing?

## How would you like to be remembered?

I hope to look back in 20 years and be remembered for helping shift the current dominant paradigm about perfume. But, of course, mostly, I want to look back and see that I could be a good parent to my daughter and role model. I want her to see the world through her own lens.

## Where can we follow your work?

Website: pomaresstolenperfume.com
Social:    Instagram @pomaresstolenperfume

# CHAPTER 11

# Nancy Volpe Beringer

ৡ৶৵

*Education is key, but some important traits that can't be taught and are just as valuable, such as flexibility and a sense of humor, are priceless assets. The pandemic proved the need to be flexible and pivot to respond to consumer needs. In addition, my sense of humor and positive outlet served as lifelines during the pandemic. As an example, I personally had to create a very tight safety pod. And therefore, as a 66-year-old who had not been to a hair salon for over a year, I decided that I might as well keep growing my hair and donate it once I returned to my regular salon appointments. FYI: Because I opted not to go to a salon, I still supported the salon and pre-paid for appointments I would normally have kept.*

At age 64, Nancy Volpe Beringer, a Philadelphia fashion designer, made Project Runway's history as its oldest ever contestant. She left her corporate-type job at the pinnacle of success and enrolled in Drexel University's three-year graduate fashion design program, graduating at the top of her class at 61. As one of the final four in Project Runway's Season 18, her finale collection reflected her brand's mission of inclusivity, adaptive design, and sustainability.

**Share with us a bit about your upbringing.**

I grew up in a traditional middle-class family as the middle child of five girls and one boy who was the youngest. I lived in Levittown, PA, a new suburban planned community with mostly one-income households where families had one car.

**What is your favorite life lesson quote? Can you share its relevance in your life?**

Without realizing it, I have lived my life by "making fear my friend," a quote I recently heard shared by Project Runway judge Elaine Welteroth. I have so many examples of how I quietly but determinedly have lived my life fearlessly. An early memory dates back to when I was 11 years old and selected two summer enrichment programs. Then, as fate would have it, I signed up for a sewing class. But quite surprisingly, as a timid child, I also enrolled in public speaking for my second class. It seems that "making fear my friend" and never letting a challenge stand in my way of pursuing a dream ultimately led me to become a fashion designer at age 61.

**You have been blessed with success. What are three qualities you possess that helped you achieve your goals?**

Fearlessness. It seems I thrive when I start a project, job, or task that I simply don't know how to do. For me, the opportunity provides a chance to learn and create my own vision. I find this ironic since I never really enjoyed going to school. Submitting my application to be a contestant on Project Runway the year I graduated from fashion school exemplifies total fearlessness. I knew I would be competing against more established and younger designers, but I also believed that my fearlessness would be my compass for survival.

Creativity has always been my oxygen. Without it, I simply don't thrive. Managing a five-year project to celebrate our education association's 150th anniversary (where I worked) provided the most varied and comprehensive creative opportunities. Besides the expected grand party, my continuous creative process leading multiple teams resulted in a documentary on New Jersey public education, our first permanent historical archives, and museum display; numerous publications, programs, and events commemorating our history, an original theatrical production in collaboration with the Trenton Symphony and American Historical Theater, and of course, a culminating grand ball celebration.

A fantastical imagination. I remember when I was about to turn 50, and Season 1 of Project Runway aired. I thought, "What would have happened if I turned my love of sewing when I was a young teenager and studied fashion design?" I fantastically imagined that I could have been a contestant on Project Runway. The fantasy apparently never left my imagination. Not only did I become a fashion designer, but on Season 18, I became the oldest ever competitor on the show at 64, where I finished as runner-up.

## Tell us about your career experience before your second chapter.

Based on my resume, some may say that I've had many second chapters. However, I consider my life as a fashion designer as my second chapter, as I am finally living a truthful and authentic life. Before designing, my fearless philosophy and the varied skills I accumulated along my journey provided the strong foundation for a successful second chapter as a fashion designer.

Sadly, the business ended after a few years when I expectedly found myself a single parent of a two- and a four-year-old. At this point, I decided to earn a bachelor's in business education to blend single parenting with earning a full-time income. Unfortunately, I found I had to supplement the inadequate teacher's income with multiple part-time positions and/or freelance projects.

Fate intervened, and I found myself once again with the opportunity to accept a job in an area where I had absolutely no formal training or experience. I began working in the field of communications for a leading education advocacy association. I initially worked as an editor of their monthly publication but moved into media relations and speech writing. Eventually, I transferred into community organizing and leadership training culminating in a management position after 18 years.

### How did you reinvent yourself in your second chapter?

I became a fashion designer at age 61. I accomplished this by leaving my job at the pinnacle of success and using my life savings to earn a master's of science in fashion design from Drexel University.

### Your second chapter's transition was remarkable. What was the trigger that made you decide you needed to make a change in your life?

I so clearly remember the exact hour that my life forever changed. It was three AM on another sleepless night. Instead of rejoicing in getting a much sought-after promotion, I found myself slowly suffocating as my new managerial position did not provide my much-needed opportunities to create. At three AM, thoughts about my sons and their successes consumed me. I actually felt envy towards my younger son as I observed him using the Internet to study photography and videography to supplement his income as a struggling musician. It was at that moment that I asked myself, "If I was young again, what would I want to learn?" I wanted to study fashion design. My life changed forever when I dared to not only honestly answer the question but immediately take action. Within months, I left my job at the pinnacle of success and used my life savings to enroll in the three-year master's program in fashion design at Drexel University.

## What did you do to discover that you had a new skill set you hadn't maximized?

When I walked into my first class at Drexel University, I knew I found my home. I finally accepted my destiny. I quickly understood that fashion design could provide my inexplicable need to create. Initially, I thought my lack of illustration skills could impact my success as a designer. I even signed up for a set of intense illustration classes before starting the graduate master's program.

I discovered I could learn these skills but that they did not come to me naturally. I overcame this barrier by accepting that the traditional design method of illustrating did not suit my skills or process. I did not let this awareness deter me. But instead, I embraced my approach of using the fabric to lead me. By playing (AKA draping) the material, I could discover what it wanted to be. My process became my strength rather than a weak link.

## How are things going now?

I hit the ground running as soon as I graduated. In addition to my many successes, I felt so fortunate that I had countless opportunities to achieve my never-ending goal of using my fashion to support organizations that help disadvantaged children and empower women.

Philadelphia's iconic fashion concept store, Joan Shepp, showcased my graduate collection in their holiday window the same year I graduated. Philadelphia rapper and Grammy nominee Tierra Whack selected me to design her premier Grammy Red Carpet look just a year after graduation. Philadelphia Fashion Week invited me to kick off their fashion week while the city's namesake magazine honored me with a "Best in Philly" fashion design award. Finally, I ended my 64th year when I made history as the oldest ever designer on Project Runway. As a final four, I showed the most inclusive and sustainable collection ever to walk in a Project Runway finale.

And then the pandemic hit, and just like countless businesses, I had to rework my goals, cancel events, and realize that I would not continue in-person custom designing. Mere survival became the immediate goal.

## Is there someone you are grateful for who helped you along the way?

Reflecting on my second chapter's journey, I appreciate that many of my strengths can be reflected in the unique traits of both my mother and father. I am also eternally grateful for the unconditional support and encouragement my husband of 10 years has shown. He has steadfastly cheered me on from the beginning. When I returned from New York after touring one of the top fashion schools, I remember exuberantly telling him about a one-year associate degree program. He smiled and then pulled out one of his many nicknames for me. He said, "Calm down, fireball." And then the advice he shared changed my life. He said, "I thought you were doing this for the love of learning, so why are you rushing the learning?"

My extreme goal-oriented persona took a deep breath and absorbed these wise words. I soon enrolled in the three-year graduate fashion design program right in my backyard at Drexel University in Philadelphia.

## Share an exciting moment that happened since committing to your second chapter.

One of the most exciting and proudest moments happened on Project Runway when I got to design the winning red carpet look for Para-Olympiad Tatyana McFadden. It was as though the Universe reached into my soul to use my desire and fashion to make a difference. Creating the adaptive design look for this inspirational wheelchair-user inspired my Project Runway finale collection at

New York Fashion Week and has been the motivating force behind my goal to enter the adaptive design market.

### Have you ever struggled with believing in yourself? If so, how did you overcome that limiting belief?

Yes, I have struggled with believing in myself. I lived a secret life as a victim of adult bullying. Not once. Not twice. But multiples times. And I felt shame. I felt there had to be something wrong with me to allow myself to be bullied. I found out I was not alone. Adult bullying is much more prevalent than you might think. In fact, I imagine many have experienced it without understanding it.

The actions of adult passive-aggressive bullying can seem relatively insignificant. They can be covert and subtle. They happen in the workplace, in families, and in schools. Bullying happens everywhere. But just because it is common and appears as a minor incident doesn't mean it isn't harmful. I have felt the pain and humiliation. I have felt isolated. I have had my work sabotaged. I have been ridiculed behind my back. I have been gossiped about. I have been given the silent treatment and ignored.

But it wasn't until I accepted that fear could be my friend that I could also become honest with myself. Once I acknowledged that I was being bullied, I began to stop the cycle. When I stopped being afraid and confronted by a bully, I started my road to recovery and became a bullying survivor.

### Typically, I encourage my clients to ask for support from those who believe in their vision before they embark on a new chapter. How did you create your support system?

I learned to share my dreams with my husband instead of internalizing them. From that moment, there hasn't been a time where my husband has not selflessly supported and encouraged me to be my authentic self.

**Starting a new chapter requires leaving your comfort zone behind. How did you do that?**

Once I accepted my destiny as a fashion designer, it meant leaving my comfort zone of financial security. I had survived single parenting when I worked 3–5 jobs at a time. So, resigning from my new executive position and walking away from a stable income frightened me. But once again, I made "fear my friend." Single parenting also necessitated a conservative financial lifestyle and savings plan. I decided to use my life savings to pay for my education.

Despite the already intensive 80+ hour weekly school schedule, I also accepted a graduate assistant position during the program. The 20-hour weekly position offset my tuition and provided stipends that enabled me to purchase my industrial equipment after graduation.

**What are five things you wish someone had told you before you started leading your business, and why?**

Fashion designing is extremely physically demanding. I wish I had been better prepared physically. I believe my onset of chronic arthritis in my neck while at school results from my age and the physical demands of designing.

Be prepared to share your life on social media. Social media, especially Instagram, plays an essential role in my business. For example, I have learned that while I might appreciate the professional photos of models showcasing my designs, my followers actually want to see more of me behind the scenes.

Fashion designing requires lifelong learning. I remember fitting one of my first clients and realizing I needed to learn much more about fitting my clients' unique bodies. Fortunately, I presented a confident front, and my client left feeling empowered and beautiful.

You don't need to do it alone. While I started my eponymous brand directly out of fashion school and worked solo for the first couple of years, there is so much more to success than just designing and constructing a garment. I feel fortunate that I've had the support of student interns, fashion influencers, Philadelphia industry leaders, and the public support of my brand, and perhaps most importantly of all, a young, talented, and passionate assistant.

Education is key, but some important traits that can't be taught and are just as valuable, such as flexibility and a sense of humor, are priceless assets. Personally, my sense of humor and positive outlet served as lifelines during the pandemic. The pandemic proved the need to be flexible and pivot to respond to consumer needs. As an example, I personally had to create a very tight safety pod. And therefore, as a 66-year-old who had not been to a hair salon for over a year, I decided that I might as well keep growing my hair and donate it once I returned to my regular salon appointments. FYI: Because I opted not to go to a salon, I still supported the salon and pre-paid for appointments I would normally have kept.

### You are a person of significant influence. If you could inspire a movement that would bring the best outcome to the greatest amount of people, what would that be?

As a survivor of decades of adult passive-aggressive bullying, I would like to continue to use my voice to educate others about the harm caused by adult bullying—a much too commonly accepted behavior.

### Dreams come true. If you could invite anyone in the world to dinner, who would that be?

Without a doubt, I would love to formally meet and design for First Lady Dr. Jill Biden. I have so many things in common with First Lady Dr. Jill Biden that I believe it is my fate for us to meet. We both consider ourselves Philly girls. We are both educators and advocates for refugees and immigrants. And neither one of us has let our age deter us from doing what we were meant to do. For me, being a relevant fashion designer and for Dr. Jill Biden, fearlessly taking on the role of the First Lady of the United States.

## Where can we follow your work?

Website: nancyvolpeberinger.com.
Social:    Instagram @nancyvolpeberinger

# CHAPTER 12

# Beth Campbell

ও৵ৎ৳

*Of course, there is no downtime—once you decide to open,
it is a full-out sprint. But I quickly realized that structuring
quiet time is essential. This may appear to be difficult
but putting your oxygen on first is the only way you can
help others. Although everyone wants to hear from you
personally, both internally and externally, you must set
boundaries that allow you to exhale, recharge, and sharpen
your focus on what truly matters. To aid my process,
I believe in a Rolling 90-Day Plan that allows me to align
time and energy collectively around priorities while providing
strength and avoiding details that do not serve our greater
goal. It enables us to say yes to priorities and no to items
that distract us.*

Beth Campbell is an award-winning architect and visionary leader in the industry. With nearly 30 years of global design experience, she just launched her own company, Campbell House. The firm is a full-service interior design studio focused on high-engagement design solutions for hospitality, entertainment, food and beverage, and the corporate workplace. Most recently, Beth served as CEO of Wilson Associates, a top global interior design firm. Before Wilson, Beth was EVP and head of design for Westfield Corporation and spent 16 years at Gensler as a managing partner and global account director.

## Share with us a bit about your upbringing.

I am so fortunate; I had an amazing childhood with loving parents, a great family, and exposure to education and discovery. When I was eight years old, I knew I wanted to be in the architecture and design field. As with all parents in the '70s, my parents spent Saturday nights at friends' houses for card club or a cocktail party. Of course, the kids were shuttled along and promptly placed in the yard or basement to play (Midwesterners and Easterners get it—we all had finished basements tricked out as game rooms).

Whenever I would come from the night's events, I would wait for my parents to fall asleep, draw the host's house, and promptly redraw it, with many design improvements. A few months into this pattern, I came home to find a drafting table with a T-square and table lamp. My dad had one requirement: "Please just wait until your mother is asleep; we don't want her worrying you're not getting enough sleep!"

By the time I was 10, I had worked weekends at one of my family's restaurants, and during the week, my father arranged for me to stop by a local architect's office on the way home from school. Turns out he studied under Frank Lloyd Wright and had an abundance of FLW books, all of which I worked my way through over the coming months. I was hooked.

## What is your life lesson quote? Can you share its relevance in your life?

"There is no limit to the amount of good you can do if you don't care who gets the credit."—Ronald Reagan.

Through this simple quote and fantastic way of making choices in life, I feel President Reagan set a tone that has resonated with me my whole life. It uncovered a key to many people's success; although you must be diligent and committed, you can go much further with a strong cast around you. The former President's comment also sheds light on how my ability to understand people and reading situations is actually a gift, which has opened countless doors for me.

Inside this formula, I have had a great opportunity presented to me that has allowed me to go farther, much faster; exemplified most adeptly via our launch of the Campbell House. We have compiled an exceptionally talented team who is quick to lead, while they are quick to take a position of followership when needed. While it does indeed take a village, sustainable success is achieved when all players understand that the credit goes to the collective.

## You have been blessed with success. What are three qualities you possess that helped you achieve your goals?

I genuinely believe that the person you see before you today is based on growing through the example of those who went before me, who surrounded, challenged, and encouraged me. And hard work and the blessings of good fortune.

Inside this understanding that we are all an amalgamation of time, people, and circumstances, I would say a true gift I am fortunate to possess is the ability to read a situation. I have always been able to see people for who they are and not just how they choose to show up. Combining this with the ability to quickly understand a situation, much like Tiger Woods reads a putt or one sees the edges of a puzzle take shape, I can see events, conversations, design projects, and business scenarios all as a series of pieces that are meant to fit together.

Another quality people have noticed in me is staying calm in a storm, choosing to see the scenario as a set of variables versus a personal afront or obstacle. Realizing that if I slow down and study the situation, there is always a pathway forward. This honed skill expresses itself in perseverance, in good times, and bad.

Even as a young child, I held a passion and commitment to exposing the good in everyone. For reasons beyond my comprehension, I see opportunity inside everyone with whom I interact. I can tell you that this occasionally ends in disappointment, but most of the time, my belief in them as a person resonates so profoundly that they unleash their full potential.

A great example of all these gifts, skills, and abilities coming together would be when I lived in Chicago. We had a major client that was extremely important to the firm, but tensions boiled over, and the client was planning to terminate us. My boss, Lamar Johnson, asked me to go with him to size up the situation. We listened to the client's complaints and frustrations, which included yelling and fist-pounding on the table. Throughout, I asked multiple questions to ensure we understood their frustration. Finally, after an hour of taking copious notes, Lamar and I asked for a 15-minute reprieve to formulate our response. We came back in the room with a complete list of changes we would implement immediately, each addressing the concerns that we surmised from our line of questioning. The client was so happy that we heard them and that we were able to fully acknowledge the real problem, which until that day had been unspoken, they not only reinstated our entire contract—they doubled our scope.

## Tell us about your career experience before your second chapter.

I have had the great fortune to work with some incredible people and clients throughout my architectural career. From starting in smaller firms straight out of university to my 16 years with Gensler, I was able to gain exposure to a breadth of project types, and more importantly, an extensive range of leaders, all of whom had an imprint on my evolving leadership style.

My most vital learning moments were experienced while working at Westfield Development. I learned the focus and pressures of the Developer/Owner's side of the design equation, all while being exposed to the most influential boss I have ever had—Bill Hecht.

Bill embodied development prowess, design sensitivity, operational knowledge, and passion for bringing out the best in his people. In addition, Bill showed me a model of success built on providing a culture that allows your collective team to grow and shine. I cherish these lessons.

Through these relationships, I have been able to express my passion for design excellence around the globe. Further, my extreme desire to learn and grow has built a global business, design, and executive coaching skill set that has served me very well in honing my craft. Bringing to bear my passion for design, my appreciation for global cultures, and my in-depth industry knowledge will allow us to build the Campbell House brand successfully.

## How did you reinvent yourself in your second chapter?

I see my life as an endless series of evolutionary steps, but this stride into entrepreneurship was the most significant change yet somehow the most natural. During this all-important transition, I worked very closely with my Executive Coach, focusing on developing my entrepreneurial skills, working on high-impact activities, and setting solid parameters on my vision to easily decide where to spend my time and energy.

## Your second chapter's transition was remarkable. What was the trigger that made you decide you needed to make a change in your life?

The decision to take the plunge was an evolution, a series of events, discussions, and opportunities. But in all good storylines, there was a specific conversation that changed my line of thinking. While in Cabo for a friend's 50th birthday, I had a conversation with Jill, who brilliantly asked, "Beth, is this something you can fix, or are you riding this to the bottom." Then and there, overlooking the Pacific Ocean with coffee in hand, I realized that although I had solutions to revive the brand, I was faced with a leadership board that had no desire to have the brand succeed. So, on that February morning, I knew I had to make a sizeable change, that I had to leave.

Through the Spring of 2020, I was interviewing for similar CEO positions and quickly realized that my goal and passion for impacting our industry, influencing lives, and making a difference meant I needed to form my own team on my terms. So, by July, I realized I was going to launch my own Creative House, based on learnings from all my experiences, both good and bad, to create an environment that fosters collaborative, flexible, and meaningful work. And to this day, all my files are labeled "Project Cabo."

Being fortunate to have an insatiable desire to learn has continually opened my world of opportunity. While living in San Francisco and working on a global optimization project with the most extraordinary team, I realized that I am not just an operationally driven project manager. My passions were evolving to include broad set problem solving for major design projects, which could be solved by applying people's skills and desires with the proper focus towards their own growth opportunities. Through my MBA and my Executive Coaching curriculum, I realized that blending design, management, and emotional intelligence in one brain is a potent cocktail.

Most recently, the realization that I thrive on the entrepreneurship side of the leadership equation has served as a powerful accelerant in my personal fire to make a difference. Pushing the boundaries of all my skills and vision to create a collective of market leaders and revolutionaries that are customer-oriented and personally vested in the wholesale opportunity impacting people through the built environment has proven to be quite intoxicating.

## How are things going now?

The launch and start-up process has been overwhelmingly astounding. The wave of support and encouragement as we embark on our new path has been nothing short of inspiring. I realize that it shows signs of hope in a difficult time for many by us striking out. Alongside us taking a sour opportunity born from the collapse of a once-great brand and building up a new House that will provide innovative services for the clients while fostering a culture that will develop and grow talent, has received words of support from around the globe.

To begin with, I feel I am one of the fortunate ones on this earth. I have the most amazing family; I am truly blessed with exceptional parents and siblings. Being adopted at birth, one cannot stop considering that I could have ended up anywhere, or even never taking a breath—I believe every step that I have taken in life to be an opportunity to fulfill my destiny.

Further exposure to a long list of fascinating life influences has to be topped by Lamar Johnson, an architect, friend, and awe-inspiring family man I had the fortune of working for in Chicago. Lamar encouraged me to lean into my "odd in design world gifts" of emotional intelligence, business sense, and design appreciation. He also taught me the invaluable lesson of the importance of authenticity and transparency in leadership. And, he taught me that brilliant, caring humans can make a difference.

## Share an exciting moment that happened since you committed to your second chapter.

I have found it interesting how excited everyone is for us in our breakout moment. Still, more interesting is how the conversation always goes to "creating an environment of freedom for designers to pursue passions while keeping personal priorities in sight" and "getting away from the bureaucracy that drowns passions." I find this front of mind for so many in our industry as we emerge from the constraints of the pandemic; we are all longing to reconnect and ensure we maintain flexibility in our work while contributing to meaningful pursuits. And typically, size is quickly translated to oppressive bureaucracy, but I believe it lies in the culture, leadership, and corporate behaviors. While it is true that many large firms are focused on profit which drive individualist rewards for slaying the dragons, firms of any size have the choice to set priorities that emphasize teamwork and collaboration while rewarding focus on qualities and characteristics of the group rather than an individual. I feel strongly that this pivot will be one of the beautiful outcomes of a dark season in our global history.

### Have you ever struggled with believing in yourself? If so, how did you overcome that limiting belief?

The first is to acknowledge that we've all been there; we question ourselves or our ability. And we all need to recognize we are driven by some type of fear. So, the question one needs to ask—is the fear moving you forward in motivation or causing you to be shy and in the shadow of what you can truly become?

Throughout my career, I have had the good fortune to see the positives that crop up from what is perceived as a lousy situation, which has oddly driven behavior in me that fosters excitement when things seem to be going sideways. During the chaos, I have learned that the brightest opportunities lie, so instead of backing away, I fill with adrenaline and lean into the uncertainty as I know with certainty that something spectacular is waiting on the other side.

**Typically, I encourage my clients to ask for support from those who believe in their vision before they embark on a new chapter. How did you create your support system?**

I am fortunate to have learned early in life the power of building a solid network of people around you. People who complement your skill sets and challenge you to be better while knowing when to encourage and guide you. I took extensive strides leading up to the launch of Campbell House to set our core leadership team, which is a highly skilled and widely diverse set of players that all complement and constructively push each other.

The other willful and concentrated effort I made before launching Campbell House was to tap into my circle of deep and distinguished advisors. I spent hours running through business plans, branding strategies, scenario planning, disaster planning, and vertical integration models. Each person brought their own perspective and insights. But most importantly, as I communicated my vision through these series of conversations, it forged a crystallization of my purpose and mission. These conversations have proven priceless.

**Starting a new chapter requires leaving your comfort zone behind. How did you do that?**

Interestingly, at this turn, I found it terribly uncomfortable to "stay the course" or "stick to a conventional career path." During the evaluation and discovery phase, the evolution that took place quickly opened up to one answer: to open my own Creative House. With the pent-up demand due to the pandemic, adding openings in the marketplace created by underperformance or competition closing shop, I knew in my heart of hearts that the time to act is now. So, I did.

## What are five things you wish someone had told you before you started leading your business, and why?

Breaking constraints. We all bring our learned behaviors with us; most of these learnings are good but, in some instances, what served us in the past will hold us back in the future. For some, it was the belief that the individualistic survivor mentality is the road to success; protect my personal assets, and I will win. Others feel that corporate hierarchy is at play no matter what leadership states. Then others cannot break the patterns of "this is how it has always been done." No matter the mindset or how great the individual players might be, as the leader, you must set clear expectations with solid definitions of success and repeatedly share the vision and mission to provide all comfort they are valued, not alone, and that together we are stronger.

Structuring your time and energy spend. Of course, there is no downtime—once you decide to open, it is a full-out sprint. But I quickly realized that structuring quiet time is essential. This may appear to be difficult but putting your oxygen on first is the only way you can help others. Although everyone wants to hear from you personally, both internally and externally, you must set boundaries that allow you to exhale, recharge, and sharpen your focus on what truly matters.

To aid my process, I believe in a Rolling 90-Day Plan that allows me to align time and energy collectively around priorities while providing strength and avoiding details that do not serve our greater goal. It enables us to say yes to priorities and no to items that distract us.

Hyper-uncertainty. Uncertainty, everyone deals with it differently. This we know. But uncertainty in a start-up compounded with the excitement of adventure is a new cocktail for me to consume. It is a hyper dose that drives all players to extremes, almost into "violent agreement" at times, myself included. Recognizing this and openly talking about it—both cause and effect—is a sure recipe to get everyone into "harmonious agreement."

Run your race. We have all dealt with stressors in our careers, ones that change as each season evolves. In my most recent stint, I found an incredible amount of negative stress, constantly digging out of problems created by someone else. Yet, although it sounds overwhelming, there was an odd comfort in the consistency and pattern. As an entrepreneur, the stress is very different; it undulates wildly and is highly positive. Although this feels more positive on the surface, adrenaline pushes 24/7 can be terribly exhausting. But I am here to tell you, I fall asleep each night with a smile on my face, both from the knowledge that I will not wake to a fresh stack of issues created by someone else, but more so by the sense of accomplishment and impact, we have each day.

Run with purpose. I have found a deep need for daily reminders to avoid distractions. The guiding voice is not to fight battles that are not on your doorstep and do not engage in battles between you and your purpose. Instead, I have found it almost therapeutic to recognize distractions and use them to take a minute to step back, reframe their top priorities, and then choose to act. Winston Churchill said it best—"You will never make your destination if you stop to throw stones at every barking dog along the way." Daily, and sometimes hourly, we need to remind ourselves that we are on this earth once, and we cannot keep wasting energy on frivolous distractions. Keep your mission and purpose front of mind at all times.

## You are a person of significant influence. If you could inspire a movement that would bring the best outcome to the greatest number of people, what would that be?

Be kind. I feel so strongly in today's political and global economic environment that we need to be better to our neighbors. Our world needs to realize that we are better together and focus on the greater good and not just our own self-interests. Fight the urge to delve into polarizing actions and conversations.

It can start with one person—with you, by being nice to a stranger with an authentic compliment, a moment of caring, a text of encouragement, and a simple smile. Then, it can be dramatically contagious. As we are on this earth one time, we owe it to ourselves and others to make the most of our contributions. So today, choose to be positive and know that every interaction is a chance to learn and give back. You cannot always choose your circumstances, but you surely can choose your reaction. Make a difference, live the "no, not me; you first" attitude.

Kindness is contagious, start a new pandemic today with the love and respect of humankind.

## Dreams come true. If you could invite anyone in the world to dinner, who would that be?

We are so fortunate to live in a time of brilliant and inspirational leaders—players with a wide variety of skills, talents, and passions. So many I would enjoy having dinner with—Warren Buffett, a superb businessman who is always led by his grounding core values. With her incredible fashion and business sense, Anna Wintour jointly displays the epitome of arts fundraising at the Met Gala each year. Brené Brown courageously shares her emotional rawness and keen ability to constantly capture the human desire to become better. And Elon Musk, a risk-taker, entrepreneur, and visionary all in one pair of perfectly selected Nikes. Need I say more?

## Where can we follow your work?

Website: campbellhouseco.com
Social:   LinkedIn - Campbell House Company Page Admin
            LinkedIn – Beth Campbell

# CHAPTER 13

# Lindsay Yaw Rogers

ॐ∞

*Understand your mission and work from there. I made
the mistake of focusing strictly on the execution and
production of work, and it landed me in a place where
I was not attracting the clients I enjoyed working with.
Instead, focus on the impact you ultimately want to have,
then work backward to figure out the "how."*

Lindsay Yaw Rogers is a brand story strategist and owner
of Raw Strategy. She coaches entrepreneurs, athletes, and
business owners to leverage their personal and brand stories
to stand out, position themselves as leaders, and inspire authentic
relationships with their customers.

## Share with us a bit about your upbringing.

I am a storyteller. It started when I was three—my parents took
our family of six on a sabbatical to some of the most remote
places in the world—trekking across Kashmir, sailing in Tonga,
and visiting tribes in Kenya. Rinse and repeat in 1988 when we
traveled around Europe in a VW van stuffed with road bikes, hiking
shoes, and baguettes, and we met the most fascinating people
along the way. These memories were seared into our cells and

would inform how I perceived experiences from age three on—normalcy was the enemy; people and their stories were the gifts. These trips embedded something in how I see and approach life's dynamism—stories can shape and impact our lives and our future.

We grew up in Aspen, Colorado, and amid those trips, I was a student, a friend, a nature lover, and a ski racer. Starting at age 13, I traveled throughout the US, then internationally, primarily in speed events (downhill and Super G), which means I'm most comfortable at speed in the cold. I formed relationships with people from all over the world, and it helped me understand that people are my fuel as I loved them as much as I loved the idea of racing at the elite level.

That has formed much of how I have pivoted my business—helping people understand that bravery and confidence in their story will ultimately cause far more impact and stronger relationships than if they chose not to share their story.

## What is your life lesson quote? Can you share its relevance in your life?

"Tell the story of the mountains you've climbed. Your words could become a part of someone else's survival guide."—Morgan Harper Nichols.

I reread this quote daily as it gives me license to feel that what we go through in life, relationships, and business is worth it—if not to us at the moment, perhaps to someone you connect with in the future. So, share the stories, share your insight, reflect on what you've learned and be honest and transparent as possible, quite literally, become someone's guide to overcoming their own monster.

**You have been blessed with success. What are three qualities you possess that helped you achieve your goals?**

I believe that you never learn less. It is a concept my dad taught me that has allowed me to obsess over my craft and not feel like it is wasted time. It allows me to take miniature tangents in life that always beget so much knowledge, insight, and experience that I lean on often, in part because I've come to understand that a narrow path means a limited perspective.

I strive to be more interested than interesting because people remember what questions you asked them, not how much you shared about yourself. Recently, I was messaging someone I viewed as a mentor on Instagram, and I was sharing how she inspired me and why. I asked her a few out-of-the-norm questions, expecting nothing in return as she has hundreds of thousands of followers. Instead, she wrote back and said nobody had ever asked her that, which spurred a longer conversation, an interview, and now it is becoming an article on *Business Insider*.

I believe that the back of the statue matters. In other words, the unsexy stuff that happens on the backend of your craft, business, and life matters. It matters how you communicate with your audience, employees, and peers because that will become your legacy. The front of the statue—the side everyone sees—is just the byproduct of the precision of the backend of your unfun stuff behind the scenes. This, again, harkens back to relationships— take care of the ones nobody will see, and they will take care of you.

**Tell us about your career experience before your second chapter.**

I've never wanted a boss, so I've made decisions along my career to make sure that doesn't happen—or if it did, it was brief, and I extracted all the knowledge I could from experience. In that, after college, I landed magazine editor jobs at *Outside* and *Skiing* magazines. A few years in, I ached to travel, so I launched my freelance career, which took off. I traveled across the globe as a freelance journalist for *Outside*, *National Geographic Adventure*, *Skiing*, MSNBC, Yahoo! and many more. I traveled to Annapurna in Nepal documenting Ed Viesturs' final 8,000m peak; to northern Norway retracing the steps of Jan Baalsrud, a forgotten war hero; to Utah where I was buried in a simulated avalanche to report on the physiological repercussions of oxygen deprivation and hypothermia; to Canada, Chile, India, and numerous locations around the world. In that time, I learned what mattered to people and why. I learned how to use language to connect and translate highly personal stories into universal truths. In essence, I learned how stories can transform people.

At a certain point, I began being approached by larger brands to build story-based content that would resonate with their audiences on a deeper, more personal level. So, I worked with MSNBC, Yahoo!, Twitter, Toyota, Aetna, and NBC on several Olympics projects, plus many more on building sophisticated and strategic content programs. It was exciting, and I loved it—at the beginning. It looked like a fabulous and lucrative career from the outside, and it was for a while. I was traveling to incredible places all over the world. I was interviewing fascinating people. And working with iconic brands the world was familiar with. But I was trading time for dollars and not building a business I was proud of, nor a legacy I could point to for my kids. Plus, I was away from my two young children, and the guilt was overwhelming as I felt I wasn't doing anything well—working, nor being the mother I wanted to be.

### How did you reinvent yourself in your second chapter?

So, in 2019, I took a break, stopped traveling for work, and started taking an uncompromising look at what I wanted in my life, how I could leave a lasting legacy that changed people for the better. I took courses, hired coaches, read every personal development and business book on the shelf today, and realized several things.

First, I wanted to help people, not just brands. Second, I wanted to give them a holistic transformation in themselves, in the stories they told the world, and how they were perceived by others. I came up with a brand story framework for entrepreneurs, coaches, athletes, and businesses that allows them to discover that their own story is aligned with their values and strategic business goals and share it with the world to stand out and build movements. That is what Raw Strategy is all about today.

### Your second chapter's transition was remarkable. What was the trigger that made you decide you needed to make a change in your life?

This may sound trite, but I was sitting in a hotel room in Washington, D.C., exhausted from working all day, and I called my daughter to tell her good night and that I had to stay an extra day to do some more work. She started crying on the phone, so disappointed I would miss another soccer game, another dinner, another book at bedtime, and she refused to talk to me. I started crying and decided this life that looked so successful on the outside wasn't worth it on the inside—she was. And so were my husband and my son. If you don't have your relationships, you have nothing. So, I decided to build a sustainable business that allowed me the flexibility and freedom to share valuable time with my family and friends while investing heavily in the growth of others. In that time, I realized that what my business was not giving back to me was that sense of discovery and service—how I could develop something substantial to change someone's life for the better.

### What did you do to discover you had a new skill set you hadn't maximized?

Up until this point, I had worked with giant corporations and teams within those organizations. And, I was always the hub of the content wheel, project managing the process of content production, so my communication had to be excellent. However, when I pivoted my business to work in a teaching and coaching capacity, I found that I was far more influential and compelling and had a greater impact. Speaking with my clients allowed me to delve deeper into their challenges, empathize with their struggles, then put systems in place to solve them right then and there. With larger brands, it is harder to be as effective in a short time frame than small and medium-sized businesses or even individual people.

The other thing I discovered is that, over time, I had created a process framework that I used with clients that made the projects immensely successful—but it was in my head. So, as soon as I catalyzed that into a step-by-step roadmap to bring clients through, I saw immediate results, and I wanted to make sure smaller companies and entrepreneurs had access to this framework.

## How are things going now?

So tremendously great! This year has been a foundational year for my business, and I feel fortunate that it has also brought in so many clients that I am thrilled to be working with. With my brand story framework, I have attracted people during a major pivotal moment in their life or business, or at their inception, along with several large and thriving brands. And the process I bring them through tends to eradicate their fear of change, fear of not being successful, and fear of not having meaning and purpose in their lives and businesses.

For example, I'm working with a Muslim woman who is launching a new business training and coaching families on keeping the Muslim faith embedded in their children's lives. She has taught me so much about her faith, and she has had massive epiphanies about her business and her life that have massively transformed how she sees her future. That, to me, is the greatest gift a client could give me.

I'm also working with a professional athlete and major influencer in England who has arrived at a point in her career where she wants to pivot her message, her offering, and how people perceive her. So, we are working together overhauling her personal brand story and documenting every step of her journey together through IG lives, Clubhouse rooms, and social posts. It is so much fun!

And I'm also working with a major brand in the construction space, creating a brand anthem video that will break with so many norms in that industry—we hope to disrupt the status quo in an otherwise very conservative space.

### Is there someone you are grateful to who helped you along the way?

A few people have become mentors for me, all of whom I owe a debt of gratitude to as they have unknowingly guided me down this new path. Unfortunately, due to the constraints of COVID-19, I lost my biggest client in early 2020. As I picked myself back up during the lag, I started listening to podcasts and reading books by Brendon Burchard, Amy Porterfield, Tim Ferris, and Seth Godin— all of whom have radically different styles, teach on radically different topics, and have radically different skill sets. But each one provided a tiny step I could take to regain my footing as I pivoted my business.

### Share an interesting or exciting moment that happened since committing to your second chapter.

People keep finding me, and it surprises me every time. As I shared previously, the biggest surprise I've had is reaching out to a huge influencer and having them respond so favorably that we have partnered on guest posts for prominent business publications together. When in doubt, don't be afraid to ask—you might just be surprised with the answer.

**Have you ever struggled with believing in yourself? If so, how did you overcome that limiting belief?**

This is not a moment in time as it is a perpetual problem that all entrepreneurs face continually because you are constantly creating and innovating new things. That said, a few years ago, I had come off of a vast, all-consuming project, and I was struggling to land projects that I was inspired by (I had plenty that just paid the bills). I wondered why, what was wrong with me, my approach, my style, etc. I happened upon a few books (*High Performance Habits: How Extraordinary People Become That Way* by Brendon Burchard) and two programs (from Seth Godin and Bo Eason) where I honed my skills articulating stories, as well as nailed down the lessons and reasons for my own journey, then encapsulated my experience into a specific and results-driven framework. I also worked future-casting what I wanted my business to look like and how and who I wanted to be in it. Once I had a clear visual of my mission and my company's mission, from there, it was less about me and more about execution.

**Typically, I encourage my clients to ask for support from those who believe in their vision before they embark on a new chapter. How did you create your support system?**

I've struggled with this because I'm intensely independent. But, in the past two to three years, I have joined several mastermind groups that have allowed me to let my guard down, learn how to grow my business in new ways, and accept precious feedback on how to do that. It has given me a massive boost of confidence in scaling my business.

**Starting a new chapter requires leaving your comfort zone behind. How did you do that?**

I love risks. I grew up ski racing downhill, and my dad was an entrepreneur who always instilled the idea of exploration being the root of all great teachings. In that, I don't find myself intimidated by being out of my comfort zone, but that doesn't mean I am always in my comfort zone. I'd say one of the ways I am frequently out of my comfort zone is by trying to teach to new audiences every month. Whether on Facebook teaching someone else's FB group or at a conference, or on a podcast, I have had to force myself to come off as confident and fully in control when I sometimes feel entirely out of place. To offset that, I typically overcompensate and tend to be overly prepared for anything!

**What are five things you wish someone had told you before you started leading your business, and why?**

Understand your mission and work from there. I made the mistake of focusing strictly on the execution and production of work, and it landed me in a place where I was not attracting the clients I enjoyed working with. Instead, focus on the impact you ultimately want to have, then work backward to figure out the "how."

Be prolific from day one. I spent years focusing on executing large projects but didn't think strategically over the long term. So, I wasn't producing content across multiple platforms that allowed others to see how I work and think, what frameworks I use, etc. Being prolific pays off as it will enable people to find you more readily, trust you, and ultimately buy from you. Since becoming a guest poster on *Business Insider*, *Medium*, *Thrive Global*, and numerous large Facebook communities, I have seen a considerable uptick in revenue.

Position yourself as a leader. Building on number one, once I pivoted my business, I began to see the importance of positioning yourself as a leader in your own space. So, get on podcasts, write guest posts, and teach to other people's audiences as frequently as possible to be seen as a leader in whatever industry you're in. Of course, that means you have to build it into your schedule every single week.

Never burn a bridge. Nobody had to tell me this, but I live by it as I firmly believe that relationships are the root of all happiness and success in life. Even if a client isn't as enjoyable as you wish, treat them as you want to be treated, and it will come back to you tenfold. For example, I had an experience a couple years ago where I was tapped to be the content lead for a large national brand. I declined the job offer but sent them a document outlining several key strategies I would have used to accept the job. That company became a client since and has referred several clients as well.

Accepting help is a key to growth. Nobody is their strongest alone. My hubris when I was young made it so that I had the bullheaded mind of someone who didn't want to admit that I didn't know anything. So, I'd fake knowing anything, and I believe it cost me a couple years of growth in my business. Instead, adopt a learner's mindset and know that asking for help is what will skyrocket your personal and professional aptitude and ability to grow.

## You are a person of significant influence. If you could inspire a movement that would bring the best outcome to the greatest number of people, what would that be?

I want people to find confidence in themselves by discovering the most compelling parts of their story—then sharing it with others as a social contribution. The primary way we all learn is through knowledge transfer, and sharing stories is the way our brains are designed to receive that information. I suppose Oprah made a career out of encouraging people to share their stories. I'd like to piggyback on her movement and allow people in the business space to find the confidence, and critical paths, to sharing their insight as a way to guide others on their journey.

## Dreams come true. If you could invite anyone in the world to dinner, who would that be?

At the moment, I'd love to sit across the table from Tim Ferris or Guy Raz. I've been studying how Tim Ferris asks questions in his podcast interviews as he is the master, and therefore tends to get unique answers out of his very practiced guests. Guy Raz is another master interviewer, but his style is so different than Tim Ferris'. I appreciate in Guy Raz his humility as it transcends the questions and makes the interview feel like you're sitting across the table from whomever he's interviewing. I'd love to sit across from both of these guys and ask them about their interview process and how they've honed their craft of becoming, quite literally, a craftsman of questions.

## Where can we follow your work?

Website: rawstrategy.net
Social:   Instagram @rawstrategy / LinkedIn - lindsayyaw

# CHAPTER 14

# Droz & Lord

જાૐ

*You will need to lean on others and ask for help. We are a scrappy, bootstrapped start-up, and we love that about ourselves. When something needs to get done, our initial inclination is to learn and save money by figuring it out ourselves. There's a YouTube video for everything these days! This spirit brought us a long way but could only take us so far. We were determined to create a beautifully designed, high-performing, natural product. For that, we needed to hire experts. And, as mentioned above, we've begun to outsource those pieces of the puzzle better accomplished by others. Stay scrappy as long as you can, but understand you will need to invest in the experts for some things. There are so many incredibly talented freelance professionals to take the burden off of you; it will pay for itself in the long run. Plus, it's fun to have a few collaborators.*

Lindsay Droz and Kristi Lord, founders of L'AVANT Collective, are on a mission to create high-performing, plant-based cleaning products safe for families, pets, and the planet in thoughtfully designed, countertop-worthy packaging. Lindsay and

Kristi set out to create a new generation of hard-working, eco-, and design-friendly household products. Not satisfied with the status quo of choosing between harsh cleaners that do the job (yet are harmful to people and the environment) or plant-based cleaners that lack the performance and aesthetic appeal, these executives-turned-entrepreneurs left their jobs, invested their savings, and took a chance on a second career to provide better options—one sustainable choice at a time.

## Share with us a bit about your upbringing.

Lindsay: I grew up in Seattle with my parents and my younger brother, Chase. I'm beyond blessed to have been raised by loving, encouraging parents who instilled kindness and the belief that our dreams could come true. It was a great childhood, and to this day, my best friends are girls I played soccer with when I was six, met in middle school, and grew up with. While my brother and I were always provided with life's necessities, my folks encouraged us to work for those extras things we wanted. When I was 15, I was obsessed with clothes, couldn't get enough of them. So, I obtained a work permit and got a job at the local GAP store (in my teenage mind, GAP was a luxury brand!). Because of my age, I could only work 10 hours a week at any one job, so I went around the mall and picked up a couple of additional jobs and soon could afford those clothing items my parents didn't quite consider necessities.

Kristi: I was born in Billings, Montana, the middle child of two siblings and two step-siblings. My parents divorced when I was in elementary school, and when it came time for high school, I opted to move with my dad to White Salmon, a small town in Washington state. Dad was a full-time teacher and an avid outdoor enthusiast, so I was on my own a lot of the time. This lifestyle afforded me plenty of freedom, but I was also expected to take responsibility for my own schedule, transportation, and finances.

I landed my first job as a dishwasher at age 14 and worked

various other positions throughout high school, from food prep to front desk clerk at a sports club to accounting work at the local insurance company. I was a hustler, working two jobs my senior year to afford gas to get around and the clothes I wanted to wear. I learned early on to figure things out with little guidance—mission-critical skills to where I am today.

### What is your life lesson quote? Can you share its relevance in your life?

Lindsay: "If you believe it, you can achieve it."—Napoleon Hill

This has been a daily mantra in my life since I was young. To successfully make a change or reach a goal, it's important to visualize what you want and see yourself getting there. With visualization and an innate belief that I can achieve whatever I set my mind to, I have a clear picture of where I'm headed and can chart my course. It's never let me down.

Kristi: "You create your thoughts, your thoughts create your intentions, and your intentions create your reality."—Wayne Dyer.

I firmly believe that what you put out in the universe creates your path through life. Likewise, your intentions set you in motion, whether you're consciously aware of the thoughts behind them or not. For example, since leaving college, I've wanted to own my own business and create something I could feel passionate about. Did I know it would be launching a sustainable cleaning product company at age 40? No way! But every decision, conscious and subconscious, has brought me to where I am today.

### You have been blessed with success. What are three qualities you possess that helped you achieve your goals?

Lindsay: Belief in myself that what I dream is possible can become a reality. I never doubted that L'AVANT could create the superior plant-based cleaning products so needed in the marketplace. I believed Kristi and I had what it would take to launch an innovative brand and change the perception of earth-friendly cleaning options in the consumer's mind.

Positive attitude. I've always had the mindset of finding the positive in every situation. However, there will be times when things aren't going your way or fall short of your goals. It's easy to slip into negativity and focus on what's gone wrong. Staying positive can be challenging, but persistence pays off. There's always a way to work things out to achieve the desired outcome; you just have to stay open to the possibility.

Surrounding myself with incredible people. I never needed to be the most intelligent person in the room, but I was always smart enough to sit next to them. From early childhood through college, career, and today, I've tried to surround myself with people I admire and whose examples I want to emulate. So much of my success in life has come from being humble enough to say I don't know and quiet enough to learn from those who do.

Kristi: Discipline. Once I set on a course, I'm head down and focused. Of course, unexpected setbacks and distractions will inevitably pop up along the way, but I deal with them and never let the noise disengage me from the task at hand.

Goal setting. At a young age, I learned the value of defining goals and setting priorities. I may not always get the end result I shoot for on the first go-round, but I know how to determine the steps that will take me there and don't waiver from that path (there's that discipline again).

Problem-solving. I was described by a boss early on as possessing the skill set of "knowing how to get things done." Well, that sounds a bit dull. I didn't have an appreciation at the time for the compliment (or even think it was a compliment!), but I've grown to realize that it was high praise. That get-things-done approach has been essential to my success, especially with the launch of this new enterprise.

**Tell us about your career experience before your second chapter.**

Lindsay: Before starting L'AVANT Collective, I spent 20 years in medical device sales. It was a job I loved, and I was really good at it. I started out as a pharmaceutical sales rep, working up to becoming an associate rep and ultimately a principal sales representative. At that point, I was running my own territory and managing an entire team. For years, the work was challenging, and I never lacked motivation. I was also fortunate to be surrounded by some incredible people, which made the job even more rewarding.

Kristi: My career has zigzagged a bit more than Lindsay's. I started out as an auditor at Deloitte, obtaining my CPA license that first year and spending five years auditing some of Seattle's largest public companies. I credit my time at Deloitte with honing my professional skills, thanks in part to their structured soft and technical skill training. The hours were long and the work grinding, but it solidified my professional foundation.

Next, I continued in operations and finance, with positions at two alternative investment companies. Enjoying the analytic side of things, I studied hard and passed the CFA (chartered financial analyst) exam in 2009, the most rigorous financial certification you can earn. I was incredibly driven and worked long hours. I was paid well and had my sights set on scaling the corporate ladder. But after my first son was born in 2011, things changed, including my perspective.

On my LinkedIn profile, I jokingly list the period I stayed home with my firstborn as "CFO of the Lord Household." I wouldn't trade a moment of that time but also spent much of it fretting about my shelf life as a professional. Looking back, that was a big waste of mental capacity, but it's the curse of the working mom. After two years at home, I picked up my career with a new role as an investment advisor working directly with clients. With no direct experience and a two-year hiatus, I re-entered the workforce at a 50% reduction in pay. The money was less, but there's more than one bottom line. I embraced my new role with a feeling of purpose that filled that wage gap. I discovered I liked helping individuals make better financial decisions and soon observed a common thread among my clients. Most generated their wealth by owning their own business. This was a revelation, especially in Seattle, where the classic success story is one of making millions on your tech IPO. While still at this firm, I had the opportunity to join a small start-up investment fund as a partner and COO. It was a chance to get in on the ground floor of a new enterprise. It also allowed me to work remotely and be my own boss for the first time. By now, I had three young children, and this flexibility was invaluable. That job ticked many boxes for me, but something was lacking: I wasn't passionate about it.

## How did you reinvent yourself in your second chapter?

Lindsay: While growing up, I had a front seat watching the careers of both my parents. It was undoubtedly a terrific life lesson about how I wanted my personal life journey to play out. Redirecting my life and career was something I knew was in the cards for me just by watching my mom and dad. Both my parents were employed by others.

My dad (social work) and mom (insurance) had to reinvent themselves to remain relevant and satisfied in their chosen fields to advance in their respective careers. My mom reinvented herself mid-career from being an "in-office" insurance underwriter and manager to becoming an "outside" national marketing executive. My dad evolved from a nurse to a social worker to an entrepreneur. Both of them encouraged me to find a job that I loved, made me happy, and feel fulfilled, but also encouraged me to be open to changes. I found a sales career that I loved, and it prepared me for my second chapter. By starting a business of my own, I could apply the marketing and sales skills I had learned working for others and put them to good use to benefit my company and me.

Kristi: I always knew I wanted to be a passion-led business

owner. I didn't know how or when, but every new position I took helped prepare me to realize that dream. Even when I wasn't completely enamored of my job, I knew I was honing the skills that would someday allow me to fulfill my aspirations. So, when I stopped viewing my career as a ladder but instead as a journey of self-exploration that would lead me to this day, there was no turning back.

## Your second chapter's transition was remarkable. What was the trigger that made you decide you needed to make a change in your life?

Lindsay: The fear of regret. I went on my own to a Tony Robbins four-day seminar a few years back. The theme was working through fears that hold you back and prevent you from achieving what you want in life and how to visualize the life you genuinely deserve. There was one moment in the seminar when I was challenged to imagine and feel what life would be like five, 10, 20 years on if I didn't make the changes I wanted if I stayed in the same job and continued doing the same things that no longer made me happy. The exercise allowed me to feel the regret I'd experience if I didn't follow my dreams. I can still taste that visualization of regret, and it's something I never want to experience again. From that day forward, my mindset and my life changed. Regret was not an option. I was going to start a company with Kristi. We were going to start L'AVANT Collective.

Kristi: As mentioned, I'd always wanted to start my own business. But it wasn't until I met Lindsay that everything clicked, and I knew I could make it happen. Lindsay possesses the attributes I struggle with. I've got the business and operational skillsets, whereas she's a force to be reckoned with when it comes to sales and marketing. We met 10 years ago and formed an instant connection that strengthened over the years as our families grew. We each have three kids and have been dreaming, and scheming ideas since our first babies were born. We watched and studied others in similar circumstances who had started businesses or created something unique. Before long, our weekend dinner discussions began to evolve into concrete ideas that led us to seek out meetings with people to discuss those ideas. We were on our way. What feels now like a natural transition started with the belief we were ready and a series of baby steps toward our goal.

## What did you do to discover you had a new skill set you hadn't maximized?

Lindsay: Over the last few years, I've taken time to reflect on my life experiences and lessons learned. Revisiting those times when I was happy and successful, what kept coming up was a pattern of setting a goal and pursuing it relentlessly. I would think about it day and night. Nothing was going to stop me from making my dream a reality. I wanted to buy a house—I became obsessed with saving money for a down payment. I wanted to get a job in the medical device industry—I was obsessed with learning everything about the field, spoke with anyone I could about it.

For L'AVANT Collective, I had to become obsessed with the conviction that our product was needed, the company possible, and Kristi and I were the ones to bring it to life. Obsession (in a good way) has always been a part of my makeup; I just needed to harness that energy toward this new purpose.

Kristi: Creativity is something I convinced myself from an early age I didn't possess (my only C was in Art!), and I chose a pretty non-creative career. I spent 20 years crunching numbers, analyzing data, and combing through legal documents. I was paid for my accuracy and precision, and I was good at it. Unfortunately, when you tell yourself something long enough, you convince yourself of it. Though I'd suppressed any natural leanings toward creativity, I craved it. Every time I got the chance to do something imaginative, I was energized.

Creating L'AVANT Collective from nothing has allowed me to exercise a different part of my brain. And the more I exercise it, the more that side of me blossoms. It really is the best part of the job. Sure, I can set up our operating system and analyze cash flow, but setting the strategy for a new product, connecting with influencers and customers who love what we offer, and navigating the course for the long-term vision of this company with Lindsay has been thrilling.

## How are things going now?

Lindsay and Kristi: It's been exhilarating. Before launch, we were so excited about what we'd created and equally nervous about taking that last step into the marketplace. We knew we'd made something unique and essential, but would the consumers out there embrace it? We were releasing our baby into the world. The launch day was full-on emotion, a heady mix of excitement, adrenaline, nervousness, and fear. When the orders started coming in that first day from friends and family and then — gasp — complete strangers . . . well, we won't deny there were a few happy tears. Each ding on our phone represented not just a sale but an affirmation that what we'd believed in and worked hard to bring to life was a reality. The initial feedback from friends and family was incredible. Then, a couple weeks post-launch, comments from complete strangers who loved their L'AVANT Collective products started coming in. The positive response about the performance, the comfort of knowing the products were all-natural, the scent, the look of the bottles — it was overwhelming. People loved our baby just as much as we did! We write thank-you notes on each packing slip as a way to connect with our amazing customers who've chosen to spend their money with us. We are beyond grateful. It's so validating to receive five-star reviews and customer testimonials sharing how well the products work and the joy using them brings to folks. That's been a lovely surprise how we're creating an entirely new experience for our customers. Cleaning is traditionally mundane, something you get through as quickly as possible and put behind you till next time. But, through our fresh scent and design-forward packaging and our lack of harsh chemical ingredients, our products bring much-needed joy to a necessary chore. They make you feel "fancy," as one customer put it. We love that! And couldn't we all use an extra dose of joy these days?

## Is there someone you are grateful to who helped you along the way?

Lindsay: 100%, my parents. Growing up, they told me I could accomplish anything I desired and instilled in me the belief that "I can do it." To this day, they're my biggest cheerleaders, constantly believing in me and confident I'll achieve anything I set out to do. My parents taught me that the only limits to my success were the limits I placed on myself. So, when I told them I was going to quit my full-time career, start a business, and create fine quality, plant-based cleaning products, they didn't bat an eye. They told me to go for it and never doubted I'd make it happen. They've been incredible mentors, and I live their words and encouragement every day.

Kristi: It's hard to choose just one; so many helped me on my journey. I had no idea what I wanted to do after college until I sought the counsel of one of my professors at Washington State University, Glen Johnson. He helped guide the decision process that landed me that first job at Deloitte. I worked for incredibly supportive but equally challenging partners at Deloitte: Mike Williams, Tom Robins, and Sally Buckles. Each one saw things in me that I didn't. They pushed me far out of my comfort zone and never let me skate by. I have a fitness trainer, Tony Moses, whom I've worked with on and off for 15 years, and he pushes me physically and mentally to move beyond what I think I'm capable of. When I feel I can't do something, it's Tony's face and his words

I typically see and hear on repeat, pushing me over that hurdle of doubt.

My siblings and parents have been my biggest fans, cheering from the sidelines and letting me know how proud they are. And my biggest fan, my rock, is my husband. He listens, he supports, and I look to him for guidance on so many things.

## Share an exciting moment that happened since committing to your second chapter.

Lindsay: The realization that people want to help and are happy to do it has been so wonderful. You just have to ask! After all, if you don't ask, the answer is always no. For the three years leading up to launch, Kristi and I met with anyone and everyone, asking advice, soaking up all the knowledge we could. We gleaned nuggets of learning from each meeting and encounter that culminated in where we are today. I am beyond humbled and grateful to everyone who graciously responded to our requests to meet and has continued to help us grow. It's something I will never forget. When people ask me for advice or get together to discuss a project, I am so happy to give back.

Kristi: The most interesting year leading up to launch was 2020. COVID-19 brought challenges we never could have predicted, trying to establish a cleaning product company when the entire world suddenly needs cleaning products more than ever. We were hit with significant supply chain slowdowns, both for raw materials and components. But some blessings came from our timing, and we've been able to move forward in some unique ways because of it, especially in getting our operation set up. Many large brick-and-mortar retailers moved their retail online during mid-2020. As a result, we purchased everything from shelving to prep tables, bins, office supplies, chairs, ladders, and shipping paper, all at significant savings. Also, because the changes in the ways people work and shop have resulted in more empty commercial spaces, we could negotiate reduced, month-to-month rates for office space. It hasn't always been easy, but launching in 2020 added a level of resilience to our company that will serve us well going forward.

### Have you ever struggled with believing in yourself? If so, how did you overcome that limiting belief?

Lindsay: Constantly! When I graduated from college, I had my eye on the prize of getting a job in pharmaceutical sales. But everyone I talked to said the pharma industry didn't hire people without field experience. After hearing this repeatedly, including from a professor who said I should go sell copy machines and "cut my teeth" in outside sales, I was prepared to give up on the idea that I could step from college to my dream job. As a new graduate, maybe I wasn't ready for this "big job." But I didn't give up.

I went to a career fair and was declined an interview with the pharmaceutical company screening rep. As I turned to leave, I saw a sign indicating that Johnson & Johnson held interviews on the 4th floor. I hopped on the elevator, found where Johnson & Johnson was interviewing and got in line. When the manager told me, he wasn't interested in seeing me because I didn't have sales experience, I told him he could at least give me five minutes of his time to hear me out; I had just waited in that line and wouldn't take no for an answer. Five interviews later, I got the job.

Kristi: Sure, I struggle with self-doubt. During some periods of life more than others, and plenty of times during the three years leading up to launch. I was a CFA charter holder and a CPA. I spent 20 years building that career, working really hard, and now I was leaving it to make soap? Fortunately, the older I get, the more confident I become. Looking back on all the times I proved to myself that I can make my own success when I set a goal and do the steps is a tremendous resource during times of uncertainty. In addition, I've teamed up with an incredibly positive cofounder who constantly repeated that this was going to work. It helps to surround yourself with positive people who can help pull you out of the occasional self-doubt spiral!

**Typically, I encourage my clients to ask for support from those who believe in their vision before they embark on a new chapter. How did you create your support system?**

Lindsay: This is a constant. As I said earlier, I am a massive fan of surrounding myself with incredible people, those I can learn from and who help me grow as a person. When I was about to start L'AVANT with Kristi, I sought out as many people as I could who had started their own companies. What were their recommendations? Pitfalls? Experiences? I entered this new chapter with a wealth of knowledge and guidance from those who'd taken a similar route before me. What I learned from others allowed me to make the best decisions for myself and for the company.

Kristi: First and foremost, I needed to ensure I had the full support of my husband. I wouldn't have taken this on without his endorsement, and I feel so fortunate as he's given me the gift of time. I invested our savings without a clear road map of how we would get this enterprise off the ground. I just knew I wanted to take the leap. He supports our family financially as I tackle this, and he's L'AVANT's biggest fan. In addition, I have a fantastic community of women in my neighborhood who I bounce ideas off of, my college best friends who openly listen to the emotional side of the journey (sometimes calling them multiple times a week!), and my sister. She is fiercely loyal and supports us with volunteer labor and spreading the word in her community.

**Starting a new chapter requires leaving your comfort zone behind. How did you do that?**

Lindsay: I try to be out of my comfort zone every day. Throughout this journey in life, I've found the only way for me to constantly grow and learn is to allow myself to be uncomfortable. Though I had loved my previous career, I came to a point where I stopped learning and growing at the pace I had in the beginning. The days became routine and lacked challenge; I was no longer thriving. To get out of that rut, a change in my comfort level had to happen. For me, that became a complete shift and starting L'AVANT Collective. Now I'm in the place I'm supposed to be—challenged daily and continuing to grow and flourish.

Kristi: In general, I thrive in roles with no road map and prefer to be uncomfortable. I find I'm more driven, focused, and productive when I'm kept on my toes. It was easy to turn the page to this new chapter, but I'll tell you, the three years leading up to launch were very uncomfortable! Every year we would set a goal to launch, and for three years, we didn't hit our target. For a goal-oriented person, this was tough. We live in a society of instant satisfaction, where new companies seem to be born overnight. There was a lot of learning, waiting, failing, pivoting, and struggling during those years. But looking back, that time taught me patience and grace. I can't control every outcome, and we certainly made plenty of incorrect decisions along the way. But, as it turns out, we launched just when we were meant to, and lessons learned from every setback contributed to our successful debut.

## What are five things you wish someone had told you before you started leading your business, and why?

It is going to take a lot more time than you think. Three years ago, when we came up with the idea of L'AVANT, we wrote our business plan and confidently said we'd launch nine months later. Looking back, it seems a bit naïve, but we were enthusiastic and determined. Little did we know, between formulation, packaging, identifying partners, manufacturing, freight, website development, brand development—everything takes longer than you think. We finally launched in December 2020, three years after we started on this journey and more than two years after that first target launch date. Our passion for our products and the difference they would make in the world helped fuel us through the peaks and valleys of getting to launch.

There will be people who will tell you it's not going to work. When we started the idea of L'AVANT Collective, we told everyone about it. For the most part, people in our circles were supportive and encouraging. But, like getting that one nasty comment on social media when you have 50 positive ones, it's human nature to focus on the negative. Some said they'd never use plant-based cleaning products. Others said there were already options on the market, so why add to it? Some flat out hated the idea because it was a consumer product and not a tech idea (here in Seattle, new tech companies seem to launch daily). The concept that plant-based cleaners could work as well as conventional cleaners were met with some skepticism, as was the notion that a new brand could break into the marketplace. In the face of doubt, we never lost belief in ourselves and our dream. We started this journey because we wanted safer products to use around our loved ones and pets. Surely, we weren't alone.

You are not going to have enough time to get it all done. Every day, we find ourselves with a to-do list of 100-plus items—all of them vital. Right now, it's still just the two of us. How do we prioritize when every choice seems like a critical business decision? Do we continue to innovate and work on developing new products, fixing a website code issue, photographing new assets, and seeking new businesses to partner with? If we pause any one of those, we're putting an area of the company on hold. So, we set priorities, assign workload, and have begun to outsource those elements we don't have the time or expertise for, like digital marketing and web development. It's a daily struggle, with three kids each (all doing some variation of remote learning), to accomplish everything that needs doing. But, writing down goals, priorities, and tasks has helped keep us on track. There are many online tools, even something as basic as Excel, that can focus and move you forward.

You will need to lean on others and ask for help. We are a scrappy, bootstrapped start-up, and we love that about ourselves. When something needs to get done, our initial inclination is to learn and save money by figuring it out ourselves. There's a YouTube video for everything these days! This spirit brought us a long way but could only take us so far. We were determined to create a beautifully designed, high-performing, natural product. For that, we needed to hire experts. And, as mentioned above, we've begun to outsource those pieces of the puzzle better accomplished by others. Stay scrappy as long as you can, but understand you will need to invest in the experts for some things. There are so many incredibly talented freelance professionals to take the burden off of you; it will pay for itself in the long run. Plus, it's fun to have a few collaborators.

Take time for yourself. In this first year of launching L'AVANT, and amidst COVID-19, we left our full-time careers, became homeschool teachers for our kids, and fulfilled the roles of a house cleaner, full-time cook, and laundry maven, all while trying to get a business off the ground. Working until two or three in the morning became the new normal, and all prior healthy routines seemed like a luxury of time we couldn't afford. Self-care became a thing of the past, and health issues starting creeping in. Now in our 40's, we had to take a beat and look at where this new normal was leading us from a personal standpoint. L'AVANT is providing an amazing new chapter, but we also want to be our best selves and be able to enjoy all the good things it's bringing to our lives. So, we make time for ourselves, whether it's working out, preparing healthy food for the week, or just carving out a little unstructured "me time."

**You are both people of significant influence. If you could inspire a movement that would bring the best outcome to the greatest number of people, what would that be?**

Lindsay and Kristi: It ties in with that element of joy we mentioned, and also the conscious choice to incorporate the word "collective" in our name. What happens in the home and the social environment you create defines your family, and your family impacts your community's health. As communities thrive, the world changes for the better. Sustainability doesn't just refer to the ingredients in our products and our production, packaging, and distribution methods. We want to be part of changing perspectives regarding the domestic workload, creating a more sustainable model of home care that expands what was once considered "women's work" to include every member of the household. Our products elevate the experience in a way that makes it easy to recruit everybody into the process. As a result, we see what was traditionally considered drudgery evolving into a positive shared experience that everyone naturally takes part in. Changing the old paradigm from "this is what mom does" to "we all live here let's all take part and have fun doing it" can set the tone for how every member sees their role in the family. Those beginnings can create an attitude of cooperation they'll bring with them to the larger community.

**Dreams come true. If you could invite anyone in the world to dinner, who would that be?**

Lindsay: Sarah Blakely, queen of the second career and founder of Spanx. She began her career in sales, so I can relate to her journey. Rejection after rejection is commonplace in that world, no matter what you're selling. The grit and resilience it takes to get up every morning, knock on doors, and hunt for your next sale—it can be demoralizing, but Sarah never gave up on herself. She knew her idea could turn into a multi-billion-dollar corporation. I try to read every article (I set up google alerts!) about her, taking notes on how she's charging through the entrepreneurial journey and continuing to innovate and grow her company. She is Wonder Woman in my eyes.

Kristi: Emily Weiss, the founder of Glossier. What a powerhouse! She has been nothing but perfection at bringing forth an e-commerce brand that's been wildly successful at connecting with the consumer. And it's been done in such a genuine, authentic way. So many incredible female founders inspire us daily to keep moving forward, and Emily is my North Star.

## Where can we follow your work?

Website: lavantcollective.com
Social:　　Instagram @lavantcollective

# CHAPTER 15

# Michelle Edgar

ॐ ॐ

*Throughout my career, I've always had a hunger for growth
and challenge. I am relentless in my pursuit of passion and
purpose. A week before the COVID-19 shutdown, I returned
to Los Angeles after losing a parent and was at a point of
personal and professional self-reflection. At my core, I felt
that I was not living my best life, and something was lacking.
I had lost touch with my life force and was depleted of
energy. I acknowledged that something needed to be done,
and I had to pivot and change something in my life. At the
time, it was difficult to tap into my energy and passion. I was
mourning the loss of my parent and fearful as I transitioned
out of a marriage. I recognized that this was the time for
my rebirth, but I was scared. So, I began running and
committed myself to this and quickly came alive. I started
running six miles a day at the UCLA track, where I began
my second chapter. Run for life became my mantra, and I
embraced a new perspective that allowed me to discover
my true power as I pushed out of my comfort zone and took
the first steps to heal, letting me get closer to
my true purpose and mission.*

A s an executive in the entertainment business, over the last 10 years, Michelle Edgar has helped artists build out their brands and accelerate their reach. Her passion for supporting her clients stems from a lifelong love of music. At age five, she played the piano and grew into a trained concert pianist. She applied that same diligence and focus to her love of sports and discovered her inner athlete on the track. Today, she has achieved her athletic goal as an All-American sprinter at the age of 38. "Just Do It" is her mantra and the way she lives her life.

Her goal when the shutdown happened was to get back on track and connect with her purpose and passion while challenging herself both mentally and physically. As a woman in business, advancing into leadership roles in corporate America is fraught with hurdles and ceilings. However, she felt pursuing her law degree focused on entertainment, media, and sports at UCLA Law would strengthen her skill set and further her path in being an unstoppable force in business.

## Share with us a bit about your upbringing.

I was born in London, raised in New Jersey, and came to this country at the age of five with a strong British accent, which sadly I lost along the way. I always had a solid work ethic, as my family instilled this in me. We always held the immigrant mindset that anything is possible if you worked on it with discipline and focus. That philosophy was ingrained in everything I embraced and has carried throughout my life.

At the age of five, I discovered the piano and fell in love with the sound as it was a creative outlet that enabled me to express myself. I would sit and study at the piano for hours. My mother recognized that I had a gift, and she invested in me through professional lessons to unleash my talent. I studied at the Manhattan School of Music for 13 years.

I then went to Northwestern University to train as a concert pianist while double majoring in journalism with a business minor. My father always told me to have a backup plan, and I ended up following in his footsteps as a businesswoman. I always knew in my heart that with my business acumen and understanding of my craft, I could uniquely help shape artists' careers through the lens of marketing and branding. My journey to the entertainment business was unconventional as I spent a summer in a talent agency mailroom and interning for Vanity Fair in London. My job in London led to an opportunity at Vanity Fair in New York, and I started my career in publishing, which led to my career as a journalist and beauty editor at Women's Wear Daily.

One day my boss said to me, "Follow the music," and at that moment, I realized that music was missing from my life, and I had to get back to my roots and passion.

## What is your life lesson quote?

My running coach always says, "It's not the age; it's the stage."

This always stuck with me. It's never too late to find your true purpose and calling. However, it wasn't until 38 that I tapped into the inner athlete in me. After eight months of training, I set a goal with my coach to train to attain All-American status, and after seven days of training at six AM for two hours a day, we achieved our goal when I ran 60 meters in 9.60 seconds.

Looking back, I will never forget the day this all manifested when one day I asked the coach to drive down to the Olympic Training Center with me. I wanted to visualize what it would be like. It was the only day I left Los Angeles in the past year, and the day culminated with Coach saying to me that we should earn All-American status, and we did just that.

Sports was not something I grew up with. My typical week was, I went to high school and then spent nine hours on Saturdays at music school. I was prepping for concerts in my free time, which was practicing for more than three hours a day on top of school, making it hard to have time for anything else. I once tried playing basketball and volleyball in school but fractured my finger, ending my high school athletics. Twenty years passed until I competed in my first track race in July 2020.

### You have been blessed with success. What are three qualities you possess that helped you achieve your goals?

Passion. You always have to pursue your passion with purpose. It's something you need to eat, sleep, breathe day in and day out—that's the magic because then it never feels like work. That's how I've built The XX Project and Music Unites. My passion for this drives me to continue creating and building, and there hasn't been a day in the past 10+ years that I haven't woken up excited to contribute to both organizations. As Jeff Bezos always says, "Every day is Day 1."

Focus. I train every day with my coach from 6–8 AM. My training and morning run sets the trajectory of my day and gives me the strength and power to perform at my best at work, law school, and every other aspect of my life. My focus allows me to get out of my comfort zone and confront my fears. But, focus does come with sacrifice—as Coach says, there's only so much you can put on your plate before you begin losing your ability to accomplish your goals.

Determination. Be relentless in your pursuits of goals to see them through. When I set out to be an agent, nothing could stop me from achieving this goal. I lived in a culture of "yes" and wouldn't take no as an answer and truly believed in myself and what I could offer my clients.

### Tell us about your career experience before your second chapter.

I feel very fortunate to have had an unconventional career journey across the entertainment, music, and media business. The common thread has been my love for marketing and working with talent to launch impactful strategic partnerships and branding campaigns. I purposefully wanted to experience all facets of the entertainment and music business, from working as an agent at International Creative Management (ICM) Partners to positions at Epic Records and Warner Bros. Records.

I moved to Los Angeles almost 10 years ago to work in artist management at Red Light Management. I have worked with wide range of exceptional artists from Travis Scott and Mary J. Blige to Andra Day and Gary Clark Jr. to H.E.R. and Anderson Paak. It has also been my passion to help the talent I work with to amplify their voices to impact change through social impact work and artists' philanthropic initiatives, from women's empowerment to voting and music education.

Serving and building community and impacting change through my non-profit and women's empowerment work has always been something I continue to focus on tied to my non-profit work Music Unites and women in leadership membership community, The XX Project.

## How did you reinvent yourself in your second chapter?

Throughout my career, I've always had a hunger for growth and challenge. I am relentless in my pursuit of passion and purpose. A week before the COVID-19 shutdown, I returned to Los Angeles after losing a parent and was at a point of personal and professional self-reflection. At my core, I felt that I was not living my best life, and something was lacking. I had lost touch with my life force and was depleted of energy. I acknowledged that something needed to be done, and I had to pivot and change something in my life.

At the time, it was difficult to tap into my energy and passion. I was mourning the loss of my parent and fearful as I transitioned out of a marriage. I recognized that this was the time for my rebirth, but I was scared. So, I began running and committed myself to this and quickly came alive. I started running six miles a day at the UCLA track, where I began my second chapter.

"Run for life" became my mantra, and I embraced a new perspective that allowed me to discover my true power as I pushed out of my comfort zone and took the first steps to heal, letting me get closer to my true purpose and mission. I then double-downed and committed to pushing myself intellectually and then started law school at ??. As Coach says, "If you change your mind, you can change your life."

**Your second chapter's transition was remarkable. What was the trigger that made you decide you needed to make a change in your life?**

My stepfather's last words to me were, "Will you move on with your life already?" This was the catalyst to my transformation. It took a series of traumatic experiences before I took control of my life and decided to invest in myself. I am transforming every day, through every step, and by every mile. I found that running and athletics were universally positive ways to heal and ignite a fire inside me. For the first time in a long time, I felt liberated. I ran over 1000 miles in 2020! Coach called me the female Forrest Gump. My goal was to better myself and live my best life across all aspects—physically, mentally, emotionally, and intellectually. Through hardship and a very challenging time, after losing a parent and getting a divorce, I took control of my life and went on my mission to "Run for Life" to find my life force and true calling and purpose.

This led to my journey at UCLA Law School, finding my coach and turning into an All-American athlete while totally transforming my mind and body. I tapped into my core and inner strength, which changed my body physically, losing 30 pounds.

## What did you do to discover you had a new skill set you hadn't maximized?

I was always very active, but I never tapped into my actual athletic ability. Also, to learn an entirely new sport while starting law school at the same time created a new set of challenges. I always welcome new ways of thinking and feel that if something is challenging and makes you uncomfortable, you need to dive into it further. My coach said that learning track is all about overcoming life's hurdles. If I could push myself out of my comfort zone, I would reach a new level in my personal and professional growth.

When I race, I'm competing with myself. It's not winning a race against your competitors but breaking your best time. The training, discipline, and focus I felt would enable me to grow as a leader as I learned new success strategies through my training that I could apply to my business.

## How are things going now?

Next week, the Olympic Training Center! When I visited the training center with Coach in November and saw how far I've come six months, I realize most things are within reach if you are willing to commit. I'm also excited for my future journey into the business side of sports and seeing how I can help contribute to athletes and apply the same passion and expertise I have developed in the music business. I'm grateful to have discovered this passion as part of my second chapter and am excited for the journey ahead.

## Is there someone you are grateful to who helped you along the way?

Coach Rucker always tells me that "Life is a marathon, not a sprint," and I'm grateful to have him shed his expertise as an incredible coach but also as a thoughtful mentor to me who has taught me so much about life. I'm grateful each day that he's on this journey with me as we set out to achieve our goals. I believe my stepfather sent Coach to watch over me.

## Dreams come true. If you could invite anyone in the world to dinner, who would that be?

I would love to take a run with Phil Knight and hear about his incredible life journey and lessons on building his legacy, and building the most impactful global brand and business. I want to learn what excites him and is on his mind today. I would be honored to spend a day in Phil's life and have him put me to work and give me a challenge.

## Where can we follow your work?

Website: thexxproject.com / musicunites.org

# CHAPTER 16

# Ruth Elnekave

ক্ত ৵

*Hire for culture. In the early days of a startup, it's easy to focus disproportionately on skills and experience when hiring, mainly because the team is so lean (often you plus one), and everyone needs to hit the ground quickly. However, an experienced team member who isn't fully committed to your vision and the culture you're trying to build is all but guaranteed not to work out. No doubt, a certain level of experience is crucial for specific roles, but the team members that will be the greatest asset for your organization are those who genuinely believe in what you're building and who share your values.*

Ruth Elnekave is the founder and CEO of JOYÀ, a botanical functional food brand on a mission to help people feel, think and live their best every day. After almost a decade practicing corporate law and a previous career in marketing, she changed course and returned to her culinary roots to pursue her passion: bringing joy to people's lives through food. Ruth holds a Master of Business Administration (MBA) from the Schulich School of Business, a Juris Doctor (JD) from Osgoode Hall Law School, a Bachelor of Arts (BA, Honors) from McGill University, and a certificate in Classic Culinary Arts from The International Culinary Center, and is a Certified Nutritional Practitioner (CNP).

## Share with us a bit about your upbringing.

Creating and sharing food has been a key part of my life as far back as I can remember. In fact, I'm sure that a passion for all things culinary is in my DNA. At home, my mother cooked delicious meals with global flavors from scratch daily, and I was her sous chef by the age of four. I'd also spend summers in Israel watching and helping my grandmother prepare her Middle Eastern delicacies that we'd then share as a family of 20+ people. As a child, I even created cookbooks when my friends repeatedly requested my baked goods recipes.

My other lifelong passion is wellness. Athletic from a young age, I was always kicking, climbing, throwing a ball around, and coaching tennis as a teenager while on every girl's high school sports team. Today, most of my travel is active and adventurous, and in my adult life, daily movement is something I crave and need. And the way the body and mind function and the role of nutrition have always fascinated me.

## What is your life lesson quote? Can you share its relevance in your life?

Oh! There are so many that deeply resonate with me, but here's one: "The work you do while you procrastinate is probably the work you should be doing for the rest of your life." — Jessica Hische.

My entire life, escaping to the kitchen (usually to bake or cook for others) was what I did when I didn't want to study, organize, and work.

As the CEO of JOYÀ, my career still entails far more time than

I'd like on a computer. But now, my work and its purpose revolve around bringing people joy through food. And when I escape to the kitchen to develop a recipe, it's often to share on JOYÀ's blog and social media channels.

## You have been blessed with success. What are three qualities you possess that helped you achieve your goals?

I'm truly blessed and so grateful for my career accomplishments. But my real blessing—what has played a significant role in my accomplishments—is the support, advice, guidance, and patience I've always received from my family, friends, mentors, and sponsors. I think I'd need to pose this question to all of these people to know for sure! But if I had to guess—thirst for knowledge. I always want to know more about things, to dive deeper. For example, growing up, I never intended to work in a restaurant or kitchen, yet I went to culinary school purely due to my desire to take my self-taught skills to the next level. (Funny enough, this knowledge ended up directly influencing the concept for JOYÀ.)

Perseverance. In law school, I had decided that upon graduating, I wanted to practice at one of the large corporate law firms on Bay Street (Toronto's equivalent of Wall Street). Every person in my JD/MBA class received numerous interviews and at least one offer for law firm internships, but I had two interviews (not at top firms) and zero offers. My grades were far below what these top-tier firms would typically consider, and I didn't have a resume stacked with impressive extra-curricular activities working in my favor. But I fully believed that I should and would succeed. I did everything I could think of, from networking and joining academic committees to focusing on business law courses (and getting better grades in those courses). I ended up working at one of the country's top corporate firms.

Initiative. I've always approached challenges by thinking outside the box, and I take the initiative to get things done. I guess you could say that I don't like waiting around for something to happen (or likely not happen). For example, following my last story, when I needed more exposure to my top choice law firms while in law school, I created new student events with these firms to make that happen. More recently, when I struggled with health issues and couldn't find products on the market that were effective and enjoyable to consume, I hit the drawing board and developed them.

## Tell us about your career experience before your second chapter.

As we discussed earlier, until my 20's, food, athletics, and wellness were driving forces in my life that you would have thought would inspire my career choices. Yet, I wasn't drawn to one career and never knew what I wanted to be "when I grew up." I was in marketing in the consumer-packaged goods industry after completing my first university degree. Still, while it was an interesting job that fed my creativity, it never felt like something I wanted to pursue long term.

Eventually, in my late 20's I took what I was advised was a "practical" route, studied business and law, and then found myself burning the candle at both ends as a corporate finance and mergers and acquisitions lawyer. It was a career that resulted in working nights and weekends, little (and poor) sleep, minimal physical activity, and rushed and often skipped meals—a lifestyle that wore me down. Yet, there was something about the challenge and intellectual stimulation that hooked me. So, despite resenting the hours and missing any semblance of a life outside of work, I continued to practice law for seven years.

## How did you reinvent yourself in your second chapter?

I've always had an entrepreneurial bug. My parents are entrepreneurs, so executing an idea and building something from nothing has always been in my blood, or at least my life.

After leaving the law and having had spent a good part of my young adult life in a bureaucratic, non-creative environment, I realized that I wanted to pour my energy into making people happy, not making them money. While I didn't yet know exactly what I wanted to do next, I knew that I couldn't stay in the corporate world and that this was the moment in my life to completely change gears and do something that I was genuinely passionate about.

**Your second chapter's transition was remarkable. What was the trigger that made you decide you needed to make a change in your life?**

When I left the law, I decided to take a year to clear my head, dig deep into what makes me "tick," and do things that my 24/7 legal career didn't allow for. I had discovered a one-year program in holistic nutrition. As I'd been disconnected from food and wellness for many years, I dove in with no intention initially to pursue a career in this space but instead feed my soul.

Just as I began the program, a few months after leaving the law, I began to experience debilitating health issues that I soon realized resulted from a body shut down due to chronic stress. Of course, there's never a good time to get sick, but if there ever was, my studies in holistic nutrition introduced me to various forms of traditional medicine and the healing and strengthening power of certain botanical ingredients. These modalities helped me heal.

Experiencing these health challenges was a blessing in disguise, as being reunited with food in such a personal and powerful way was the lightbulb that made me realize that I was meant to bring people joy through food.

**What did you do to discover you had a new skill set you hadn't maximized?**

I don't think I actively discovered any particular unutilized skill set before starting my new career path. Rather, part of what gave me the confidence to dive into a field so utterly unrelated to the profession I had studied and excelled in was that I knew that through all of my experiences to that point, I had developed many skills that would be transferable to founding just about any business: analytical and problem-solving skills, drafting and negotiating contracts, leading teams, managing projects, structuring financing and more.

There was also one key thing that I felt profoundly lacking in my legal career: a creative outlet. Sure, you need to think creatively to successfully negotiate deals and facilitate your clients' business goals in the face of legal obstacles. But I'm an artistically creative person, and working 15+ hour days left no time for artistic activities. Luckily, I've been able to apply my creativity daily building a brand, from the early seeds developing JOYÀ's brand identity, website, and packaging, to ongoing projects related to photography, social media, and advertising.

## How are things going now?

Since we launched just over a year ago, it's been a roller coaster of a ride filled with an array of obstacles, wins, failures, and excitement almost daily! Building a new business is always challenging, and throwing a pandemic into the mix doesn't help. But it does make you even stronger and more agile and forces you to learn very quickly how to roll with the punches.

Some considerable obstacles have included extreme supply chain delays that prevented us from getting ingredients needed for production, pivoting and completely restructuring our packaging solution, and figuring out how to connect and build trust with consumers with canceled live events. Some of our wins and developments have included launching an innovative and truly sustainable packaging solution, creating partnerships with principal retailers, and preparing to launch in Canada and on Amazon. And we've got some exciting new products in the works!

## Is there someone you are grateful to who helped you along the way?

I'm truly blessed to have so many people in my life who have been a source of unconditional support and have provided invaluable guidance and mentorship. But there's one particular person without whom I don't know if—or when—I would have discovered the entrepreneurial path that I'm now on.

While I was still practicing law, I worked with a brilliantly talented career coach. At the time, the goal was not necessarily to completely switch careers but rather to grow as a professional and find more fulfillment, whether in law or another field. She pushed me to look deep inside and be honest and vulnerable and helped me uncover parts of my true nature that I had become oblivious to because I was so all-consumed with my career.

My life-changing work with this coach made me realize that nothing brings me more fulfillment and gets me more fired up than helping people in ways that bring them well-being and true joy. And what do you know? Drafting contracts and structuring deals were not accomplishing that. Yet, without the guidance and friendship of this coach, I may have never left the law.

## Share an exciting moment that happened since committing to your second chapter.

Things happen daily that would make an interesting (and very entertaining) entrepreneurship book. But what immediately comes to mind for me is an experience from JOYÀ's pre-launch days that resulted in a pivot from the original concept to where the business is today, in the herbal supplement space.

JOYÀ was initially conceived as a wellness café offering beverages, including the elixirs and herbal teas we now sell. We planned to open in my old backyard, Toronto's financial district, where I knew the lawyers, bankers, and busy professionals wanted delicious yet nourishing food to support their health in the face of their demanding lifestyles. There were no options at the time. Landlords were excited about the concept, but locations I considered suitable were not becoming available.

We scoped locations for almost 10 months, which gave me time to reassess. I realized that as excited as I was about a business that would allow me to interact with customers daily, I was even more excited about sharing the power of our offering with a much larger audience, well beyond just Toronto.

And talk about a blessing in disguise! This "lack of success" finding a location led to pivoting JOYÀ to what it is today and away from owning a restaurant in a neighborhood that the pandemic devastatingly turned into a ghost town.

### Have you ever struggled with believing in yourself? If so, how did you overcome that limiting belief?

Absolutely. I have my moments regularly, particularly when we're facing challenges or something isn't going right. I learned very quickly on this entrepreneurial journey, mainly from speaking with other entrepreneurs and first-time founders, that having moments of doubt is normal. It's a challenging and a demanding, and draining ride.

Each time I find myself struggling or even feeling like an imposter (which happens!), I remind myself that I'm not alone. Every startup founder experiences immense and ongoing challenges, and I've got an incredible and growing network of peers and experienced mentors who are there for me with their support, advice, and, more importantly, their tales from the trenches.

### Typically, I encourage my clients to ask for support from those who believe in their vision before they embark on a new chapter. How did you create your support system?

I wouldn't say that I consciously set up a support system or knew I had one in place before embarking on this journey. Instead, as questions and challenges arose, I started to ask for all kinds of support—time, advice, and information—and realized how many well-positioned people I knew who wanted to help, even if it meant connecting me with their own network. And now that I know how crucial a robust support system is, building and strengthening mine is something I work on every day.

I've always loved to support and mentor others, whether coaching sports, teaching culinary skills, or mentoring students or law firm colleagues. Not only do I get so much fulfillment from helping people feel empowered and joyful, but I always learn a fair share from the process myself. My experience with my support system is no different. I love connecting with founders just starting their journeys and others in similar stages to mine. There have been very few chats, if any, in which I haven't learned something valuable just from being there to support others and hearing their stories.

## Starting a new chapter requires leaving your comfort zone behind. How did you do that?

My transition from corporate lawyer to wellness CPG (consumer packaged goods) entrepreneur was gradual, but deciding to step out of my comfort zone for good was not. I knew I had to leave my role at the firm seven years in, but I was emotionally and mentally consumed by the position that I couldn't figure out my next step while still practicing. So, I left before I had a game plan and decided to take time to clear my head and figure out what my next adventure would be.

As soon as I distanced myself from that intense, 24/7 environment, I immediately realized after spending over a decade studying and working in an area that brought me no joy, there was no way my next move would be back to "big corporate."

This decision did mean that I would be leaving what I had worked long and hard to excel at to venture into the complete unknown.

But I was approaching 40 and wanted to finally pour my energy into something that I was truly passionate about—that would allow me to feel like when I leave this world, I will have done something good.

### What are five things you wish someone had told you before you started leading your business, and why?

Hire for culture. In the early days of a startup, it's easy to focus disproportionately on skills and experience when hiring, mainly because the team is so lean (often you plus one), and everyone needs to hit the ground quickly. However, an experienced team member who isn't fully committed to your vision and the culture you're trying to build is all but guaranteed not to work out. No doubt, a certain level of experience is crucial for specific roles, but the team members that will be the greatest asset for your organization are those who genuinely believe in what you're building and who share your values.

Connect with peers ASAP. As we discussed earlier, a strong support system is vital, and having one in place from day one that explicitly includes other start-up founders in your space is invaluable. I wish I would have known this as I was preparing to launch JOYÀ. These are the people who are going (or have gone) through your exact early-stage challenges, and had I had those connections earlier, I would have saved myself a reasonable amount of time and headaches spinning my wheels in the early days.

Keep questioning and iterating. As they say, perfection is the enemy of progress. In fact, nothing will ever be "perfect," but if you constantly hold back and don't just get out there and test and try, you'll never learn or know what does and doesn't work. I got stuck in this vicious circle in the early days, and as a result, missed out on the opportunity to beat several competitors to market.

That said, never get comfortable. There's always room for

improvement, and if you don't stay inquisitive and open-minded, you'll miss out on great opportunities to grow and improve.

Don't forget to enjoy the journey. While your future goals (including what you want your culture to be) should guide your decisions and actions, don't get so caught up in planning that you forget to savor and enjoy each moment of the ride. The experiences of today are what determine the organization's culture tomorrow. The entrepreneurial journey doesn't get easier. No matter how much you learn, new (and often more complex) challenges continuously arise. But if you're on the path you're meant to be on, it gets more fun.

**You are a person of significant influence. If you could inspire a movement that would bring the best outcome to the greatest number of people, what would that be?**

I sincerely believe that one of the most straightforward and meaningful opportunities for increased wellness in society is the emotional and psychological wellness derived from experiencing many small moments of joy throughout the day. How incredible would it be if people would stop for a few minutes a couple of times a day to truly savor and appreciate something that brings them joy—a hug, a view, the sunshine or fresh air, a steamy and delicious latte, a selfless act for another person? I'd bet that the effects would be so impactful that people would find themselves practicing "joyous savoring" more and more until it became a habit.

**Dreams come true. If you could invite anyone in the world to dinner, who would that be?**

Oh, wow. Just one? I am in complete awe of Brené Brown and her eye-opening work in such essential areas for humanity, including equality and empathy. I've learned plenty from her (and her podcast's guests' discussions) about authentic leadership and the importance of vulnerability as a leader. I don't think one meal with her would be enough!

## Where can we follow your work?

Website: joya.ca

Social:     Instagram @thejoyalife

               LinkedIn and Clubhouse @ruth.joya

# CHAPTER 17

# Leena Alsulaiman

ॐ ॐ

*Set boundaries! When we run our own businesses, the boundaries are ours to set. And it can be hard not to fall into the trap of wanting to do everything a client asks for in fear of losing work. But as an entrepreneur, it's your responsibility to set the boundaries and work only with people who respect them.*

As a lifelong creative, Leena Alsulaiman's career path has taken her from jewelry designing to conscious image and brand consulting for women across the globe. The California-based entrepreneur mother of three is devoted to cultivating change and building confidence for her diverse clientele. Whether they're starting a new career path or simply need a wardrobe refresh, Leena's keen eye for transformation helps her clients put their best foot forward into the next chapter.

## Share with us a bit about your upbringing.

Growing up as a female Saudi/American hybrid in the Middle East, I craved and searched for all things creative in a time where it wasn't necessarily an easy thing to find. However, when I was choosing what to study in college, I landed on Jewelry Design as it ticked the creative box and was accepted as a career path by my family. In those days, creative fields and careers were uncommon or not widespread, and as I look back on my diverse career history, I see that I found ways to infuse creativity into everything I have done.

For many years, I took the entrepreneur's path and unconsciously always brought a side of creativity to my roles. And while that was my "day job," my passion led to color outside the lines, and I offered my expertise, guidance, and knowledge to women that were starting their own ventures, growing their brands, or making career moves.

### What is your favorite life lesson quote? Can you share its relevance in your life?

"Being selective—doing less is the path of the productive."— Tim Feriss

Focusing my attention on what's truly important in my life by protecting and conserving my energy has been the most productive thing I do. Moving away from the mindset of needing to be busy to feel validation has kept me from hitting walls and feeling burnt out or unhappy. Focus on the important few and ignore the rest.

### You have been blessed with success. What are three qualities you possess that helped you achieve your goals?

Knowing my "why." Once I could identify my purpose clearly and define the impact I would like to have in creating a business, it shifted everything. I am deeply invested in service, which makes motivation and inspiration easy to access.

Resilience. Being able to integrate and learn from challenging experiences. Taking all those stories, mistakes, and learnings and choosing to keep creating and serving. Understanding that a single experience doesn't define you . . . how you react and move on does.

Optimism. I'm relentlessly optimistic—a silver linings collector. The glass is always half full. This doesn't mean that I'm shiny and happy at all moments of the day. What it means is that I can look at a situation, and while it might be challenging, I'm able to see around that corner and see the possibility versus the difficulty. As Marie Forleo says, "Everything is Figureoutable."

**Tell us about your career experience before your second chapter.**

My career has had many, many chapters before this point. All different but also very much the same. So, this is why I do feel that at this point, I am truly in my second chapter. Pursuing a career up to this point for me has been rooted in response mode. Not knowing exactly what I wanted to do and craving the experience, I took on many different roles and tried it all, from being a jewelry designer, wedding planner, health coach, and communications manager, to a fashion stylist. The only constant was that I was helping and guiding women entrepreneurs on the sidelines.

**How did you reinvent yourself in your second chapter?**

I wouldn't call it reinventing. I would say it was more of a blossoming. When you reinvent something, you change it so that it appears to be entirely new. That's not what I did at all. My second chapter has come to life through acceptance and fully embracing my gifts and the things that bring me joy.

**Your second chapter's transition was remarkable. What was the trigger that made you decide you needed to make a change in your life?**

The plunge was a byproduct of being furloughed and working from home. I had unknowingly planted the seed of this new chapter months ahead of the furlough, but then the world slowed down; I had time to sit with myself to assess what I wanted my life to look like post-pandemic. And the more I sat with it, the more it became clear that the time was now.

## What did you do to discover you had a new skill set you hadn't maximized?

Truth be told, I have had people coming to me for help with their ideas, brands, and creative start-ups for years, and I've always obliged, helped, and gotten involved, but in my mind, I was helping a friend or doing it as a favor.

Launching my website and finding the language to communicate authentically helped me put my clarity and consulting services out there; I realized that I could add value and make a career out of it! My platform caters to creatives, and I expand and tailor each service based on my clients' needs. I am always listening.

## How are things going now?

It's been such an expanding and beautiful experience. I have recently updated my website to reflect all the growth since the launch in June 2020. The services and iterations of how I work have unfolded and evolved in such a way that I could never have imagined! In just this last year, my clients have been inspirational women creatives from all corners of the globe—India, the Middle East, Africa, Greece, and the US. Ranging from artists, jewelry designers, fashion editors, makeup artists, and entrepreneurs, I have guided women through the journey of creating and showing up with purpose.

## Is there someone you are grateful for who helped you along the way?

Honestly, it took a village! But three extraordinary people have lifted me through this journey—my children. They have been my motivation to create a career that brings me joy. As my biggest cheerleaders, they believe in what I do and what I give to the world through my work.

A defining moment in this chapter dates back to last March when COVID-19 arrived on the scene, and I was signing the contract hiring my website designer. I was conflicted by the uncertainty of the time and making a move that big. My kids sat with me at the dining table and said: "You always tell us that there is no perfect time. So, you need to do this. Now." And the rest is history!

## Share an exciting moment that happened since committing to your second chapter.

I would have to say the most unexpected thing that has happened since I started this chapter would be the shift in how I work with styling clients. It has evolved and taken a different iteration based on my growth. I am now a style coach, and I work with women by blending creativity, style tips, shopping strategies, and guidance to help them uncover and find the authentic style that's unique to them. Defining style from the inside out!

## Have you ever struggled with believing in yourself? If so, how did you overcome that limiting belief?

I am a recovering perfectionist, and the limiting belief that everything had to be perfect before I could share it with the world was a huge obstacle and challenge that I had to overcome.

Once I started my consultancy, it quickly became apparent how much my drive for perfection hindered my growth. I'm not a perfectionist—I'm scared of putting myself out there! It was frustrating for me because the fast pace I was trying to create was always bogged down by my doubting how it would "look," and it finally dawned on me. So, in reframing it this way, I have been able to share more openly and authentically.

**Typically, I encourage my clients to ask for support from those who believe in their vision before they embark on a new chapter. How did you create your support system?**

My support system is like a beautiful abundant garden. Over the years, I have cultivated deeply rooted relationships. I have planted the seeds, watered, nurtured them, and watched them blossom and grow. As a single mother, I am blessed to have an entire community of women in my support system. In her own unique and memorable way, each of these women showed up and lifted me through the birth of this chapter.

**Starting a new chapter requires leaving your comfort zone behind. How did you do that?**

All my life, I've been much more comfortable being behind the camera than I was in front of it. But when I started this consultancy, I understood that I needed to show up and be on camera. People needed to connect with me, and in the era of all things virtual, it meant being on camera and Instagram posts, IG lives, and interviews.

I am happy to report that after speaking in a virtual conference, conducting numerous Instagram live interviews, and even taking part in the TikTok Creator Learning Fund, I am much more comfortable showing up!

**What are five things you wish someone had told you before you started leading your business, and why?**

There is more than one way to succeed. There will always be a program, a webinar, or a course that promises to teach you the secret and formula to success. But there's no quick fix or fast pass to success. No one is you, and once you understand that, you can create something that works for you! Your path is your own.

Delegate more. Protect your time and energy for things within your skillset and that you enjoy—delegate the rest. Think about time management and let go of things that take too much of your precious time.

Rest up. Rest creates space to listen to your body and quiet your mind. When you run straight into things without slowing down, you will miss details and need to come back and course correct, which is not the end of the world, but taking a break saves time and energy on going back and forth.

Set boundaries! When we run our own businesses, the boundaries are ours to set. And it can be hard not to fall into the trap of wanting to do everything a client asks for in fear of losing work. But as an entrepreneur, it's your responsibility to set the boundaries and work only with people who respect them. Your brand isn't for everyone. And that is OK. Trying to please everyone through your work is not a good strategy. In business, if you take on being a people pleaser, you will get lost in your attempt to gain acceptance, which will lead you to lose your voice, message, and authenticity.

**You are a person of significant influence. If you could inspire a movement that would bring the best outcome to the greatest number of people, what would that be?**

I would love to inspire a movement of celebrating women in the second chapter of their careers and lives. A collective that inspires and lifts. Women that start something new in this unique stage of life would benefit from a supportive community celebrating and cheering them on while also exchanging success strategies, tips, and experiences unique to this chapter. Today too many people hold information close to their chest. We shouldn't be afraid of sharing because someone else knowing what we know will not take anything away from us.

**Dreams come true. If you could invite anyone in the world to dinner, who would that be?**

I would love to have dinner with Oprah. She's an inspiration of resilience and perseverance and such an expander of how to live authentically and do anything you can dream up no matter your age!

**Where can we follow your work?**

Website: leenaalsulaiman.com

Social:   Instagram @leena.alsulaiman

# CHAPTER 18

# Janet Wischnia

ৡ৵ ৶ৡ

*It's the value of listening to customers. American Blossom has only been selling for about two years. In this time, I have gotten to know some wonderful customers. I make it a priority to speak directly with customers at every opportunity. I read every review, and I have involvement in any problem that occurs. This gives me an early warning about anything I need to improve. I also get lovely suggestions, which help to improve the product. For example, Lynn, a UX writer, has placed several orders with us and volunteered to help us improve our website navigation. As a result, our IT director made several of the changes she recommended.*

Janet Wischnia is the founder of American Blossom Linens, a high-quality, sustainable, organic, 'Made in the USA' bedding company. Its origins spring from the family-owned textile manufacturing business she grew up in, ATD-American Company. Started in 1931 by her grandfather, the business was passed down to her father Jerome and uncles Spencer and Arnold, and she became president in 2003. Janet is a graduate of the University of Pennsylvania and Drexel University (MBA).

**Share with us a bit about your upbringing.**

My dad introduced me to this business when I was five years old. He brought home scrap work papers to scribble on while he did his own work at night. He would bring me to the office during school holidays, where he taught me how to fold pillowcases. I would deliver folders to other people in the company so that I would get to know them and they would get to know me. I worked in my family's business, ATD-American Company, for almost 40 years. I became president when my dad retired in 2003. (By the way, my dad passed away in July at nearly 95, and he still came to the office every day up until a month before he passed away.)

My grandfather started the company in 1931 with one retail linen store in the downtown area of Philadelphia. When my dad and his two brothers joined the business, they opened a second store. Over the 90 years we have been in business, the company has been reinvented several times. Under the leadership of my dad and uncles, it transitioned from a retail business to a wholesale manufacturer and distributor of textiles and other products to government agencies.

As the company grew, we expanded beyond bedding products to the healthcare and hospitality markets. Those markets grew to be larger than the government market. We sold so many sheets that it became cost-effective to start doing the manufacturing in-house.

Right after 9/11/2001, we bought one of our major competitors, Thomaston Mills, who had declared bankruptcy. They had a much larger facility, more automated equipment, and a highly trained workforce. It gave us the ability to produce higher volumes at a lower cost and a faster turnaround.

Much like now, the period after 9/11 was filled with uncertainty. The hospitality industry was heavily affected by a general decrease in travel. We also faced challenges due to changes in the global trade policies and the drive for "cheap" products where low cost rather than better quality became the prime consideration. During this period, more than a million textile jobs left the US.

We have survived these difficult times because of our quality and speed. We have developed the ability to provide customized, quality products quickly, enabling us to continue manufacturing in the USA.

## What is your life lesson quote? Can you share its relevance in your life?

My favorite life lesson quote is from Winston Churchill, "Success is going from failure to failure with no loss of enthusiasm." It is relevant because success is all about the journey. If you never try to get out of your comfort zone, you will never get better and succeed, and a big part of that is dealing with the failures that inevitably come. So, you need to embrace the failures.

## You have been blessed with success. What are three qualities you possess that helped you achieve your goals?

The three qualities that I possess are persistence, faith, and constant learning. A great example of persistence is our company's insistence on manufacturing in the USA. With increased global trade in the 1980s and 1990s, virtually all textile manufacturing moved primarily to India, Southeast Asia, and China. At that time, our business sold to the government, healthcare, and hospitality trade. We had been using contractors to manufacture the bedding that we sold to these customers.

As our business grew, we began to sell more products than our contractors could successfully provide. In 1992 we started our first small manufacturing facility in Virginia. My husband and I moved to Virginia along with our children to start this facility. We hired and trained the people and purchased the necessary equipment. As time went by, we began to outgrow this factory. In 2001 one of our previous contractors, Thomaston Mills, went bankrupt. We decided to buy them out and to buck the trend of manufacturing jobs leaving the US. We continued to employ these incredible American craftsmen and sell products made in the USA.

Faith is the hardest of these three qualities to maintain, but it is so important to have. We started the American Blossom Linens brand in 2019, and sales were good, but I hoped to grow much bigger. 2019 was a year of learning, and in 2020 I planned to take all of the lessons learned and rachet up our growth. Then the pandemic hit in March. Like every other small business, I was worried that sales would come to a screeching halt, and we quickly tried to slow down production so that we would not have an overabundance of inventory and no one to buy it. The funny thing is that about a month later, the exact opposite situation occurred. Because people were working from home and wanted to enhance their bedrooms and all of the publicity concerning the lack of PPE resulting from our reliance on China, more people wanted to buy 'Made in USA' bedding. Our sales skyrocketed by 400%, and we had to quickly build up our production. I had to have faith that sales would materialize and that my team could quickly fulfill the demand we were blessed with.

The last quality is constant learning. Throughout my life, I have found it exciting and helpful to always read and learn. I constantly read books on business. My current favorite is *Building a StoryBrand* by Donald Miller. Currently, I am reading about how to do better email marketing. I also read books about self-improvement. My current favorite is *The Book of Joy: Lasting Happiness in a Changing World* by the Dalai Lama, Desmond Tutu, and Douglas Carlton Abrams.

At the age of 43, I decided that I needed more business training. I had three children, the youngest was three, and I decided to go to an executive MBA program. I was working, studying, and raising children. It was a fun but busy time.

When we started our brand, my team members and I knew nothing about selling online or retail marketing. As a team, we learned how to do it by reading, watching video tutorials, and seeking out people who knew more than we did. Together we learned how to build and optimize a website and do SEO (Search Engine Optimization). We faced and overcame many obstacles.

## Tell us about your career experience before your second chapter.

As I said earlier, my dad took me under his wing when I was five and started to train me in business. Although I did go through a rebellious stage when I was in college (more on that later), I graduated from the University of Pennsylvania. I started work at the family business two weeks later. At the time, our main business was selling textile and furniture products to government and quasi-government agencies. I started as an entry-level customer service associate, worked on quotes to customers, became a product manager, and became the manager of the contracts department, the national sales manager, and eventually the president in 2003.

## How did you reinvent yourself in your second chapter?

I reinvented myself by doing what I always do: set goals, set up tasks, learn all I can, ask for advice, work with my team, persist in my efforts, and try very hard to keep the faith. One of the skills I learned that helped me reinvent myself was analyzing and looking critically at a situation. This was something I developed by working on government contracts for many years. You have to understand what the contract requires and analyze the situation to find the best way to meet the customer's needs and get the sale of the right product at the right time at the right price. This analysis applies to most situations in business.

## Your second chapter's transition was remarkable. What was the trigger that made you decide you needed to make a change in your life?

I turned 60 in 2019 and had been doing a lot of thinking about what direction I wanted my career to take. Two of my three children are married, and I had two grandchildren. I did not want the responsibility of being president, but I wanted to stay with the business. I had the itch to learn something new.

With all of the publicity about 'Made in America,' the growing concern about sustainability and the environment, and the direct-to-consumer model's growth, I thought I would try to take our company back to our retail roots. Caring and responsible stewardship are essential values in our family. Thomaston Mills, our manufacturing plant, had been in business since 1899, and our company had been in business since 1931. How could we protect some of these last remaining American textile manufacturing jobs and satisfy the demand we saw for American Made products? It became my mission to create 'Made in the USA' products that consumers could trust that were made to last, using only safe and sustainable manufacturing methods. I stepped down as president, turned that job over to my very capable cousin Robert Zaslow, and began to plan our new brand, American Blossom Linens—bedding 'Made in the USA' from 100% organic Western Texas cotton.

### What did you do to discover you had a new skill set you hadn't maximized?

When you are an entrepreneur with a mission, you develop the skill sets to do the job. You build a motivated team and help the people around you develop skills you may not be good at. I searched for people that could teach me online advertising. I learned social media, video, and photo production while other teammates learned how to build and optimize websites and email marketing. You overcome barriers by hard, thoughtful work, teamwork, and brute strength. You just do what you have to do. One habit that helps to maintain my will, perseverance, and courage is exercise. I find that when I regularly exercise, I have less fear, and my mood is calmer. My exercise of choice is spinning. After my gym went out of business, I bought a Peloton. That bike helped me get through 2020!

## How are things going now?

It is going great. As I said earlier, in 2020 our sales went up 400% over the previous year. Of course, the pandemic did cause a few supply issues, as experienced by most manufacturing companies. Demand was greater than the supply, but that is a good problem to have. The best and most surprising aspect of this has been that I have gotten to know some great people. I have become friends with many of our customers. We email, text, and I have even taken a socially distanced walk with one of them. When my dad passed away in July, many sent me condolence emails. The support for our products has been overwhelming. People email me to tell me that they have been looking for bedding like their grandmother had and want to buy only USA-made products. We have close to 500 very positive reviews.

## Is there someone you are grateful to who helped you along the way?

Frankly, it is hard to choose just one. I have wonderful sisters, children, friends, cousins, and coworkers who provide me constant encouragement and ideas. When he was ill, the people who took care of my dad have helped me with support and even ironed sheets for my photoshoots. I would say that I am particularly grateful toward my dad, Jerry, and my husband, Eric. My dad started training me in business, and he taught me the meaning of being responsible, dedicated, and trustworthy in all aspects of life and business. He encouraged me to learn from the ground up about business and had me do almost every entry-level job at the company during my summer vacations.

Like many teenagers, I did go through a rebellious stage. When I went to college, I decided to take liberal arts courses, but no business courses. When I was nearing the end of my senior year at the University of Pennsylvania with no idea what I would do upon graduation, my then-boyfriend, now husband, Eric, said you should work at the family business. He said you have an excellent mind for business, and you like it, so why not do it. I am very thankful to both of them for their encouragement. It has been fun so far (most of the time), and I look forward to seeing where this new venture will take us.

## Share an exciting (or interesting) moment that happened since committing to your second chapter.

The most interesting thing that has happened has been working and becoming friends with Sally Fox. Our brand prides itself on sustainability. I had been looking to introduce a new color to our line at the end of 2019. A colleague who works at a weaving plant introduced me to Sally, who created a brand of cotton called Foxfibre®. She is a "cotton pioneer"—in the 1980's she was the first to develop the systems to grow and promote organic cotton in the USA, which started the conversation about organic textiles. The naturally colored kinds of cotton that Sally works with have existed for centuries and can be traced back at least 4300 years and originated in the Americas. Heirloom cotton was once abundant and grew in a rainbow of shades, including green, yellow, blue, and brown. She did what no one thought was possible. She hand-bred ancient, naturally pest-resistant varieties of cotton that can be grown using organic and biodynamic farming methods. She developed long-staple lengths that allowed the cotton fiber to be spun into high-quality yarn. Together we created our Latte Linen fabric from a blend of Foxfibre® and West Texas organic cotton.

When we introduced the product, we decided to make a series of videos interviewing Sally about her journey. That was something I had never done and certainly got me out of my comfort zone.

**Have you ever struggled with believing in yourself? If so, how did you overcome that limiting belief?**

I struggle every day to believe in myself. Every day I don't feel up to the task and the mission of this brand, but then I just get up and go do it. I take one step at a time and one thing at a time. Frankly, having a mission is crucial because it helps you get over the self-doubt and get you back on track. The mission outweighs the doubt. So, I just keep pushing forward. My husband says that I am courageous because fearless people have it easy, but I have to constantly fight my fear and do what I do despite the fear.

**Typically, I encourage my clients to ask for support from those who believe in their vision before they embark on a new chapter. How did you create your support system?**

One of my strengths is networking, so this really helped in this new endeavor. Cultivating teamwork is crucial. It has been so important for me to gather experienced, motivated individuals within our company to handle manufacturing, packaging, shipping, and building our website. I also have friends helping—my best friend from college writes blog posts, and another friend helps with line art, yet another does photoshoots. My family—husband, sisters, and cousins have tested the product and given me so much encouragement. Experts outside of our company help with design, advertising ideas, strategy, and implementation.

Tanya, the wife of one of our salespeople, has her own graphic design company, which helped me develop the brand's look, and I have had such fun. We even went on a road trip to do a photoshoot together before COVID-19. After working with three online advertising companies, I found Uri at Adjust Media, who has been wonderful to work with and a perfect advisor. I feel blessed to have such a talented and supportive network to help me bring my idea to market.

**Starting a new chapter requires leaving your comfort zone behind. How did you do that?**

The truth is I never get comfortable getting out of my comfort zone. I make it tolerable by continuing to learn and exercising to reduce stress. The main thing that keeps me moving forward is focusing on our mission to create jobs in the USA and gratitude for all those on the team and customers who care and support us. The whole journey has been an exercise in getting out of my comfort zone. Remember, I knew nothing about retail marketing or building a website!

**What are five things you wish someone had told you before you started leading your business, and why?**

The value of listening to customers. American Blossom has only been selling for about two years. In this time, I have gotten to know some wonderful customers. I make it a priority to speak directly with customers at every opportunity. I read every review, and I have involvement in any problem that occurs. This gives me an early warning about anything I need to improve. I also get wonderful suggestions which help to improve the product. For example, Lynn, a UX writer, has placed several orders with us and volunteered to help us improve our website navigation. As a result, our IT director made several of the changes she recommended.

The value of listening to employees. Not being very experienced with retail packaging, I went to our sewing supervisor, production planners, and plant manager for guidance. It was their idea to make the box from recycled cardboard and not use any plastic packaging. We have less waste which is, of course, better for the environment and is appreciated by our customers.

The value of listening to vendors. I was looking to make an environmentally friendly product and different from other products in the marketplace. One of our long-time partners introduced me to Sally Fox, the breeder, and supplier of FoxFibre® organic cotton grown in color. It enables us to produce a fabric that is colored and dye-free. I have had the opportunity to visit Sally at her farm, and now we have become friends.

The value of listening to your gut. I started this process because I wanted to make sustainable, 'Made in the USA' bedding that I personally would love to sleep in. Using organic cotton, heavier, more substantial fabric, deeper pockets, and more generously sized flat sheets was the right decision. Customers are ordering; we have 96% 5-star reviews. Best of all, customers call me just to tell me how much they like the product.

The value of not listening. When the going gets tough, don't listen to "it can't be done." Throughout my career, I have been told many times, "You cannot do that,"; "it's cheaper to make bedding overseas,"; "no one will pay the price for the American Blossom quality." Well, after two years, we have proved them wrong. We will make this a success because it is a great product, and it is also the right thing to do to keep jobs in the USA.

**You are a person of significant influence. If you could inspire a movement that would bring the best outcome to the greatest number of people, what would that be?**

This is a very easy question for me. I would start a movement to educate people on the importance of buying products 'Made in the USA.' For over 30 years, we, as consumers, have allowed our manufacturing jobs to be sent overseas. This has affected most industries, from medicine, electronics, equipment to furniture, clothing, and bedding. Unfortunately, the American people have continued to support companies that have moved production to China and India in pursuit of "cheap." Economists say that if things cost less, everyone benefits, but is this really true? Is "cheap" really the best?

In times like this, with COVID-19 threatening supply chains and jobs, maybe we should rethink our buying habits. We pay the price for these "inexpensive throw-away" items in lost jobs, environmental problems, ever-larger landfills, and lack of control of products that we rely on to live our lives.

Manufacturing here in the USA certainly helps our economy. USA manufacturers are held to much higher wages, environmental and safety standards, making price competition difficult, but the benefits are worth the extra cost. While most textile manufacturing left the USA, as a family business, we felt it was essential to take care of our larger community, so we decided to do what it takes to continue manufacturing in Georgia. It has not been easy, but we have been committed because it is the right thing. In the process, we have built up our manufacturing capabilities, using technology where we could, partnered with other American suppliers, and most importantly, worked hard, and just kept pushing forward.

## Dreams come true. If you could invite anyone in the world to dinner, who would it be?

There are two entrepreneurs that I would love to meet. First of all, I am a Shark Tank junkie. It is practically the only show my husband and I watch. We have watched most episodes more than one time. I would love to meet Laurie Greiner. She is intelligent, hardworking, persistent, and still remarkably kind to all of the contestants—and I love the way she dresses! The second person is Peter Thiel. He believes in avoiding competition by thinking in unique ways that overcome the status quo. American Blossom bucks the trend of chasing after the lowest price at the expense of quality, sustainability, and responsibility.

## Where can we follow your work?

Website: americanblossomlinens.com
Social:   Facebook / Instagram / Pinterest @
          americanblossomlinens

# CHAPTER 19

# Belinda Huesman

࿇

*Begin now! Do the work, even if you do not see results right away. The grant proposal I wrote for the arts center led to the coaching experience; the coaching led to my decision to transition out of my position and take a leap of faith, which allowed me to pursue and honor my talents. That leap connected my passion with my purpose, a purpose that is bigger than me. I wish I had connected years ago with the network I am now building. It's never too early or too late to follow your dreams!*

Belinda Fraley Huesman is The Menopause Outlaw, a motivational singer-songwriter embracing wisdom to erase ageism in the music industry through the power of story and song. She is the founder and CEO of Menopause Outlaws LLC and The M.O. Network, a digital community empowering women to connect their passion to their purpose, age fearlessly, and defy boundaries. She is the author of an inspirational children's book titled *Wings*, currently on Amazon, as well as her new book release, *Becoming the Hero of Your Own Story*. She is partially responsible for "Loretta's Law," Maryland Uniform Power of Attorney Act in 2010. She was recognized as one of The Daily Record 2018 CEOs of the Year and "Women Who Make a Difference" from the Chamber of Commerce of Northern Anne Arundel County, Maryland.

## Share with us a bit about your upbringing.

I grew up on the outskirts of Baltimore City, in a small town called Brooklyn. Growing up, life seemed idyllic, with mom always home and in a neighborhood with all the small-town American conveniences. We did not want for anything.

Our lives changed when I was about ten. My father was successful and bought a bar and a big house on a hill. We all worked at the bar, which might not have been a good thing because that is when things started to change. The stresses and power of owning a bar invaded my parent's marriage and our lives. It turns out my father somehow became connected to some shady characters, and our parents feared for our lives as well as their own. His success came at a cost to our entire family.

My parents started fighting, and this period was the beginning of the end. I remember my sister and I would blast the music and sing and dance to drown out the fighting. Our childhood hinged on whatever was happening with my parents at the moment. Then, fifty years ago, Carole King released the album Tapestry. It would be the album that changed the course of my life and my dreams. The song "It's Too Late" repeatedly played in the front row as I viewed my parent's divorce.

## What is your life lesson quote? Can you share its relevance in your life?

Instead of quoting another person, I will share with you my own mantra. These are words I live by and are the pillars of my platform—"Passion illuminates the path experience has yet to walk."

I believe my passion for writing songs had shed light, even during those moments when I had to put my dream on the shelf.

Continuing to act on and acknowledge our passion lights the way, even though we may not be aware of the next steps in the present moment. I believe when it is the proper time, the path will appear.

## You have been blessed with success. What are three qualities you possess that helped you achieve your goals?

Common sense, optimism, and confidence in our understanding of purpose. Having common sense is a quality that is not so common. From an early age, watching my father (who only had a fifth-grade education) become a successful businessman was a life lesson. It helped me to see that it is essential to rely on our sensibility and our intuition.

During the struggles in my own life, I remained optimistic for the chance of a better future. Relying on my passion and sensibilities, I literally wrote my way out of a bad marriage. I reminded myself, through my writings, that I am the hero of my own story. That I had control over my destiny. This helped me to manifest a positive outcome. I have always believed that positivity prevails. I think two thoughts cannot occupy the same space. Therefore, one can choose to either dwell on the positive or the negative of any situation. I choose positivity.

I believe confidence is instilled from an early age, but we all struggle with maintaining self-confidence during our lifetime. However, placing ourselves in an arena that builds continued confidence is essential. It helps us to acknowledge our gifts and purpose and provides us the courage to follow our passion.

## Tell us about your career experience before your second chapter.

As I said earlier, passion illuminates the path experience has yet to walk. I never stopped writing songs (and honing my craft) amidst the job change and life challenges I faced. This passion drove me to constantly write. As my father had a business, and my mother was the bookkeeper, we all worked in the family business at one time or another. In my senior year of high school, I worked part-time at UPS in the payroll department. It was there I realized I had a natural aptitude for numbers. I then took a job at the Hyatt Regency, Baltimore, in the accounts receivable department. Once I married and had my children, my husband's career was deemed more important. We transferred to Dallas, where I worked from home raising two sons.

In 1997, after my divorce, I moved back to Baltimore and worked obtaining construction permits for my twin sister's company. I then remarried in 2002. After my father passed in 2006, my family wanted to carry on his legacy. So we opened a construction management firm. I was then asked to sit on the board of the local art center (a position my twin sister graciously turned down). I jumped at the chance! That position led me to my next job; I became the executive director and CEO of the Chesapeake Arts Center. Transferable skills, common sense, and my love of numbers were vital for managing the non-profit center.

## How did you reinvent yourself in your second chapter?

I have to say, it took me years to reinvent myself. I first had to own my talents and be thoroughly grounded in my purpose. It was always my dream to follow my passion for singing and songwriting. However, there were expectations in my family; you got a job and married, settled down, and had kids. I did just that, but it did not turn out the way I planned.

It was not until my mother passed away (at the age of 54) that I took action to pursue my dream. I was thirty. Before she died, she said to me: "Don't be like me, go after your dreams. Even if you fail, it won't be because you didn't try." After she passed, we found a book of her poems. My mother literally kept her dreams on a shelf. I knew I had to honor her and myself. So I started traveling back and forth to Nashville, attending any and every event to learn about the music industry.

In 2010, my husband and I made the decision to get a place in Nashville. A co-writer and I were writing songs for our demographic (over 40). We called ourselves The Menopause Outlaws™, with a plan to become a brand. We felt that no one was cutting songs that spoke to our audience; we knew there was a void to fill by sharing our wisdom and life experiences. It took ten years, during which I took over the entity and formed the LLC of Menopause Outlaws™.

**Your second chapter's transition was remarkable. What was the trigger that made you decide you needed to make a change in your life?**

As I have shared, my career path was built organically around the ups and downs of my family life. I worked in my position at the arts center for seven years (which operated out of the high school I attended). Roaming those halls each day as a professional with a demanding job brought me back to *The Girl I Left Behind* (which became the title of one of my songs). During that time, the center received a Bloomberg grant which included money for professional coaching. In these coaching sessions, I realized I was not fulfilling my God-given talents, nor was I connecting my passion with my purpose. I discovered I had what I refer to as the gift of encouragement and my voice and words as a singer/songwriter. I knew it was time to leave my position.

In my final months, during the transition period, I hosted a fundraiser with a one-woman show. I told the story of my life story through my songs. The event was entitled: The Hero of My Own Story. At the event, I appealed to potential donors by sharing stories of my childhood within those same walls. I told them, "You never know what heroes are in the making walking these halls."

During this performance, my purpose was illuminated by my passion. I shared how Carole King's song "It's Too Late" had inspired me as a young girl. I shared how I escaped into the art of music during a stressful time in my life. I explained how the arts center provided that same escape for at-risk students when the opportunity to attend our programming. After the show, I had so many people come up to me and tell me how my story resonated with them. It was brave, and I realized I could empower others by sharing my story; by being my own hero. I knew then it was time to become The Menopause Outlaw. I knew she was inside of me, more empowered than ever.

Honestly, the pandemic helped to clarify my goals and the underlying message further. As I began my entrepreneurial next chapter, I realized that I can address ageism through the power of story and song as a singer-songwriter. This second act is more extensive than mine. Embracing wisdom and erasing ageism is a huge undertaking. It takes a network, a community. So why not use the universal language of music to accomplish our goal?

### What did you do to discover you had a new skill set you hadn't maximized?

The most crucial skill set I have maximized is setting goals. As Benjamin Franklin said, "If you fail to plan, you plan to fail." I wrote the plan for Menopause Outlaws™ years ago, but now I am taking action to accomplish our vision. I am bringing it to life. Setting goals, along with the three qualities (common sense, optimism, and confidence), has served me well. Prioritizing the one most important thing each day that will move us closer is key to achieving our goals.

Looking back, 1997 was a tumultuous year. After experiencing a divorce, losing my home, relocation, menopause (due to a total hysterectomy), bankruptcy, and a custody battle, I realized I can do anything I set my mind to. I drove away with $300 and a tank of gas when I left Texas. What did I have to lose? Now in 2021, I have a plan, and it is coming to fruition!

## How are things going now?

This movement is still very new. However, I am grateful to John Leal (Brace Artist Management) and Katharine Poole, journalist and author, for their belief in this movement. Last year, they joined my team, working pro-bono, to galvanize this message and actively support Menopause Outlaws™. I believe this changed the direction of their paths and inspired them to combine their passions with purpose.

Our podcast, *Real & Raw* with the Menopause Outlaws, is gaining momentum. We have had the opportunity to interview iconic women, including Beverly Keel and Tracy Gershon of Change the Conversation. Like our network member, Lisa Neville Ambler, we have inspired others to branch out and take entrepreneurial steps of their own. Most of all, we bring together a community of women to share our stories, wisdom, and expertise. Our voices are being heard and respected, and valued.

I receive words of empowerment from our network/community members daily. One upcoming *Real & Raw* podcast guest, Virginia Brick of SESAC, wrote, "I feel completely humbled to have been asked to be a part of the vision you ladies have for the M.O. tribe . . . Thank you for making me feel enough! Thank you for lighting that fire in my soul to go after my dreams and aspirations even more . . . Your light and love are felt (even through a Zoom camera), and the words from the emails are so encouraging. Honest space with women who build each other and empower others through their own highs and lows through each chapter of life they have written already."

## Is there someone you are grateful to who helped you along the way?

I would have to credit my husband for his support in this endeavor, both emotionally and financially. He supported the decision to move to Nashville when this idea was formulated. He is my partner in life and in business with Menopause Outlaws™, LLC. Menopause Outlaws™ (along with our partner company, The M.O. Network) and strives to outlaw ageism in the music industry through the power of song and the enlightenment of stories and conversation. My husband has continually encouraged me to take a leap of faith and follow my dreams every step of the way.

### Share an exciting moment that happened since committing to your second chapter.

There are so many stories . . . I am blown away by the caliber of women my co-host, Katharine Poole, and I interview for our podcast Real & Raw. Our first two guests were Beverly Keel and Tracy Gershon, co-founders of Change the Conversation, Nashville. Their example and story have given me more confidence on this path; I am encouraged to change a paradigm. In addition, we are being contacted by incredible women who want to be included in our interviews. This tells me that we are on the right path, and many women want to be part of it.

### Have you ever struggled with believing in yourself? If so, how did you overcome that limiting belief?

I sometimes have imposter syndrome. I read about it, and I understand this is true for many women. I try not to dwell on limiting beliefs for long. I roll up my sleeves, push those thoughts aside, and get back to work.

### Typically, I encourage my clients to ask for support from those who believe in their vision before they embark on a new chapter. How did you create your support system?

In September 2019, before transitioning out of my role at the arts center, I went to Nashville with a gut feeling. I attended the first Change the Conversation event at the Entrepreneur Center, entitled

"Surrounding Yourself with the Right Team." After that, I knew I had to start making things happen. On a follow-up trip, I met up at SESAC and was introduced to some songwriters who told me about an event with the Arts and Business Council. I attended, and it was there that I sat next to John Leal with Brace Artist Management. I told him my plan, and he supported my endeavor wholeheartedly. He eventually introduced me to Katharine Poole. They are both now members of The M.O. Network's executive team.

## Starting a new chapter requires leaving your comfort zone behind. How did you do that?

The one-woman show fundraiser at the arts center took me right out of my comfort zone. Showcasing original songs and telling my life story was terrifying. I dreaded it. That is until I was up on stage; after about ten minutes, I finally relaxed and realized that I was the hero of my own story. I was truly living my purpose. It was an epiphany.

## What are five things you wish someone had told you before you started leading your organization, and why?

Begin now! Do the work, even if you do not see results right away. The grant proposal I wrote for the arts center led to the coaching experience; the coaching led to my decision to transition out of my position and take the leap of faith to pursue and honor my talents. That leap connected my passion with my purpose, a purpose that is bigger than me. I wish I had connected years ago with the network I am now building. It's never too early or too late to follow your dreams!

Surround yourself with winners, people that are constantly moving out of their comfort zone. My Dad had terrific gems of wisdom, one of my favorite quotes he would often say was, "You will never soar with the eagles if you are hanging around a bunch of turkeys." (Longfellow Deeds)

Find people who have skill sets you do not possess. You will waste valuable time deviating from your purpose and stay stuck in a perpetual Groundhog Day.

Words are power. What you say to yourself and others can make or break you. I write for myself first and believe my lyrics to be true for me and inspirational for others. I am the hero of my own story.

You need passion! I repeat, "Passion will illuminate the path experience has yet to walk." Your passion for something is a clue, follow it, and it will lead you to your purpose.

**You are a person of significant influence. If you could inspire a movement that would bring the best outcome to the greatest number of people, what would that be?**

I have already started it. The Menopause Outlaws™! A Musical Movement: Addressing Ageism Through the Power of Story and Song to Help "Write" the Wrong! The bigger goal is to embrace wisdom and erase ageism for those who will come behind us. I see us changing the definition of the word menopause. I hope one day Webster's Dictionary will rewrite the definition to include the word wisdom as a part of its meaning.

**Dreams come true. If you could invite anyone in the world to dinner, who would that be?**

Oprah Winfrey. She is a transformative powerhouse imbuing authenticity, vulnerability, and honesty. She is true to who she is. She changes lives.

**Where can we follow your work?**

Website: themonetwork.org / Iambelinda.com

# CHAPTER 20

# Ed Latimore

❧ ❧

*The work never ends. If you're going to work for yourself and do so with a mission, then you have to accept that there is no end. You never really stop creating and contributing. There are only short breaks that last as long as it takes for the next opportunity to arise. And if it takes too long, you have to create it.*

Ed Latimore is a former professional heavyweight boxer, a competitive chess player, a US Army National Guard veteran, and a bestselling author. Ed's work focuses on self-development, realizing your potential, and sobriety—all of which he approaches from personal experience, overcoming poverty and addiction. Many people have learned from Ed's experiences through his writing and speaking.

## Share with us a bit about your upbringing.

I grew up as a typical "at-risk youth." While I knew my father, I probably saw him once a year, and he played no disciplinary or guiding role in my life, so I was effectively raised by a single mother. We lived in public housing and cycled on and off food stamps and public assistance. The neighborhood I grew up in was full of people with a similar backstory. Areas like this are notorious for gang violence, drug use, and high crime rates.

I was fortunate enough to avoid getting caught up in many traps that keep people stuck in that environment. I mainly avoided falling in with the wrong crowd because I remember hating my neighborhood and the limitations of my lifestyle with a passion. While I didn't know exactly what "different" looked like, I remember that I wanted to have a different life than what I grew up with and in other surroundings than all I had known as a child.

## What is your life lesson quote? Can you share its relevance in your life?

I have two: "The difficulty of a task is irrelevant if it's vital to your success."—Mayur Bardolia. And, "Given enough time, you can learn anything."

This combination of ideas made it possible for me to improve my life, especially when things looked bleak. For example, when I was broke, I knew that it would take a long time to fix that problem and that it might be difficult. However, I improved my financial situation by enrolling in school at the age of 28 and pushing through a challenging physics major.

When I decided that I wanted to build a following for my writing, I expected it to take a long time to build a fan base and learn the craft of writing to the point where I could skillfully communicate any idea to my audience. It takes time to develop these and even longer to get paid for them.

These quotes were helpful to me in my darkest hours as I stopped drinking. Every recovering alcoholic understands that it takes "one day at a time," but this is tested in the face of temptation to take you back to the bad habits you're trying to rid yourself of. However, I knew that if I stuck with it over time, no matter how difficult it'd become, I'd make myself into someone I could be proud of.

## You have been blessed with success. What are three qualities you possess that helped you achieve your goals?

First, most importantly, I'm willing to take risks. Risks are generally viewed as something that you want to avoid, but that's only in the case of "pure risk." Pure risk is a risk that can only result in loss. I've succeeded because I eagerly embrace what is known as "speculative risk."

Speculative risk is a risk where you can win or lose something. The best version of this is taking a calculated risk by betting on yourself. The worst is gambling by betting on things you can't control. So, I take speculative risks—smart bets on myself.

When I was an amateur boxer, I needed to train with the best coach around, but he was 20 miles away, and I needed to drive. So, I drove a broken-down beater to the gym every day; although my driver's license was suspended, I couldn't afford insurance, and the car couldn't pass inspection. Getting pulled over once would have realistically meant jail time. However, I took the risk because I needed to train, and it paid off.

Second, you need grit. Grit is the ability to persist towards a long-term goal despite any setbacks you face along the way. Many people give up at first sight of difficulty. A few don't give up until they meet the second or third setback. But most people eventually give up. Not those with grit. Even though I have a physics degree, I nearly failed all of my math classes in high school. I failed calculus three times before I finally passed it a fourth time. I had to retake two courses throughout my degree, but I pursued my degree despite these setbacks and failures.

Lastly, you need to be grateful. Just because things aren't going well doesn't mean they'll always be that way. Looking at a situation and realizing that things could be worse is one of the most powerful things you can do for your life. It keeps your perspective positive, and a positive mind is a powerful asset for solving your problems.

When I lost my first fight by first-round knockout, I remember being worried about how I'd pay my bills and dealing with public embarrassment. However, rather than focus on that, I looked at all of the good things in my life. I even told myself that one day it would be the best thing that ever happened to me. I truly believe it was because of this mentality that I could leverage that experience into a way to grow my popularity as a writer.

## Tell us about your career before your second chapter.

Before my second chapter, I wasn't doing much with my life outside of amateur boxing. I worked whatever jobs allowed me to make enough money to live and afforded me the freedom to train.

## How did you reinvent yourself in your second chapter?

The first thing I did was get my alcoholism under control. I've been sober since December 23rd, 2013. I consider this the first full day of my second chapter because I decided to build a better life for myself. Shortly after, I enrolled in school and set out to make sure that I could do something other than box and work low-level customer service jobs.

These are outcomes of a change in my internal process. I decided that I would stop trying to be liked and try to be respected. People like a person they can always drink and party with, but they may not respect them. I think it's important to aim to be respected because it tends to be a better proxy indicator for the progress you're making in the world.

Being respected forces you to build a life of value and substance. But, on the other hand, being liked merely demands you to be entertaining, and very often, being entertaining forces you to behave in a counterproductive way to making progress.

**Your second chapter's transition was remarkable. What was the trigger that made you decide you needed to make a change in your life?**

I remember one night I went out drinking with some friends. I woke up at a friend's house, and I couldn't remember how I got there. This wasn't an uncommon occurrence, but I finally had things I was trying to accomplish. I had just enrolled in school, started military service, just turned pro as a boxer, and I had just met the woman who'd go on to be my fiancé. I finally had something to lose.

I looked at my future and decided that I wanted it to be better than my past. So, I always tell people that this moment in my life was akin to the part in *The Matrix* where Neo is trying to escape from the car on his way to meet Morpheus, and Trinity stops him and says, "You have been down there Neo. You know that road. You know exactly where it ends. And I know that's not where you want to be." I looked into the future of someone on a path of continued drinking and decided that I didn't want to be there. Then I started to change.

**What did you do to discover you had a new skill set you hadn't maximized?**

I learned that my unique talent is teaching and writing. I learned that I really enjoyed using my platform to help people deal with the challenges, make similar life changes, and overcome substance abuse. I initially started by simply writing articles on my experiences with sobriety and the benefits I gained from it in my own life.

This was primarily therapeutic, but then people started to tell me that they were using my articles to help them in their journey. After seeing the effect, I was having just by casually sharing, I decided to write a book about dealing with the emotional changes that accompany sobriety and the positive benefits that come with it.

## How are things going now?

The best part is about living a life where I use my platform, experience, and writing to help people with the same problems I've overcome. I'm consistently receiving messages from people on social media, giving me credit for them making it one year without alcohol. Even better are the people who say my books gave them the courage to walk away from alcohol.

## Is there someone you are grateful to who helped you along the way?

There is no particular person who helped me get to this level. Instead, several people are responsible for the success I have. First, I'm grateful to all the people who recognized that I had a problem, and they called me out on it. Second, while I'd like to think I would have made the changes in my life on my own, I'm grateful that I had people around me to help out.

I'm grateful to the people who have taught me everything about SEO and online marketing. Without those skills, I'd never been able to grow a following, make a name for myself, and make a living being able to help people. It's not just enough to have something to say. You also need to be able to make people listen to you.

I'm grateful to the platforms and people who have given me opportunities to discuss my work and story and believed in me to recommend my work to their audience. I would not be anywhere without all of these influences.

## Share an exciting moment that happened since committing to your second chapter.

I always told people that I'd be more famous as a writer than a boxer. I don't think I even appreciated how true that might be. So, I've learned to not mention where I'm traveling to if I don't want to turn people down for meeting up. This has happened in places where I figured no one had read my writing—in places like Juneau, Alaska, or Marrakech, Morocco. I even got waived through by the TSA once because the agent at the airport gate recognized me.

I don't tell these stories to brag. I am far from famous. I only mention it because it's pretty exciting and unique that I can have this type of far-reaching effect by simply trying to help.

### Have you ever struggled with believing in yourself? If so, how did you overcome that limiting belief?

I've never really struggled with believing in myself because I don't believe in notions of talent. I know that if I apply myself to whatever I'm trying to achieve, then it's basically impossible to fail. At the very least, it's impossible to not make any progress and learn something that will help get me closer to my goal. Because I lean on this idea, I never struggle with believing in myself. I'm confident in my ability to learn, and I know that I won't quit, so there is no doubt that something good will happen from me sticking to the goal.

### Typically, I encourage my clients to ask for support from those who believe in their vision before they embark on a new chapter. How did you create your support system?

Support is nice but isn't always feasible. I was very much "baptized by fire." The two significant rebirths in my life were both without support systems. When I got sober, no one around me was not drinking that I could ask for advice. I didn't know anyone who stopped drinking so late, went back to school so late, or joined the military so late.

Likewise, when I started the transition from professional boxing to my writing career, I didn't know of anyone who did that either. The connections from one world don't really translate well to the other world. Therefore, I figured out a lot of "best practices" for self-promotion on my own.

## Starting a new chapter requires leaving your comfort zone behind. How did you do that?

While I enjoy writing, much of my most successful content has been through audio or video medium. I am still struggling with making the transition because writing is comfortable and relatively easy for me. Still, I can't deny the power of reaching more people via these other mediums. Therefore, I will continue to step outside of my comfort zone and embrace them even more.

## What are five things you wish someone had told you before you started leading your endeavor, and why?

Your effort and reputation get you the opportunity, but your follow-through and results are how you keep it. When you start any new venture, you don't have any previous results to rely on. Instead, you have to rely on your reputation and some marketing. This is how I got some of my first coaching clients. They read my writing and decided that I could do a good job of helping them solve their problem.

The quality insight that comes from experience will help someone out. I have some high-profile clients, and my first thought used to be, "How can I possibly help you? You're far more successful than I am." The reality is that no one is perfect, and sometimes the area where you're successful is the exact area that someone needs help in.

Leverage will allow you to do more things faster, but you've got to learn how to let go. Content creators and business owners are deathly afraid of letting someone handle any part of their business. However, the only way to make progress past a certain point is to bring in help and learn to depend on them. This requires you to become more like an employer, but this is an inevitable step if you want to continue to grow. I would not be able to run my memberships, website, and programs if I did not bring in partners and hire people to outsource to.

The more money someone spends, the more forgiving of mistakes they tend to be if they don't happen often, and you fix them immediately when they do. This is a surprising observation. The more money someone spends, the more laidback they tend to be and less anxious about getting an immediate return on their investment. This is almost certainly because to get to a position where you can spend a lot of money, you likely learned that it takes time to produce a good outcome.

The work never ends. If you're going to work for yourself and do so with a mission, then you have to accept that there is no end. You never really stop creating and contributing. There are only short breaks that last as long as it takes for the next opportunity to arise. And if it takes too long, you have to create it.

**You are a person of significant influence. If you could inspire a movement that would bring the best outcome to the greatest number of people, what would that be?**

I'd want people to practice forgiveness and come to a deep understanding of it. We need to realize that justice and forgiveness are two separate things, not meant to replace one another, and both are necessary to progress our world and heal it. Our greatest problem right now is that we can't let go of the past.

**Dreams come true. If you could invite anyone in the world to dinner, who would that be?**

I'd love to dine with Naval Ravikant because I've enjoyed the significant insights that he's made on social media while also picking his brain about how he sees the future. A successful venture capitalist is likely to have a unique perspective on the direction the world is taking and how to prepare for it.

**Where can we follow your work?**

Website: edlatimore.com

Social:    Twitter and Instagram @edlatimore

# CHAPTER 21

# Vickie Aigner

৵৶

*Positivity and always seeing the glass half full. I am endlessly optimistic. I dream, and for me, the dream is my new reality. From all the challenges I have been through, positivity is the one thing that has kept me going. Losing a husband, creating a career from scratch in my 50's, raising six children on my own—I could not have made it past these challenges without waking up every morning and reminding myself of the positive things to look forward to.*

Vickie Aigner is a health and wellness expert turned start-up founder of Alive, Fit & Free, where she provides virtual classes and events for seniors. Her path was anything but ordinary. After being widowed at 48 with six children, she started her career and finally turned her passion into a social start-up at age 66.

## Share with us a bit about your upbringing?

I grew up as an only child in California, and I always longed for brothers and sisters. All my friends had them, and I wished so badly to have a "normal" family. However, I was awkward around the brothers and sisters of my friends and didn't really know how to relate. I think my longing for being a part of a community started at this stage. I grew up in a predominantly Asian neighborhood in Sacramento, and I was the only non-Asian girl in my group of neighborhood friends. I absolutely loved being a part of the community, but I had no idea that I didn't necessarily fit in at that age. I thought I was Japanese until one day while dancing in a bazaar at the Buddhist Church, all decked out in my kimono and finger clackers, someone commented on my pretty blonde hair and blue eyes. I was devastated. All of a sudden, in my six-year-old eyes, I did not belong to the community I was so excited to be a part of.

I remember the holidays; my mother and a group of her friends would always plan big get-togethers for anyone they knew that didn't have a family. Our celebrations were open to anyone that needed a place to go; it was a group to call their own. These celebrations were the highlight of my year, as I had more than enough friends to play with, and everyone was welcome.

Looking back, my desire to be a part of a community definitely started at a young age from my childhood.

## What is your life lesson quote? Can you share its relevance to you in your life?

"The love in your heart wasn't put there to stay; love isn't love 'til you give it away."—Oscar Hammerstein.

I always wanted to be around people from a young child, interact with them, and share my passion for life. This quote encompasses what is important in life. We can say, 'I love you,' a hundred times a day, but if our thoughts and actions don't align with those words and aren't actively showing it, it's relatively meaningless. After my husband passed away, I realized that we are never guaranteed another moment other than the present. So, if it is in our hands to do something nice for someone and show them that we care, even if it is just a smile or a pat on the back, then we need to do it. It might be our last chance to warm someone's heart!

Saying, 'I love you,' is not loving someone—love is a verb, and we have to make sure that person has received the love you have for them. And isn't it just so fun to surprise people with something that uplifts them?

## How would your best friend describe you?

Energetic, caring, compassionate, hard worker, dedicated, enthusiastic, loving, high energy, positive. Of course, there is the other side as well—I can be impatient, unplanned, impulsive, and too sensitive. For me, life is about getting to know yourself, the good and the bad, and balancing those characteristics in how you interact with the world around you. At the end of the day, I'm happy to accept the flaws that make me part of the person I am.

## You have been blessed with success. What are three qualities you possess that helped you accomplish your goals?

Positivity and always seeing the glass half full. I am endlessly optimistic. I dream, and for me, the dream is my new reality. From all the challenges I have been through, positivity is the one thing that has kept me going. Losing a husband, creating a career from scratch in my 50's, raising six children on my own—I could not have made it past these challenges without waking up every morning and reminding myself of the positive things to look forward to.

Perseverance and dedication to my passion. It's hard to start a business. It's hard to get rejected time after time and still keep going, but perseverance is what gets you there. You will find those you are meant to serve, but it won't be without rejection and discouraging days. Keeping my vision front-of-mind and persevering was vital in helping me get to where I am today.

Energy. I am very high-energy. I actively keep my positive energy high through various meditation practices, and it's the one thing that people comment on the most, 'How do you have so much energy?' Energy is what gives you the tools you need to keep going when times are tough, to have enough fuel in your tank to work hard and do the things you need to do daily, and to power through challenges as they come at you and move on to the next. At 67, I teach multiple fitness classes a day, have my own personal practice in the morning, and (in non-COVID-19 times) enjoy going out with friends at night. I can't say enough about how having lots of positive energy contributes to your success in life.

**Typically, I encourage my clients to ask for support from those who believe in their vision before they embark on a new chapter. How did you create your support system?**

Until the age of 48, I was a stay-at-home mom to my six children. After my teenage years, I moved to Northern Idaho with a dream of living off the land. I homesteaded 60 acres with no running water or electricity. I befriended the old-timers and gleaned all I could from the land while growing and preserving my own food. After I lived there for ten years, I felt I had accomplished my dream, and I was ready for something new. During this time, I had taken some certification courses in health and wellness, but I never practiced in the industry.

I then moved to Oregon, where I met my husband. After we married, we eventually joined the Mennonite Church, which is a God-fearing religious community with a particular code of rules to live by. As we had been searching for a community for so long, this tight-knit, caring community drew us in. As a woman in the Mennonite Church, my job was to be a submissive wife and mother, which I did for the good part of 10 years. Before my second chapter, my prior experience for the last 15+ years was as a stay-at-home wife and mother in a very religious community.

## How did you reinvent yourself in your second chapter?

After about 10 years as a part of the Mennonite community, it became more and more apparent that this lifestyle was not for us. We had just moved to Mississippi and had started building our own home. I was the contractor, and my husband and two sons were the builders. The plan was to complete the house, sell, and move, leaving Mississippi and the Mennonite community. This would not be an easy feat as they must 'expel' you from the community for you to go, and they don't do that easily.

Life, however, had different plans. Halfway through building our house, my husband had a severe heart attack and passed away within a week. So here I was, a grieving widow, with six children ranging from 3–18 years old, in Mississippi, in the middle of building a house amidst the Mennonite community. I had no reserves or savings and began cleaning houses for a living, hauling some of my children along with me. After surviving on cleaning houses for a year, I realized that this would not cut it and went back to what I knew—fitness and nutrition.

That was the year of reinvention. Finally, I mustered up the courage to leave the Mennonite community. I began pursuing my personal training certification and other fitness certifications and started studying for my Wellness Coaching and Holistic Nutritionist degrees.

We then moved to Arizona so my oldest son could pursue his degree in architecture, and that's where my career in health and fitness began. I worked at several fitness clubs before becoming a Wellness Coach for a company where I coached hundreds of people a month—and I loved it! So, I decided to start my company, Alive, Fit & Free, to help people get healthy and happy. I wasn't sure what that looked like, but I kept walking through open doors and following the trail that led me to where I am today, targeting the senior industry.

**Your second chapter's transition was remarkable. What was the trigger that made you decide you needed to make a change in your life?**

I had a couple of triggers.

When I was 25, I developed cervical cancer, which I healed naturally. That was the first trigger that got me passionate about health and wellness.

My second trigger was when my husband died in 2001. I was forced to go to work cleaning houses, and I determined this was not what I wanted to do for the rest of my life.

My third trigger was perhaps the most important to defining what Alive, Fit & Free is today. After my husband died, I threw all my energy into surviving. I never addressed the elephant in the room, processing grief and prioritizing my mental health. After I crashed emotionally in 2007, I attended a self-development school, which provided me with that missing piece. As I grew and healed from the grief, I realized the vast role mental and emotional health play in overall wellbeing. As a health and wellness practitioner, I could give you all the right foods and teach you how to move your body, but if we didn't start from the inside out, with healing and changing beliefs about who we are, we aren't addressing our whole health. We are holistic beings. We cannot separate our emotional, mental, and physical aspects; they are intertwined. This gave me a renewed passion for the direction I wanted to take Alive, Fit & Free.

Finally, my most recent trigger was in late 2019. I was still providing fitness and wellness services as an independent contractor under Alive, Fit & Free, but I started experiencing more demand than I could fulfill. At the same time, I had this feeling that it was time for something bigger. I wanted to scale Alive, Fit & Free to reach as many people as possible. My daughter, a tech entrepreneur, decided to partner with me to make this happen, and we took the plunge to launch Alive, Fit & Free as a social start-up in early 2020.

**What did you do to discover that you had a new skill set you hadn't maximized?**

For me, it was more of a rediscovery of who I was. By now, you've understood how community and others' opinions played a significant role in my life for a long time. The fear of what other people thought of me and my longing for the approval of others was crippling. I hid my true self because I was afraid of disappointing others. I needed to gain confidence and trust in myself and find the courage to act on it. It took me a long time to move past that fear and actually let myself shine through, but when it finally happened, that's when I noticed the greatest pivot in my life. And seeking the approval of others to validate oneself? Such bondage. I'm so happy to be myself freely, although it's often easier said than done.

**How did you find that, and how did you ultimately overcome the barriers to manifest those powers?**

In 2007, I attended a self-development program that taught me how to embrace myself and find my full power. All of those qualities that made me 'me,' I gained a new respect for. My whole life, I had tried to place myself in a box, reasoning that if I could be like everyone else and follow all the rules, I would be worthy of love and acceptance. But I had it all wrong. I am a free-spirited person. Boxes and limitations do not fit me. I am happiest when I am free and flowing. In a sense, I gained permission to be me. Then, I started meditating and seeing the life I wanted. I would say daily affirmations to encourage myself. I was, and I still am, my own cheerleader and take time for myself daily with my morning routine to get myself ready for the day with the right mindset and attitude.

**How are things going now?**

This whole journey has been absolutely amazing! At Alive, Fit & Free, we created a platform that offers affordable, accessible classes and events for those most impacted by the loss of human connection while giving class instructors and event facilitators a way to quickly scale their businesses. We mainly target seniors, but we are open to anyone!

We are very passionate about two things. We are passionate about defining what "senior" really means. Even though we are technically classified as seniors once we turn 60, society currently paints seniors as people simply sitting around, needing to be taken care of, with no more individual interests. Instead, senior should mean having the freedom and flexibility to learn new hobbies. For instance, try ziplining for the first time, take up aerial yoga, indulge in fashion addictions, and truly live life to the fullest. We aim to show the world what senior means by actually giving seniors the options to live alive, fit, and free at any age or ability.

Community! Remember my childhood and the deep desire to always belong? I want everyone to feel accepted and welcomed, and we have created a community that allows just that. The sense of isolation that happened this last year was horrendous for us all. When we began our virtual classes, our community started to develop naturally and organically, and it has been so rewarding to watch it unfold.

When we started planning Alive, Fit & Free's pivot in late 2019, we had a strategy to be a completely virtual platform. When COVID-19 hit in early 2020, it was the perfect time to launch. We started with just five weekly classes early last year and now offer over 60 live classes and events every month. We work with individuals and senior living facilities across the country and have instructors and facilitators worldwide. We provide fitness classes, creative workshops, virtual tours with international tour guides, language classes, and dance classes, just to name a few. We launch the next version of our platform next month, and we can't wait! Of course, it was challenging to get started, but momentum is definitely picking up, and we are in full growth mode.

## Is there someone you are grateful to who helped you along the way?

My daughter Sophie, now business partner, saw the potential of where Alive, Fit & Free could go. We talked about it and brainstormed for a few years before taking the plunge. Then, when the time was right, we said, "Let's do this."

Sophie is an entrepreneur, and her expertise is in social tech ventures. We are just about polar opposites: she's calm, cool, collected, has an incredible mind, and strategizes and plans precisely. And I am open and jump right into things as they pop up without stopping to think about them. My talents lie in creating the vision, encouraging and inspiring others, driving sales, and designing engaging, well-loved classes. When you combine the two, it's an outstanding balance.

When we first began working together, I was used to just doing whatever I wanted, and when I'd get an idea, of course, I would run with it. But, as she manages the business and tech side and I manage the day-to-day operations, we now work very well together, both playing into our strong suits.

## Share an exciting moment that happened since committing to your second chapter.

There are quite a few, but one of my favorites is when I was learning what an incubator was. Earlier last year, when we were deciding whether to raise investment or go the bootstrapping route, my daughter forwarded me some emails about some incubators in Silicon Valley. I had no idea what Silicon Valley was (or meant) and even less idea about incubators. After she explained it, we both had a laugh, imagining a 67-year-old start-up founder sitting with all the 20-something college dropouts at a Silicon Valley incubator. We decided not to go in that direction, but I haven't ruled it out, although I may be even older by the time that happens!

## Have you ever struggled with believing in yourself? If so, how did you overcome that limiting belief?

Once I started that self-awareness journey, I realized I lacked self-confidence and was self-conscious and fearful of others' thoughts. I am one to get an idea, say to myself, "Wow, that sounds fun!" and dive in without thinking. That would often come off as self-assured or self-confident, but I never felt that way on the inside. I just knew I could do something and went for it. Everything would be good until I took my eyes off of the goal, and then I would get fearful. My lack of self-confidence would send me down a rabbit hole of 'I'm not good enough, everyone thinks this or that, why would they listen to what I have to say,' and on and on.

What has really helped me are my daily affirmations, which I continue to this day, that speak the truth of who I am to me. I also read books that build me up and help me to remember who I am. I've worked many long and hard hours reframing beliefs that no longer serve me or that are just not true. I think we continually need to grow in our self-awareness and create that arsenal of tools that works for us to continue to grow and gain the self-respect and self-confidence we need. Then, we can keep our eye on our goal, on our 'why,' and take the focus off of ourselves.

## Typically, I encourage my clients to ask for support from those who believe in their vision before they embark on a new chapter. How did you create your support system?

I had a great networking group I had worked with for many years. We all encouraged each other to pursue our dreams. That was huge, as it kept me going and dreaming and moving toward my vision over the years.

I also have family and friends that can be supportive. The operative word here, can. Sometimes the ones we are closest to are not the most supportive when we embark on a new journey. You can't take it personally. Listen to their concerns, but follow your heart. I also keep joining groups that are pursuing their goals. You can learn by simply exposing yourself to others that are also pursuing their dreams. Listen to motivational speakers, TED talks, or whatever you can find to keep yourself motivated. Surround yourself with others that are becoming and transforming. Once you find a suitable business partner and team, you have that support system built-in, and you are all working toward one amazing dream.

## Starting a new chapter requires leaving your comfort zone behind. How did you do that?

I'm not afraid of change. I get bored quite easily, and my personality is to just get inspiration and jump right in, full speed ahead. Now, in some respects, that's wonderful. If I stopped to think things through, I probably wouldn't bring to life half of the ideas I get. However, there is a healthy balance. You do need to stop and get a strategy before diving in. When I was 19, I had a dream of homesteading a piece of land. So, I put my mind and energy into it, and away I went to live in Northern Idaho on 60 acres with no power and no running water for 10 years. That is how I lived—I had a dream, and I jumped right in.

For me, jumping in is what I do. I now embrace my 'jump in' nature and learn how to balance it with strategic planning.

## What are five things you wish someone had told you before you started leading your business, and why?

Dare to dream. For me, dreaming and having a vision is crucial for all of us. It expands our possibilities, and it allows us to look forward to something that resonates deep within us—and then bring it to life. I personally love creating vision boards. It is a visual representation of my dream and what I am working towards every day. In my experience, that daily reminder of the goal always gets me there in the end!

It's said things are created twice—once in thought, then bringing that thought to life. I recently had the privilege of meeting Clara Knopfler, a ninety-three-year-old Holocaust survivor, author, and speaker who still speaks and shares her story any chance she can. She said these words that stuck in my memory: "The script stays; the words fly." When having a dream, it is imperative to let the words fly—out of these words, you will gain inspiration and perhaps use them to help define your way of working later. So, every day, speak your vision out loud as if it is already happening, and make sure your emotion is behind it. You'll find out just how powerful dreaming and surrounding yourself with that dream truly is.

Have a daily self-care routine. You can't pour out of an empty cup! As leaders, our number one job is to keep ourselves functioning at our highest potential. So how do you keep yourself filled up, encouraged, and ready to share whatever it is that you do? I have a few tools that I use daily and others I pull out when my tried-and-true dailies aren't cutting it.

I teach wellness and fitness classes to seniors. My classes are known for being upbeat and fun. We laugh and get excited about life. However, some days I just don't want to—the energy and motivation aren't there. On those days, I get up and put on a motivation meditation. Then, I speak through a list of affirmations to encourage me. I do some specific movements that change my vibration and increase the release of those feel-good hormones that change my brain's chemistry. I move my body, I become my own cheerleader, and I can root myself on, "Come on, Vick, you got this! One more step, put that smile on your face, clap it out, now laugh." I move my body in a purposeful way that helps fill me up for my day. I also try to take at least one day off where I'm not allowed to do any business. I take myself off the schedule and do whatever I want whenever I want—and I take plenty of me-time!

Keep your eye on your passion, and just keep going. When we first get a vision, we're fired up and excited and passionate about it. We see where we want to be and how it will look when we get there, so we begin doing what we can to move forward. But, often, we don't anticipate that hard part between "Let's go!" and reaching your goal. Maybe we feel like the growth isn't happening the way we imagined it, or the results aren't immediate, and we get very discouraged. It's the reason that most entrepreneurs give up, and most businesses fail. We then need to stop, step back, and focus on the passion and excitement we had initially; we need to remember our 'why.' I know—everyone says that, but honestly, that's where our focus needs to be. Not on the money, not on the results or the ROI, but remembering the outcome we are trying to achieve. Remind yourself why you are doing what you are doing, how you planned to get there, and why you planned to do it this way. Adjust course if necessary, but most importantly, just keep going. As you stay consistent and keep going, that snowball gets bigger and bigger as it rolls down the hill, and soon the speed picks up.

Trust your team to do their job. After 15+ years working on my own, one of the hardest things for me was learning how to work with a team and delegate responsibilities. I was a lone leader doing what I wanted, how I wanted, and when I wanted, answering to no one. Don't get me wrong, I wanted and needed a team to help shoulder the growth and expansion. There was too much for me to handle. So, taking my grimy little fingers off of everything as I delegated tasks and responsibilities was and still is a learning experience. The right people joining your team, each one in the position that will allow them to bring forth their expertise and be creative, is the perfect scenario. Now you have many people with creativity and ideas working together. That's called multiplication! Let them know what the expectations are, then give them the freedom to be creative in that role.

My daughter is great at developing websites, communication, and business. Me, not so much! I like to play, design classes, create movement patterns and study the latest scientific research to see how we can change brain chemistry for the better. I was politely removed from several departments that are not my expertise, and it's nice to know that those tasks now belong to someone else and will be done correctly.

Let your personality shine through—people want to deal with people, not businesses.

There are likely many alternatives your clients could turn to instead of using your products or services. What makes them choose your company? What can they get from you that they can't get anywhere else? The answer: You! You are the only you. Yes, keep your eye on the competition so you can stay ahead of the game. Still, a considerable part of the business is your relationship with your clients, which is hugely influenced by your characteristics and personality.

People want to deal with people. If clients feel that they have a valued relationship with you, they will want to work with you and try their best to make that business relationship work. If a competitor comes up with a feature they would like, they may tell you about it to see if you can also provide it instead of instantly switching to a new company. The reason is you—your personality, your unique ways, your human-ness, how you make them feel—so make sure that you let those things come out in a client relationship.

I'm known to be the one that makes you laugh, inspires, and lifts the energy in the room. I work this way with everyone, including my clients, and have very close relationships with many of them. Be authentic—ultimately, people want to interact with a person, not a business, so be the person that you are. Let you shine through!

**You are a person of significant influence. If you could inspire a movement that would bring the best outcome to the greatest number of people, what would that be?**

It would be precisely what we are doing at Alive, Fit & Free—only a million times more extensive with worldwide reach. Creating a community that embraces and encourages all people of any age, any ability, anywhere to love on themselves, do the best for themselves, get strong and healthy, and enjoy their life.

## How would you like to be remembered?

I would love to be remembered for helping others laugh, sharing the gift of health and self-care, spreading joy, and ultimately creating a safe, welcoming community for people to simply do life together.

## Dreams come true. If you could invite anyone in the world to dinner, who would that be?

I would love to have dinner with the Instagram inspirations, the @idiosyncraticfashionistas, Jean, and Valerie. To me, they embrace who they are and share that with the world in the most out-loud way, shouting from the rooftops! They have redefined the word "senior" to be vibrant, colorful, and alive. They demonstrate courage and confidence and inspire me to do the same.

## Where can we follow your work?

Website: alivefitandfree.com.
Social:    Instagram / Facebook / Pinterest / YouTube.

# CHAPTER 22

# Melissa Clayton

ಹಿ ⚬ಒ

*"Don't try to be everything to everybody. I tried to offer jewelry to everyone, and my head was spinning. I went to bridal expos, baby expos and then tried to get Tiny Tags into a college campus store. If I started off with a specific target audience, it would have saved me a lot of time and money."*

Melissa Clayton is CEO and Founder of Tiny Tags, an online jewelry brand designing and creating fine personalized jewelry for mothers. As a former CPA who knew she had to break out on her own, Melissa is obsessed with entrepreneurship and sharing the lessons she has learned along the way. Melissa holds a BA in Philosophy from the University of Massachusetts, an MS in Accounting, and an MBA from Northeastern. Melissa is a wife and mother to three boys and resides in Acton, Massachusetts.

## Share with us a bit about your upbringing.

I grew up in a small town outside of Boston with my father, a passionate entrepreneur. I spent weekends trying to avoid "stopping by the office" because I knew I would be stuffing envelopes for hours. I was very close with my Dad, and, even as a teenager, loved spending time with him. My Dad has been my inspiration and has been my rock my whole life.

## What is your life lesson quote? Can you share its relevance in your life?

"Life's a marathon, not a sprint." — Phillip C. McGraw

I tend to get ahead of myself and want everything done yesterday, so this quote reminds me to slow down and be thoughtful.

## You have been blessed with success. What are three qualities you possess that helped you achieve your goals?

Three qualities that have helped me in my life are a positive attitude, perseverance, and resourcefulness.

Growing up, I listened to Zig Ziglar with my father, so it was ingrained in me to always view life through a lens of gratitude and that a positive attitude could alter your reality. When I started Tiny Tags, I never spent time thinking of what could go wrong. I only focused on all the great things that could happen. The fear of failure never stopped me.

Perseverance has definitely served me well in growing Tiny Tags. When I was figuring out how to scale the business and needed a manufacturing partner, the internet was not what it is today. I remember calling the Economic Development Council of Rhode Island and asking them to send me a copy of their latest report because it listed all the state's jewelry manufacturers. It was that report I used to cold call jewelry manufacturers and is ultimately how I found our current partner. After that, I wouldn't stop until I found the right partner.

In the early years of starting Tiny Tags, we didn't have the budget for advertising or to hire a PR firm, so I had to be resourceful on how to get our name out there. For example, I remember wanting to take an ad out in an entertainment magazine, but we couldn't afford it, so I reached out to another company and asked them if they would want to share the ad. Being resourceful is still critical to getting things done!

## Tell us about your career experience before your second chapter.

My first chapter was spent in corporate America. I graduated from business school with an MS and MBA in Accounting, passed my CPA exam, and worked in public accounting. I learned a great deal in public accounting because you could see all the numbers behind various businesses. I learned so much from doing audit and tax work for small family-owned restaurants to multi-million-dollar investment funds.

## How did you reinvent yourself in your second chapter?

When I was working as a CPA, there was no flexibility, and I knew I needed more life/work balance as a new mom. I never expected to leave corporate America, but after my husband and I weighed our options for childcare, we decided I would stay at home.

As a proud new mom, I started looking for the perfect "mommy" necklace. When I couldn't find one that I loved, I decided to try to make my own as I'm always up for a challenge. At this time, finding things online was not what it is today. I ordered a bunch of tools to play around with, but I didn't have much luck.

Not too long after, I started talking to the woman next to me on a plane ride. She was in jewelry design school and gave me her info. We connected within a week, and she helped me find all the materials and tools I needed to get started.

I started hand stamping necklaces and sending them to all my friends back East. It did not take long until I was getting 10-15 orders a week. The orders and personalization requests were through email, and they were sending checks to me. The reaction

I was getting from my jewelry made me feel so good, and I knew there was something there. At this time, we had our second son; I was making jewelry five nights a week and on weekends. My entrepreneurial spirit had definitely kicked in, and my mind was turning on how I could grow this "hobby" into a real business.

## Your second chapter's transition was remarkable. What was the trigger that made you decide you needed to make a change in your life?

Tiny Tags was a hobby for several years while my boys were young, which was a conscious decision. My goal was to build a foundation so that I had something to build upon when the boys started school. My youngest started kindergarten when I rolled up my sleeves and felt like Tiny Tags became a business.

That year was amazing, but I was still juggling being a mom and running the business. My husband was gone from 6 AM to 8 PM, and with no childcare support, I could only work during school hours. This was when I had the idea that my husband and I should switch roles. I pitched my plan to my husband, which was that he should quit his job and be the primary caretaker for the kids so I could focus 100% on Tiny Tags. Within three months, my husband left his job. That was over five years ago, and I'm happy to say my husband joined Tiny Tags as our CFO a year after leaving his job. 2016 was the year that when Tiny Tags went from a hobby to a real business.

## What did you do to discover you had a new skill set you hadn't maximized?

When I think back, I realize that my first chapter was the wrong career for me and that I belonged in a more creative industry where I could bond emotionally with other people, especially women. I knew my gift was my connection to people, so when I started Tiny Tags, it felt like I had found where I belonged. I overcame barriers by constantly trying to learn. I would read every business book I could find and asked everyone I knew questions.

## How are things going now?

Tiny Tags growth has been impressive over the last five years since I have been 100% focused on the business. The top strategy that has worked for us is our singular focus on mothers. Everything we do and say is about moms and motherhood. I am proud to say that most of our growth has come from word of mouth from the moms in our community. Connecting with our moms is the best part of my job and what I love to do. We started a monthly series called *Stories Behind the Tags,* where our moms share the story behind the engravings on their Tiny Tags.

## Is there someone you are grateful to who helped you along the way?

I am grateful to my dad. He has always believed in me and encouraged me to take risks. About two years into Tiny Tags, I started to market our jewelry to brides, graduates, and even dads. I felt that I had to be everything to everybody. My Dad gave me the confidence to do only what was in my heart, connecting to moms.

## Share an exciting moment that happened since committing to your second chapter.

My favorite story is how Meryl Streep ended up wearing Tiny Tags. Meryl Streep was the keynote speaker at the Massachusetts Conference for Women, where we had a table. Before the event, I reached out to the organizers and pitched them the idea of giving her a 14k gold Tiny Tags necklace with her four kids' names engraved on the tag. They loved the idea.

I hand-delivered it on the morning of her speech, and I kept my fingers crossed. Less than 48 hours later, I received a message on

Instagram from a customer saying they saw Meryl Streep wearing Tiny Tags. Sure enough, there she was in an interview with her Tiny Tags on front and center. I was running around the kitchen in complete shock. Even more shocking was that she wore her Tiny Tags necklace on two major photo shoots. I think the most moving part of it was that she is a mother to four kids who was thrilled to have a piece of jewelry with their names on it.

### Have you ever struggled with believing in yourself? If so, how did you overcome that limiting belief?

All the time! Even today, I doubt myself. My Dad used to say, "If it doesn't scare you, then it is not worth doing." When I had the opportunity to speak at a mom 2.0 summit roundtable, I questioned what I would say and if anyone would care. I gave myself a pep talk and just spoke from the heart. After I spoke, I had women coming up to me and thanking me for being vulnerable.

### Typically, I encourage my clients to ask for support from those who believe in their vision before they embark on a new chapter. How did you create your support system?

I wish I had created a support system in my early years; that's excellent advice. When I started Tiny Tags, there were not as many resources readily available as there are now. Today, I have a much better network thanks to forums like HeyMama and Rebecca Minkoff's The Female Founder Collective. Now the resources are limitless, and now it is work to determine which ones are the best fit.

### Starting a new chapter requires leaving your comfort zone behind. How did you do that?

I went from being a CPA to a jewelry designer, so that was entirely outside my comfort zone. However, I got comfortable by learning.

I joined the Jewelers Trade Association, and I took classes at the local jewelry supply store. Once I started immersing myself in the jewelry world, I felt everyone was always willing to share information.

## What are five things you wish someone had told you before you started leading your business, and why?

Don't try to be everything to everybody. I tried to offer jewelry to everyone, and my head was spinning. I went to bridal expos, baby expos and then tried to get Tiny Tags into a college campus store. If I started off with a specific target audience, it would have saved me a lot of time and money.

Dream big. My initial goal when I started Tiny Tags was to make $100 a day. Unfortunately, I spent quite a few years just living in the day-to-day and not thinking where I wanted to be in 10 years. If I dreamed bigger earlier, I would have made more connections earlier in the business.

Know your why. Simon Sinek's book, *Start with Why* was an incredible resource, and it helped me understand how important your 'why' is. Sharing my why has been a slow evolution because it is so personal. Knowing my why gives everything purpose, and it provides me with clarity, but sharing it requires vulnerability.

Trust your gut. If you don't feel like you can trust someone, then walk away. I started working with an influencer who promised me the world. She was going to have all her celebrity friends wearing Tiny Tags and share on social media. She demanded payment upfront, and once I paid her, she went dark. It turned out she was a scam artist, and I lost a few thousand dollars, but the lesson was priceless.

Start before you're ready. If you want everything to be perfect, you'll never get anything done. We have had to go live on a new website knowing that it was not perfect, but you can't always wait for something to be perfect when you're a small business with limited resources.

**You are a person of significant influence. If you could inspire a movement that would bring the best outcome to the greatest number of people, what would that be?**

I would love to start a movement where children cannot have social media until they turn 18. It breaks my heart to see the damage being done to our kids, especially young girls, with social media. We as parents need to stop bowing to pressure to allow our kids' devices and apps to harm them.

**Dreams come true. If you could invite anyone in the world to dinner, who would that be?**

I would have lunch with Ariel Kaye, Founder of Parachute; Sara Blakely, Founder/CEO of Spanx; and Whitney Wolfe Herd, Founder of Bumble. These three women have built incredible brands, and I would love to learn from them.

**Where can we follow your work?**

Website: tinytags.com
Social:    Instagram @tinytags

# CHAPTER 23

# Traci Jeske

ॐ ॐ

*Success does not happen overnight: Don't compare yourself
with others; success takes time. You may not see the results
as quickly as you like but trust me, you reap what you sow.
My success seemed to take longer than some of my peers. It
seemed like some of them did have it overnight, but as time
went on, they became one-time wonders, and when that
instant success seemed to slow down, they fell off the train.
On the other hand, I planted my seeds every day, whether I
felt like it or not. Some days bigger ones, some days, smaller
ones, but I always did. Yes, it took me longer, but trust me,
when you plant so many seeds over an extended period, you
will reap much more when it is your time.*

Traci Jeske is the director of En Vogue Stylist. This
internationally certified personal stylist helps women 50 and
beyond up-level their glamour game and unapologetically
create and live their best and most stylish second act. Blending her
Canadian background to her stiletto sharp Italian brand, she brings
30 years of fashion industry knowledge to help women find their
unique style and look and feel fabulous in every season of their
lives. Traci has been featured on Fox, CBS, and NBC.

**Share with us a bit about your upbringing.**

I grew up in a small town in Red Deer, Alberta, Canada. I was the youngest of six, so the baby of the family. I had a beautiful childhood. I grew up when there was a boom in the economy, and life was just so much fun and more accessible for so many people. We traveled a lot; we often flew to Hawaii for summer vacations in the '70s before it became the place to travel. I remember my parents flying many times to Las Vegas for long weekends; they didn't see Elvis perform, but my aunt and uncle did. My father loved country music and literally had every instrument you can imagine. We even had a stage in our house where all of us siblings and my father would get up and play musical instruments together and sing. We are a very close family and have so much when we all get together.

As a teen, I was very insecure; I gained a lot of weight in high school and literally hated everything about me and my body. There was pressure at school to be pretty, thin, smart, and I continually told myself I was none of that. All my friends were skinny, beautiful, had good grades, and cute boyfriends. I was constantly comparing myself to them, wanting to be them! I was extremely tough on myself and can still remember throwing brushes at the mirror, yelling at myself, and crying. Nobody, not even my family, knew the struggles I was going through at that time. I always used my style in high school to help me feel better about myself, and even if I didn't think I wanted to be seen, I obviously, deep down, truly did. In my first year at university, due to my insecurities and self-hate, I developed an eating disorder that followed me for 20 years until I was almost 40.

**What is your life lesson quote? Can you share its relevance in your life?**

"Style is a way to say who you are without having to speak."
—Rachel Zoe.

Moving to Italy 24 years ago, I literally felt like I was put on mute from one day to the next. I couldn't converse with anyone without knowing a word of Italian other than *ciao*, mamma, pasta, and pizza. I couldn't understand what others were saying, why they were laughing, and at times I thought they were laughing at me. This made me feel stupid, embarrassed, invisible, and unworthy of being noticed. To make matters worse, I had to have my husband speak for me and take me everywhere. I couldn't even buy groceries myself for fear of somebody asking me something I couldn't understand. This was highly frustrating for an independent woman like me and a real sink or swim moment. But I chose to swim!

I started to use my style to speak for myself by up-leveling my glamour game and elevating it to create the life I wanted. Guess what happened? I got noticed. Women began to be curious about me. They approached me, attempting to talk to me — in my terrible Italian and their terrible English. Finally, however, I started making friends. My style and clothing empowered me to venture out, talk to others, go out on my own, and follow my dreams to start my own styling business, even if I didn't speak Italian perfectly. It literally made me the woman I am today. Although I worked in the industry for many years, I hadn't realized how powerful your personal style is until that period in my life. Never underestimate the power of a good outfit on a bad day!

## You have been blessed with success. What are three qualities you possess that helped you achieve your goals?

My faith in God. I know God has an amazing plan for me, and I have learned throughout the years that his timing is much better than mine, and he knows what's best for me. I am exactly where he wants me to be. He guides me with his wisdom; when it's right, those doors and opportunities will open and come to me with ease and grace.

Courage. You need the courage to build a business and follow your dreams, as many people around you will try to keep you where you are. It was challenging for my husband and I as I have changed so much over these past 12 years. I am much stronger, more determined, and focused than before. I know he is proud of me and tries in his Italian way to understand and support me as much as he can. With both of us having our own businesses, it's sometimes difficult to get our schedules to match. But we do find time and make the most of what little we have together. I don't believe it's the quantity of time we spend together that matters but the quality.

Determination. Your business doesn't grow overnight; it takes time and resilience. I have tried different things in my styling business, endured rejections, nos, and often no clients! Yes, there were times when I said that's it I'm done, times when I had literally no money in my bank account and thought I was crazy for going after my dream. But after a good cry, a good bottle of wine, and a good night's sleep, I always got up and kept going. Every day, I always make myself plant one seed, and it does not matter how big or how small or if I feel like it or not. You just never know; maybe it's today that God is going to open that one door for you that will change your life forever! Imagine that you quit and miss out on the biggest adventure of your life because of a rough patch! I missed out enough with my eating disorder—I refuse to anymore.

### Tell us about your career experience before your second chapter.

I always loved playing dress-up from when I was a little girl (and still do today) and knew that somehow this is something I would be doing when I was older. I got my first retail job at the age of 17 at one of the first Gap stores that came to Canada, and this was the beginning of it all. I quit university to start my career, becoming assistant manager then Gap and Gapkids' store manager.

At the age of 22, after losing my father to cancer and struggling with my eating disorder, I decided to quit my job, pack my suitcases, and move to Australia. I had no job, knew nobody there, but I had to get away. Within a month, I found my apartment in Surfers Paradise. I got a job in the fashion industry and lived there for four beautiful years. Coming back to Canada to renew my visa, my girlfriend introduced me to this Italian boy working in Canada. To make a long story short, I never went back to Australia but moved to Italy. We got married in Italy after three months and have been living here ever since. I became a mother to two amazing beautiful kids. Not knowing the language well and being a mom, my eating disorder and fashion career were sidelined. When I worked, it was limited.

## How did you reinvent yourself in your second chapter?

I always dreamt of having my personal styling business, creating my very own brand and in my 40's that calling became even more potent, and I just knew that it was now or never and that I was ready. I started studying with a famous celebrity stylist here in Italy in her academy. I literally took every course she had; I went to the academy every weekend for a year, learning everything I could from her—in Italian, which was not easy for me. I eventually became one of her ambassadors, which meant I would go to events all over Italy, helping her style guests that she would pick from the audience. But this was not enough for me. I wanted more.

I went to New York to study and become a certified international personal stylist, which made me stand out in a crowd of many personal stylists. Then I got myself a mentor who was a celebrity stylist in Dubai to guide me and give me tools to build my business as she did hers. This then led to collaborating with her in Dubai and working with clients there.

To this day, I have never stopped learning in my styling profession and in my business. To run a business, you need to have a successful mindset and continue to grow. Every day I read 20 pages of a motivational book; right now, I'm reading *The Big Leap: Conquer Your Hidden Fear and Take Your Life to the Next Level* by Gay Hendricks, which I recommend to everyone. I take courses on personal styling to keep me updated. I always have a mentor who has been fundamental for growing my business, getting new ideas, getting out of my comfort zone, and being accountable to someone. If she asks me to do something and I know I have a call with her, and she will ask me how it went, it's obvious I'm going to make sure I did it.

### Your second chapter's transition was remarkable. What was the trigger that made you decide you needed to make a change in your life?

After finally breaking the chains of my eating disorder at 38, I was finally free, the woman that little girl dreamt of being but was too afraid and insecure to become came out. Now I know my eating disorder was a way for me to keep myself hidden and small as I was scared of myself and my dreams. I was going against who God destined me to be, and when my 40's arrived, I literally promised myself that I would never hide again and fear what it takes to walk into becoming and being that woman. It was stepping up to the plate and stopping pleasing and making everyone around me happy but me.

Working in the fashion industry for years but never being seen, it was time for me to become known and stand out in a crowd. I wanted to be that bold woman, have my center stage moment, and start creating my successful personal styling business, transforming women's wardrobes and their lives as well. I want to inspire them to be all they can be and look absolutely fabulous doing so! Age is just a number and should never define how we dress, look or feel.

**What did you do to discover that you had a new skill set inside of you that you hadn't maximized?**

Women were constantly coming up to me, asking me for help on their style and what they needed to do to look and feel fabulous. What I knew to be something easy and simple was a real struggle for other women, and they looked to me for advice and help. They were bewildered about what they should or should not wear, and the fear of being invisible was genuine to most of them. I had women come to me in tears, loathing their bodies and their look wanting to be and look like someone else; it was exactly the same way I felt when I was younger, and these women were experiencing it at an older age. Having so many women asking me for help, I realized that this was my calling. Everything I went through with my eating disorder, moving to Italy, and feeling invisible was for a reason; to give back to women and help them find their unique style, to sparkle and shine and feel good in their own skin.

**How did you find that, and how did you ultimately overcome the barriers to help manifest those powers?**

Imposter syndrome was a huge factor as I often felt like I was never qualified enough to help other women and always felt like someone else was better than me. Being a perfectionist, I wanted to have everything absolutely perfect in my business. I thought I had to know everything about personal styling before I could work with someone. That feeling of "who do I think I am" was constantly in my head. It was not easy to let go, but this way of thinking was holding me back and not moving me forward in my business. I was stuck, and to make matters worse, it held me back from helping those women who needed me. I had to agree that nobody is perfect, nobody knows absolutely everything; my mentor says, "better doing than waiting to be perfect as we know that day will never come!" I have always had a vision of how I wanted my life to be, but if I didn't start putting myself out there and start working, that vision would've never come true.

Through prayer, journaling, and beginning to believe and trust in me, I let go of wanting to be perfect and just started doing, and little by little, I built my confidence. I continue to look for opportunities or ways to break out of my comfort zones. If I don't know or am unsure about something, I tell myself, just like Marie Forleo (in her book), "*Everything is Figureoutable,*" and like Gabby Bernstein (in her book), "*The Universe Has Your Back,*" which is God for me. And it is true, trust me.

## How are things going now?

I cannot tell you how incredible this journey has been. Yes, it was not easy. Yes, at times, I felt like a horrible mother and partner doing something for me. But my children are my number one fans. They push me to do more and inspire me every day to go for whatever makes my heart sing. I am such a fulfilled and much happier woman now than I ever have been in my whole life. I literally have to pinch myself at times to see if I'm dreaming. But, I thank God every morning, afternoon, and evening for the strength and courage he has blessed me with, along with my dreams. I have always wanted to work traveling around the world and never dreamt I would have worked in Dubai and other beautiful cities. I have met many amazing, incredible women in my journey, and I know I have touched and changed my clients' lives and the women I have come across and, in return, mine as well.

## Is there someone you are grateful to who helped you along the way?

That would be my mother. She has always supported me in everything I do, telling me to go after my dreams no matter what they are. She has been my inspiration with her fabulous style; even at 90, she never leaves the house unless she looks perfect. To this day, people still stop her everywhere to tell her how beautiful and stylish she is. She definitely stands out in a crowd and has done so since I was a little girl. She is strong beyond words.

At 63, when she lost my father, who absolutely loved and adored her, to cancer, she was a housewife and mom and found herself not only without her partner but trying to understand, with the help of my siblings, his business. We are very blessed that my father left her with more than enough to live an incredible, fulfilling life. She has a tremendous love for life; she always laughs and smiles and is adored by all she meets. She is highly competitive at cards and loves to win! She loves her children, grandchildren, and great-grandchildren and is present and gives so much to each of us. She is an enormous reason why I am the woman I am today. She has inspired me, pushed me, and loved me through thick and thin.

## Share an exciting moment that happened since committing to your second chapter.

When I think about the woman I was before starting out on this adventure and the woman I am now, I always get overly emotional. When I think about the woman I was, that little girl inside me, who had a dream but was afraid of going after it, my insecurities and fear of how amazing and big I wanted to become was a self-destructive pathway to hold me back. I hurt myself and my body every day and told myself how ugly, fat, and unworthy I was, a failure, and that I didn't deserve to live.

However, the transformation to the woman I am today, confident and filled with self-love, who followed her dreams and stepped into that woman I was destined to be, is an incredible blessing. I thank God throughout the day for the gift and favor he put on me and my life, as I know that I wouldn't be here today as this amazing, strong, determined woman if it wasn't for him. I know I had to go through what I did to help other women to show them that no matter what their past is, no matter where they come from, it is NEVER too late to live the life of their dreams, that they can and will have their center stage moment and look and feel fabulous doing so. Age is just a number and does not define how we dress, look and feel.

### Have you ever struggled with believing in yourself? If so, how did you overcome that limiting belief?

I am my biggest critic, so yes, there were many times, especially at the beginning of my career, I would let negative comments about me really upset me. I am the type of person who wants everyone to like me, and hearing negative comments, giving value to other people's opinions and remarks was a way to crush my self-esteem and my dreams at the same time.     Living in a small village in Italy can have some pros but can have many cons at times. Everyone knows you, your family, and your business, and everyone loves to talk about you, and it seems like they are just waiting for something to go wrong to be in their glory to talk about you. When a situation came up in my personal life, everything according to the village resulted from starting the business as I wasn't home. In their eyes, I was neglecting my kids and family traveling around the world. They believed I was more worried about posting beautiful photos on Instagram than my family, which was hurtful as it was utterly untrue. If there is someone who lives and breathes for their kids, it was and still is me. The most painful part was that this was coming from people I thought were my close friends, friends I thought would ask me if I ever needed anything, and, instead of helping, they just disappeared, and, worse, they talked badly and judged me without understanding the whole situation. It was very hurtful, and I doubted everything I was doing and lost my confidence and power.

After praying, meditating, journaling, and receiving the love and support from my family and true friends, I realized that other peoples' opinions are not facts. I am the most important person, and the only opinions that matter are mine and my kids. I forgave these people as I am not a person to hold grudges or be bitter. I have learned to give no value to opinions or ideas over the years as it is a waste of time and energy. There will always be haters in the world, no matter how good you are, and often the better and bigger you get, the more these kinds of people will go against you. It's important to not listen and not give weight or importance, remember your why, and live your purpose by staying close to those who really love you and have your back no matter what.

**Typically, I encourage my clients to ask for support from those who believe in their vision before they embark on a new chapter. How did you create your support system?**

I surrounded myself with people who had similar dreams and goals and had possibly more experience than me. They pushed me out of my comfort zone. Having a mentor was a must. I needed that support and help from people who had successful careers and could show me how to build my business and support and celebrate with me along my journey.

**Starting a new chapter requires leaving your comfort zone behind. How did you do that?**

In the beginning, I tried hard not to get out of my comfort zone as it literally terrified me. But once I started and saw the growth and the results in me as a woman and in my business, I was absolutely amazed! That incredible feeling of adrenaline and excitement mixed together with fear is astounding, one that I love! So, if you ask me to do something today and it doesn't scare me, and my first reaction isn't "I can't do that," I know something is not right.

When I went on stage for the first time in my life with my Italian mentor, an important celebrity stylist, I spoke to the Italian audience. I didn't know or understand the language at the time, which was probably one of the most challenging things I had to do at the beginning of my career. All I could think of was not making a fool out of myself but, more importantly, not making one out of her. I felt like an imposter that I wasn't good enough, and of course, I thought that people would laugh at me for my accent and how I spoke Italian. And as a result of all that negative thinking, I froze and got total stage fright! I forgot Italian completely and could hardly breathe.

Then I took a deep breath, closed my eyes, and just started speaking English and Italian mixed together. I thought I made a total fool out of myself, but it was quite the opposite. I got so many compliments as I gave that international flair to the evening. The biggest lesson I learned from that was I didn't die, and no one killed me. I could have done better, but it's all part of growing up. We learn from our mistakes; they make us stronger and inspire us to keep improving. As one of my mentors told me, "Better doing than waiting to be perfect."

## What are five things you wish someone had told you before you started leading your business, and why?

You can be a good mom and have a career at the same time. In the beginning, I felt like a horrible mom wanting my own career and not staying home with my kids 24/7. But I have realized and seen firsthand that your kids want you to be happy, and you want to be happy with your kids, and being fulfilled and following your dreams is the best way to achieve that. I know I was doing it for me but also to lead by example and create a better future for them. I was criticized and looked down upon by moms around me, people talked behind my back, and I received nasty comments and DMs on my Instagram telling me I should be at home with my kids. It was awful, and it hurt me. But, it was and is my kids that push me and keep telling me to go; they are my most essential and biggest fans as I am of them. We have such an incredible and unique bond that even if I am busy or away, they know, I am with them, and when important matters come up, I am always the first to drop EVERYTHING and run to them. I am and always will be their mom who will fight their battles and celebrate each and every one of their wins.

Success does not happen overnight. Don't compare yourself with others; success takes time. You may not see the results as quickly as you like but trust me, you reap what you sow. My success seemed to take longer than some of my peers. It seemed like some of them did have it overnight, but as time went on, they became one-time wonders, and when that instant success seemed to slow down, they fell off the train. On the other hand, I planted my seeds every day, whether I felt like it or not. Some days bigger ones, some days smaller, but I always did. Yes, it took me longer, but trust me, when you plant so many seeds over a more extended period, you will reap more when it is your time. And that is what happened to me. The first two, three, even four years were very slow, almost nothing, getting just a few bites back from what I put out there, and it was frustrating as I saw my peers having success and could not figure out, "why not me?" But I kept on planting, never giving up, and then with total ease and grace, it just started happening to me too. I started getting dream clients, and opportunities of a lifetime kept coming to me; doors bigger than I ever could imagine started opening, and the right people started crossing my path, helping me get to where I needed to go. So don't get frustrated because it hasn't happened yet; if you're like me, keep going, keep planting what you put out, and it will come back to you 10x fold.

Surround yourself with people you would like to become. There is nothing more genuine than realizing that you are like the people you spend time with. Successful people only hang out with successful people. There is so much power in this, and it should never be underestimated. If you want to level up your business, life, and career, you need to surround yourself with those people. I have had to let go of many people in my life that were not helping me get to the next level. I found their comments and constant doubt and boring gossip brought me down and made me doubt myself. I have always been very selective in my life and never had a crowd of friends, and now that I have my own business, the few I had have become less. Today I have only four girlfriends that I count on for everything; we have the same goals and dreams. Our businesses may be different, but we all want to reach out and help as many women as possible and be successful at the same time. I love having these women in my life as they understand, push, and inspire me. When I need to be moved, they move me. When I need a hand, they guide and help me. I know in my heart they want only the very best for me and I for them. Sisterhood is a beautiful and powerful thing.

Have a morning routine. How you start your morning sets the tone for your whole day. The most successful people have one, and so should you. I was not a morning person at all, so the thought of waking up early to do all these things seemed impossible to me before having a morning routine. I used to wake up feeling groggy and unmotivated, trying to motivate myself without much success, and as a result, my business reflected how I was feeling. After reading and listening to many books by famous and successful people speaking about morning routines, I committed to having my own. And thank the Lord I did as I know it has made me more productive, inspired, focused, and energized than any energy drink. Now my morning routines are non-negotiable. I do not care if I have an early meeting or an appointment. I am up two hours before, so if that means getting up at 4:30 AM, I do it. When you open your eyes in the morning, thank God or whoever you believe in for blessing you with another day. Nothing is to be taken for granted. Each and every day is a true blessing. Set your intentions, get clear on where you are going today and what you want to achieve, and journal it. I always suggest writing in a diary and not on your computer. Something is compelling about a pen and paper. Exercise or move for 30 minutes. Sing out loud while having a cold shower to your favorite upbeat song. Listen to or read something that inspires you for 20 mins. Do all of these, and I guarantee you, you will be on the way to success.

Drop being perfect. You do not need to know everything before getting started; you do not have to answer everything. The perfectionist syndrome will hold you back and stop you from doing things. Trust me, you know more than your clients, and nobody ever expects anyone to be perfect or know everything. One of the best pieces of advice I ever got was, "Doing is better than perfect." We all start somewhere, and it's that starting somewhere that is the beginning of it all. My Instagram account was far from perfect at the beginning and still is, but it's much better than it was, and even if it's not perfect, it's where I have gained credibility and become known. My first styling packages were far from perfect and less professional than they are now. Everything in my business has evolved and gotten better over time as I have evolved. Nothing is perfect, nor would I want it to be. How boring is that? With experience comes knowledge, and with knowledge comes learning and growth.

**You are a person of significant influence. If you could inspire a movement that would bring the best outcome to the greatest number of people, what would that be?**

It would be the movement of sustainable fashion. If there is one thing the pandemic has taught us is that we do not need all the clothes we have in our wardrobes, they do not serve us. And buying fast fashion, which costs next to nothing, is creating an incredible amount of waste and pollution in our environment. So, I am constantly pushing my clients to invest in higher and higher quality garments than pieces that will last only one season and then need to be thrown away. We have to remember and become more conscious when buying clothes. If a sweater costs five dollars, imagine the person or worse, child in that terrible factory with horrendous working conditions, being exploited, earning next to nothing, and risking their lives every day going to work. It's an unfortunate and horrible situation that we as consumers have the power to stop.

### Dreams come true. If you could invite anyone in the world to dinner, who would that be?

My dream dinner is such an easy question for me. It would definitely be Oprah Winfrey; it has always been my dream to meet her. She has been on my vision board for many years, and I believe I will somehow meet this incredible, beautiful woman who has inspired me more than she could ever know since I was a teen. I still remember running home from school watching *The Oprah Winfrey Show* at 5:30 PM every day in the '80s and '90s. I never missed an episode. Oprah is an icon and my idol; loveable, strong, and sensitive. She created her empire from nothing, even when the odds were against her. She came out a winner and showed us that she too struggled with her weight and accepting and loving her body for how it was. Oprah is a generous, beautiful soul, and everything she did in life she did and still does with such elegance and grace.

The second would be Kris Jenner, as my kids tell me we are so alike. I admire and love how she created her empire and a larger one for each of her kids, which is my dream. I love her courage and strength, her laugh, how easily she cries. If I see myself in someone, it is definitely her. Of course, her incredible style and lifestyle.

### Where can we follow your work?

Website: envoguestylist.com
Social:   Instagram @tracijeskeofficial

# CHAPTER 24

# Mindy Keegan

ॐॐ

*It's okay to ask for help. I used to think I could do it all and should do it all, but that's not realistic, especially as a mom and business owner. I hit burnout during the holiday season last year because I wasn't prepared for the growth we had, and I didn't have help at the time. So, I hired help early this year and haven't looked back since. We can do anything, but we can't do everything!*

Mindy Keegan is the owner of Made for Mama Shop, a small business inspired by her own journey of motherhood. She is a mom of two young boys who left the corporate grind to raise her kids and currently works out of her garage to design and create products that motivate, empower and build a community around motherhood. She's been featured on the *Today Show*, *The Product Boss Podcast*, and *The Local 724 Podcast* with the hopes that her story and products will inspire other moms to stop chasing perfection and do more of what makes them happy.

## Share with us a bit about your upbringing.

I grew up in a small town in Pennsylvania and had a normal childhood. My dad worked, and my mom was home with my younger sister and me. I always remember thinking that I couldn't wait to be a mom one day and drive my kids to school, just like my mom. Looking back, I have to laugh because I had the entrepreneurial spirit in me. I remember selling Ziploc baggies of pretzels to our neighbors and thinking of names for the beauty salon I would own one day. However, after high school, I took the traditional route, went to college, landed a corporate career, and climbed the ladder for 11 years until I became a mom and knew something had to change.

## What is your life lesson quote? Can you share its relevance in your life?

My dad always told me growing up, "If you're not the lead horse, the scenery never changes." I never really understood that quote until my 30's when I started learning about leadership, change, and growth. I've learned that it's true—you've got to be brave, stand up for yourself and be a leader in your own life if there are parts of it you want to change. If you continue to follow others, you'll always be looking at them rather than creating your own path and opportunities.

## You have been blessed with success. What are three qualities you possess that helped you achieve your goals?

Drive. I know that failure will happen often, but when I'm up against it, I use it to fuel rather than knock me down. I have a drive in me that runs deep. For example, I was scammed last year by an ad agency. They pitched me and wanted me to pay them several thousand dollars to possibly be featured in local ads. I thought it was an immense opportunity to get our business seen by so many until I realized they were targeting me. I was embarrassed and disappointed, but rather than sulk, I did all the research I could on pitching myself and landed on the *Today Show* in December, which was a huge blessing to our family and business.

Growth. I am constantly learning and growing, personally and professionally. I heard once before that if we're not growing, we're dying, and I believe that to my core. So, I continue to push myself to grow in new areas every day by learning from mistakes, listening to others' stories, reading business and self-development books, and leaning into the uncomfortable feelings that come with growth.

Authenticity. I show up as the most authentic person I can be, especially on social media. I show the real moments, the challenging moments, the struggles, and the happy, joyful, and exciting moments. I've shared my business journey from the beginning, the good and the bad, and I believe that authenticity attracts the right people to my brand and life.

## Tell us about your career experience before your second chapter.

I worked in a corporate career for 11 years right out of college—the first seven years were spent in higher education, and the last four years were spent at a global HR firm. I met some fantastic people and leaders and also learned what not to do as a leader. I was promoted several times and continued to excel, but I knew that sitting in a cubicle my entire life was not for me. I would listen to moms playing with their kids in a huge water fountain outside of my building. I could see them out of the enormous windows in the building, right behind my seat. I wanted to be the mom out there, with my children, seeing their smiles, hearing their laughter, and wiping their tears, rather than the one inside who only saw my kids for a couple hours a day.

## How did you reinvent yourself in your second chapter?

I left my corporate career in 2018 to dive into motherhood. It killed me that I only got to see my kids for a couple hours every day. It was now my turn to be the mom I always dreamed of. While I took care of the kids, I also took a part-time job and worked for a network marketing company from home. I've been working since I was a teenager, so not working wasn't an option . . . it was just about finding the right fit for the stage of life I was in. When the network marketing wasn't bringing in the income we needed, I pivoted, created Made for Mama Shop, and started making coffee mugs with inspirational sayings on them. I knew that if they brought me a smile in the morning when I woke up, they could do the same for other women who were also in the thick of motherhood, feeding their babies throughout the night, changing diapers, taking care of everyone else before themselves.

**Your second chapter's transition was remarkable. What was the trigger that made you decide you needed to make a change in your life?**

Yes, I remember it very vividly. I took a vacation day from work for Christmas Eve. My manager called me and asked me to log into my laptop because they were having an issue and needed my help. I logged in and was sitting on the couch with my computer in front of the Christmas tree. My son was about two years old, needed something, and started crying, at the same time that I was trying to figure out the issue for work. I remember being annoyed and overwhelmed, then looking at his face . . . he needed me, and I was supposed to be offline that day. We both sat there crying together. I knew deep down that I had to make a decision. At that moment, I knew I needed to start thinking about a major change in my life.

**What did you do to discover you had a new skill set you hadn't maximized?**

That's a great question. I knew I had a creative side to me that I wasn't utilizing. I remember telling my boss that I wanted to look for something within the company that would allow me to be more creative, but I couldn't find the right fit. So, to discover that innovative skill set, I just started taking action. I started making coffee mugs with my vinyl-cutting machine, but I didn't like their fonts, so I learned about hand lettering and fell in love with it. I always had it in me but never knew that it was something I could do for work. I used to make signs in high school and for my children with creative lettering on it, and I've always been the cheerleader for others . . . now it's come full circle. Taking action and bringing joy to the process will help manifest what you're meant to do in life.

## How are things going now?

Made for Mama Shop has seen tremendous growth in only the 15 months that it has existed. We've built a supportive and amazing community online. We were featured on the *Today Show*. We've been featured on several podcasts about business and motherhood, and the way it has taken off has surpassed anything I've ever dreamed of. The connections we've built with other moms around the country have been amazing. They share their stories with me of struggle and how our mugs give them light and hope at the beginning of each day. We're now looking to expand into a bigger space because our garage has reached its capacity, but I'm excited for what's to come!

## Is there someone you are grateful to who helped you along the way?

I'm most grateful to my business mentors, Jacqueline and Minna, from The Product Boss. Through their teachings, podcasts, and paid programs, I built a solid foundation for my business and learned about every aspect of owning a product-based business. In addition, their mentorship program allowed me to see what was possible and what I needed to focus on to grow the business. I've also met other small business owners in their community for collaborations, promotions, and connecting on our commonalities in this space.

## Share an exciting moment that happened since committing to your second chapter.

The most exciting thing that happened since starting our business was the connections we made through the *Today Show* segment. I had strangers all over the country reaching out, calling, and emailing to tell me how proud of me they were . . . complete strangers who just saw our story and resonated with my business and my family. They shared their personal stories of motherhood, loss, and struggles with illnesses. I couldn't believe that our story would inspire and connect with so many people, but that was when I truly knew how much of an impact our business could make on others.

## Have you ever struggled with believing in yourself? If so, how did you overcome that limiting belief?

Yes, I struggled with believing in myself for a long time after being in an emotionally abusive relationship in the past. I didn't know who I was, I didn't speak up for myself, and I didn't voice my opinions for years after it ended. However, once I started learning about affirmations, mindset, and self-growth and put it all into practice, I overcame the limiting beliefs that I wasn't enough. I started saying positive affirmations to myself daily, as well as reading personal development books. After a few months of doing that consistently, my mindset started to change, and after a few years, my life changed. I saw what was possible and believed that I could make anything happen. I'm a huge believer in having the right mindset, and I know without doing that work, none of this would've been possible.

**Typically, I encourage my clients to ask for support from those who believe in their vision before they embark on a new chapter. How did you create your support system?**

My husband has been my support system from the start. Once I actually told him how I felt about missing my kids' childhoods and how unhappy I was, we started planning to see what small steps we could make together to make it work. Without me knowing, he was crunching the numbers and trying to come up with ideas too. I wouldn't have taken the leap without his support.

**Starting a new chapter requires leaving your comfort zone behind. How did you do that?**

This whole journey has been way out of my comfort zone. My comfort zone was going to a job where I had specific duties every day; I knew what the next level was and how to get there, I had a manager to rely on for feedback, and I had a set schedule. I knew all of my coworkers and was comfortable with what I was doing. Starting a business of my own has been full of uncomfortable twists and turns! Some of that includes being on video on social media, being on television, investing money and hoping that the products sell, learning new skills daily to continue to grow the business, and coming up with new ways to grow and new products to market. It's all been uncomfortable, but in the best, most exciting way possible!

**What are five things you wish someone had told you before you started leading your business, and why?**

It's okay to ask for help. I used to think I could do it all and should do it all, but that's not realistic, especially as a mom and business owner. I hit burnout during the holiday season last year because I wasn't prepared for the growth we had, and I didn't have help at the time. So, I hired help early this year and haven't looked back since. We can do anything, but we can't do everything!

Mindset is everything. It's easy to fall into comparison, negative thinking, and self-doubt when you're a business owner. There are so many decisions to make, the pressure that can build up, and everyday challenges. It's essential to take care of your mind, whether reading an inspirational book, doing a daily devotion, meditation, etc.—there are lots of options available. When I find myself getting into a mental slump, I know it's time to pick up a book or be more consistent with my meditation practice. It helps me get my mindset back to where it needs to be to run a successful business.

Surround yourself with like-minded entrepreneurs. I started this business alone. I had no mentors. I had no direction. I had no foundation. Once I found a group of people like me, who were building businesses for their families and futures, the game changed. We're able to bounce ideas off each other, lean on each other, encourage each other and be on this journey together. It makes a huge difference to know that you're not alone.

Growth will be uncomfortable. Each time I hit a new goal or level in my business, it's uncomfortable. The unknown of what will happen next makes me excited but also a little nervous. It's just part of owning a business, and you learn that something big is about to happen for you when those feelings arise. Lean into it rather than run away from it.

Let it grow. I've had a fear of success most of my adult life. I'm still unsure where it stemmed from, and if you've never had that fear, it might sound crazy. However, it's been something I've had to work on, and just a few months ago, I had a business mentor say to me, "let it grow." There comes the point where you need to feel the fear and do it anyway. If it's growing, let it grow and stop trying to control every aspect of the business. I've learned that once you are open to receiving and letting it grow, the possibilities are endless, and new opportunities arise that you may never have otherwise known about.

**You are a person of significant influence. If you could inspire a movement that would bring the best outcome to the greatest number of people, what would that be?**

If I could inspire a movement to bring good to the most amount of people I could, it would be a Real Motherhood Movement. It would be moms sharing the genuine parts of motherhood together. To unite in the journey, share our everyday struggles, celebrate the good, lean on each other, and show that motherhood is not perfect—it's messy, confusing, amazing, and fulfilling. In my opinion, we need more "real" in the world and on social media.

**Dreams come true. If you could invite anyone in the world to dinner, who would that be?**

I would love to sit down with Sara Blakely, the powerhouse behind the Spanx brand. I'd love to be able to chat business with her, pick her brain about her success and how she was able to grow her business into what it is, the steps she took, and how she balanced motherhood alongside it. The fact that she's a mom, authentic with what she shares online, and a huge supporter of other women, along with being so successful in what she does, makes her such an inspiration to me in my own life and business.

**Where can we follow your work?**

Website: madeformamashop.com
Social:   Instagram @madeformamashop

# CHAPTER 25

# Chad Hutson

ॐ ॐ

*Find the right underrepresented niche and specialize in it.
In the beginning, we were primarily visual content creators
but with a desire to use that skill to augment physical
environments. I'm thrilled to say we focused on that
desire because we saw the content production industry
cannibalized over the years due in part to in-housing within
brands and agencies, but primarily because of online and
social media. The sheer bulk of content needed for those
platforms brought production budgets way down, and
along with it, the content quality. So instead, we were an
early pioneer of experiential content, and while there's
more competition than before, we've developed a strong
enough reputation to be on many shortlists
for opportunities.*

As the co-founder and CEO of Leviathan, Chad Hutson facilitates creative strategy and all key business developments for the specialized experiential agency, including managing the company's overall operations. His efforts have led to client relationships with Nike, Disney, Microsoft, T-Mobile, Amazon, Universal, McDonald's, and Airbus. Chad continues to lead Leviathan after its acquisition by digital agency Envoy, of which he is also a partner.

## Share with us a bit about your upbringing.

Most of my childhood was spent in a rural Georgia town. We moved there after my biological father died in a helicopter accident when I was five. While there wasn't much in the way of activities, I distinctly remember three things that helped shape my future passions. For one, there were seemingly endless fields, streams, and woods to explore, driving the need to experience the world around me. Second, there was the emergence in the '80s of the personal computer, one of which I obtained at a young age and learned to program. Lastly, music and audio production, which I thrived on in high school and later studied in college. These elements of the arts, technology, and experiences still drive me to this day.

## What is your life lesson quote? Can you share its relevance in your life?

This phrase has multiple meanings to me, "Know when good enough is good enough." First, it can serve as a mental check when self-doubt plagues you during failure. When you question if you could do more or do better, it can also push you to do just that. Or after obsessing over whether the quality of your work is perfect and final, sometimes you just have to ship it as-is now and reiterate further after. "Good enough" can be the words that give you peace or drive you to higher performance, but the key is to use your own personal gauge—not others.

## You have been blessed with success. What are three qualities you possess that helped you achieve your goals?

Most commonly, when people use the term "empathy," it's focused on feeling what others are experiencing, though I like to use it more broadly—put yourself in someone else's shoes. It's still prioritizing kindness and understanding but also employs strategic tactics for diffusing tense situations or negotiations. Being empathetic helps me every day in almost all my interactions, both professional and personal.

A trait somewhat tied to empathy, I think, is adaptation. My career has taken a few different turns, and I've had the benefit of working for and alongside several professionals with such varied personalities. Being a mimic or chameleon allows you to try out tactics or personas of other successful individuals and see what works and fits your personal style, but without sacrificing your own originality. It's an inherently human quality, it's how we learn from an early age, and it's also how we survive. Employing this same mentality in business is key—not just studying your idols and opponents but also unrelated luminaries and industries to test out practices that can help you pivot, thrive, and avoid the plight of others who don't change their paths. Following the advice of "adapt or die" has allowed my businesses to endure or be reborn as something more extraordinary.

By now, there should be a single word in the English language that combines both patience and persistence because, in my professional experience, you can't have one without the other. Patience is playing the long game, which can be vital in running an enterprise, but without persistence, patience can be just waiting for something to happen, which is never the right strategy. I employ this combo—let's call it "patiently persistent" daily when engaging with potential clients, trying new management methodologies, or even navigating a global pandemic. You have to keep pushing forward while simultaneously exhibiting endurance and tolerance.

**Tell us about your career experience before your second chapter.**

After graduating college, I worked a variety of jobs in Nashville's music industry—in the Warner Bros. Records mailroom, for live venue developer, a music publishing company, an indie-folk label, and at artist Alan Jackson's management company. All of these taught me facets of the business side of the music industry. Still, it could be pretty disheartening to see creative people treated more as objects for sale, so I got out of that field (but not before gaining newfound empathy and a protective sentiment for creative folks).

From there, I moved to Las Vegas. I was an operations manager for an audiovisual integrator, an interesting mix of being behind a desk one moment to stripping speaker wire the next, followed by becoming a media and technology project manager for exhibit company MC2. This was a thrilling blend of physical environments (tradeshows, events, museums, retail), interaction, animation, and other media. Then in the wake of 9/11, the other members of my team and I broke off and started our own content and interactive production company, called eatdrink, with a handful of creative agencies and record labels as clients.

Six years and an expansion to Chicago later, the financial crisis of 2008 all but decimated the company after what had been our most successful year to date. All employees were laid off, and a sizable debt was left to deal with for several months, but as the work began to trickle in again, I was at a crossroads—keep this going or make a fresh start?

## How did you reinvent yourself in your second chapter?

So, in 2010, with debt paid, cash back in the bank, new ideas, and new partners, the company was relaunched as Leviathan. Within its first year, Leviathan came into the creative industry as an experiential powerhouse. For example, our live concert visuals for electronic musician Amon Tobin were featured in *Wired*, *Fast Company*, *Los Angeles Times*, *New York Times*, and countless creative publications, all of which led to projects for BMW, Microsoft, Disney, and HP, among others. Over the next five years, we tripled in size and notoriety, though the work was unfocused. There was too much reliance on being subcontracted by other agencies; thus, we began the pivot to becoming a more self-sustained creative consultancy that owned its brand relationships. Simple in theory, but without the experience, it was much trickier in execution.

For years our team was used to executing our own ideas and bolstering other agencies' concepts. But gaining the brand relationships, developing upfront strategies, and in particular, bankrolling larger projects with lengthy payment terms as an independently owned consultancy was nothing that could be solved overnight. This required different staff, stronger management, extending well outside our comfort zone of operations, and an infusion of investment. This could've been done by raising capital and going it alone. But the idea of joining something larger while maintaining our identity was even more appealing. Enter Envoy.

Envoy was a successful digital agency that we'd partnered with many years before that had formed a new "collective" holding company model, where operational resources are shared as well as clients but acquired companies' identities were kept. So, a deal was done, I agreed to stay on to run Leviathan for some time, and soon after, everything fell into place. The most significant contracts we'd ever been awarded landed and subsequently tripled in size. Our client roster grew to include McDonald's, Nike, T-Mobile, Universal, Amazon, and others, and the team grew as well. Instead of always hunting for our next gig, the phone just never stopped ringing with opportunity.

The company I co-founded had finally become what I'd hoped for—an industry leader in experiential design, with more stability, revenue, and the support of a more prominent family. The story was just starting to get interesting, so instead of riding off into the sunset, I chose to stick around and see what the next chapter of this book brings and doubled down as a partner in Envoy.

**Your second chapter's transition was remarkable. What was the trigger that made you decide you needed to make a change in your life?**

From my brief time in the music industry, I learned that there are two types of successful acts: those that stay in the same lane—rinse and repeat—and those that continue to forge new paths for their careers—new musical genres, acting, etc. Even though my first company had just survived the financial crisis and was on the way to becoming "normal" again, something was missing . . . and reinvention felt like the right path. That said, it wasn't a comfortable feeling; taking a risk seldom is. But my partners and I saw an opportunity to break away from the herd, and I'm so glad we took that chance.

**What did you do to discover you had a new skill set you hadn't maximized?**

Perhaps contrary to the typical CEO personality, I consider myself more of an introvert, so being the "face" of the company can sometimes be uncomfortable and emotionally taxing, such as speaking to large groups or bringing in new clients. The fear of rejection is real, especially when your livelihood depends on how confidently and effectively you present. While practice does make perfect, I finally realized one thing that helped me overcome those fears: knowledge. When you really know your craft, and you can speak not only as a knowledgeable subject matter expert but also with passion and conviction, people listen. The confidence comes from a real place and isn't just bluster, and that genuine messaging resonates with those you're hoping to reach.

**How are things going now?**

Leviathan is doing better than ever, despite the pandemic. 2020 started off strong with our largest projects before us, and when

COVID-19 shut the world down in March, our business, like many others, was significantly impacted in Q2. But we took that time to pivot our "phygital" creative offerings to include more virtual and hybrid approaches, and this is precisely what our clients needed. As a result, by the start of Q3, we bounced back and even met our original revenue goals for the year, which was a record figure for us. Again, this is proof that you can never stop reinventing your business, even when the original formula for success has worked for you in the past.

## Is there someone you are grateful to who helped you along the way?

This is a tough one! Over the years, there have been so many mentors from family to co-workers, some I've mimicked and others who've been consistent sounding boards. Two such advisors are Ric Peralta and Don McNeill, who led creative agencies Attik and Digital Kitchen, respectively, and eventually sold them to larger holding companies. Ric was the one who firmly suggested that we own our conceptual work and client relationships; his advice led to the turnaround of my business. Don was also a great coach when times were tough. Although both agency brands have since been absorbed into holding companies, and their original leaders are no longer involved (a fate I could someday experience), they've shown me more chapters can be written even when one closes.

## Share an exciting moment that happened since committing to your second chapter.

I suppose it all depends on who is listening to the stories as to which they find interesting. Of course, there are personal favorites—a feature in Communication Arts magazine, sharing a stage with those I admire, competing and winning against more established companies. But probably the most interesting to me is hearing stories on how our work has impacted others. Whether it was live concert visuals we created 10 years ago or Disney theme park installations from two years ago, there have been thousands who have experienced our work. Yet, I still meet new people who say, "that experience was amazing" or "my mind was blown; how did you all do it?" Those enthusiastic reactions of awe are unforgettable.

## Have you ever struggled with believing in yourself? If so, how did you overcome that limiting belief?

One of the most challenging moments for Leviathan was when one of my co-founding partners decided to leave for another opportunity. He was our mad scientist, always coming up with never-been-done ideas that we were actually able to make, so losing that ingenuity made me wonder how we could continue to be a technically inventive company and how I could inspire innovation in my team. But that moment made me realize two things: the spirit of that co-founder's invention still lived on in me and the organization's DNA, and that it was also a time to improve upon less successful operating methods. Adversity can bring opportunity, and after the initial anxiety came excitement to innovate yet again. If you have the drive and capable people around you, anything is possible.

## Typically, I encourage my clients to ask for support from those who believe in their vision before they embark on a new chapter. How did you create your support system?

It's indeed lonely at the top, and when you're the leader in an organization, there are few that you can vent to. I didn't realize until after I started Leviathan that I needed a lifeline. But when I reached out to the leaders I respected, it was always surprising how accommodating they were to listen and share advice. When others ask how I'd create such a support system, I suggest they be unafraid to reach out to those they admire and not ask for a job but simply talk about how that leader's career evolved. The stories and advice can be inspiring and game-changing, and now I do my best to mentor others whenever I can to pay it forward.

All this being said, you can't beat the support of your family and friends either. Both my wife and daughter are incredibly understanding of my work and can give the soundest advice when I'm overcomplicating issues.

### Starting a new chapter requires leaving your comfort zone behind. How did you do that?

This may sound odd, but hear me out. As a kid, I had a knack for impersonating others' voices and would enjoy acting like that person for extended periods. In starting Leviathan, I found myself wearing many hats and in situations outside of my usual expertise. To help myself cope, I'd create different personas for how I'd address crowds at speaking engagements or when having difficult conversations with teammates. Not long after, I recall reading that Beyoncé had created an alter ego, Sasha Fierce, for similar reasons. I was so glad to hear I wasn't crazy for having my own separate voices or personalities to cope with uncomfortable environments!

### What are five things you wish someone had told you before you started leading your business, and why?

Find the right underrepresented niche and specialize in it. In the beginning, we were primarily visual content creators but with a desire to use that skill to augment physical environments. I'm thrilled to say we focused on that desire because we saw the content production industry cannibalized over the years due in part to in-housing within brands and agencies, but primarily because of online and social media. The sheer bulk of content needed for those platforms brought production budgets way down, and along with it, the content quality. So instead, we were an early pioneer of experiential content, and while there's more competition than before, we've developed a strong enough reputation to be on many shortlists for opportunities.

Evolution is natural. Make a business plan, but be prepared to rewrite or tear it up regularly. Everything from naivety and competition to financial and health crises has caused us to alter our own business course. As long as you stay true to the core and purpose you set out to follow, the rest can change—and probably should change—all along the way.

Have a professional support system. You're not alone. Friends and family can be great sounding boards when you need to vent, but they won't always understand the complex business challenges you're experiencing. Talk to other executives in and out of your industry regularly, or join professional societies comprised of senior executives. Listen and learn, but also be prepared to teach and mentor yourself. Both are cathartic and beneficial to your professional development.

Don't be so hard on yourself. Set your own bar on what should be "good enough." If your goal is to become the next Google or Amazon, hats off to you. But what if you don't make that dream come true? Can you be satisfied with where you wind up? The answer can be simultaneous, "yes, you should be," and "now, onto what's next." Being satisfied with your level of success doesn't mean becoming complacent; you're allowed to pat yourself on the back and then kick yourself in the butt to achieve the next level.

It's going to be more difficult than you imagine, but it will all be worth it. Unfortunately, there is no single self-help or professional book that will tell you everything you need to know to run your business. Even if there was one, unforeseen circumstances would likely throw you off track. But even in tougher times where business is light and layoffs could be imminent, be patient and be persistent. The strong will survive, and you'll be glad you hung in there.

**You are a person of significant influence. If you could inspire a movement that would bring the best outcome to the greatest number of people, what would that be?**

Working in experiential design, one of our primary purposes is to evoke feelings within a given environment. At the core of this is empathy: design an environment to put people in others' shoes. If you've ever been to a museum or a memorial where you've felt wonder or sorrow, you know the power of empathy in experiential design. These same design skills could also inspire others to support war-torn or impoverished countries or act sooner to clean up our planet. You'll undoubtedly see examples of this on a smaller scale, but more powerful and widespread experiences could change more minds and affect more change in the world.

**Dreams come true. If you could invite anyone in the world to dinner, who would that be?**

If given my druthers, I'd prefer to host a dinner with modern artists like Refik Anadol, Olafur Eliasson, and Sougwen Chung alongside architectural legends like Art Gensler, Ed Schlossberg, and Frank Gehry, and perhaps throw in Bill Gates for fun. The conversations around art, technology, spaces, and visual communication would be mind-blowing and would no doubt give me some terrific new ideas.

**Where can we follow your work?**

Website: lvthn.com
Social:   Instagram / Twitter

# CHAPTER 26

# Lynn Power

ॐ ঔ

*It's 24/7. I knew that being an entrepreneur was an around-the-clock job, but dealing with a customer question at midnight or delivering a product on the weekend is pretty much the standard.*

Lynn Power is a long-time advertising executive who spent 30 years building iconic brands. She left advertising in 2018 to launch MASAMI, a premium clean haircare line. Lynn loves building high-performing teams, disrupting the status quo, and helping women find their voices.

## Share with us a bit about your upbringing.

I was raised in Chicago with my two brothers by entrepreneurial parents. My parents were small business owners (an insurance agency and a travel agency), and I got to see first-hand how hard they worked and how much control they had over their lives. Unfortunately, both industries are now almost entirely digital, so I witnessed their struggle to stay relevant. Running a small business must be in my genes; my brother does it also and works with me on MASAMI.

**What is your life lesson quote? Can you share its relevance in your life?**

"Beware, for I am fearless, and therefore powerful."—Mary Shelley, *Frankenstein*

I've found very little room for fear if you want to do your own thing. You need to acknowledge it and move on. Too much to do!

**You have been blessed with success. What are three qualities you possess that helped you achieve your goals?**

Resilience. It's so critical to not let yourself be beaten down (which is easy to do). There will always be challenges, but you need to look beyond the day-to-day to the bigger goal. I felt very beaten down by the #metoo lawsuit that happened two years into my job at J. Walter Thompson, yet I stayed another two years to see it through. I thought that was the right thing to do, even though it was grueling most days.

Empathy. Understanding and appreciating where people are coming from and what they are dealing with are beneficial to building a high-performing team. This has been especially critical during COVID-19 when we don't see each other every day. We need to go out of our way to make sure everyone has what they need to get by. We do weekly check-ins, and I'm lucky enough to work with friends, so we talk constantly. That helps a ton.

Dot connecting. I believe that dot connecting is the new "creativity." Being able to see analogies from one business to another and translating skill sets. I've always been an avid networker and have enjoyed meeting people who challenge me (usually outside my industry). Don't think of this as a time suck; think of it as expanding your universe to let serendipity happen. For example, I recently met another entrepreneur who has a seaweed nutritional business, and we are looking to collaborate, so you never know.

**Tell us about your career experience before your second chapter.**

I spent 30 years in the advertising industry, working my way up from my first job as a receptionist at a small agency to CEO of J. Walter Thompson NY, one of the oldest and largest ad agencies in the world. I loved the world of advertising, especially the ability to work on lots of different brands and categories, and I was fortunate enough to work on iconic brands such as American Express, Clinique, Hershey's, and Campari. I've worked at some of the top ad agencies throughout my career, including Ogilvy & Mather, BBDO, McCann, Arnold, and Grey.

**How did you reinvent yourself in your second chapter?**

After I left JWT, I started brand consulting—putting all of the years of knowledge I had spent building large brands to help startups. I found this incredibly fulfilling because you could see the impact almost immediately (whereas it takes months or even years for large brands and corporations to implement change).

But then, I met my co-founder, James, in 2018. He had been working on haircare formulations for almost 10 years, and when he started telling me his story, my advertising cynicism kicked in. But I tried the products and was converted. So, we decided to launch MASAMI, combining his formulation knowledge and my branding and marketing expertise.

**Your second chapter's transition was remarkable. What was the trigger that made you decide you needed to make a change in your life?**

The more senior I got in advertising, the more removed I was from doing what I loved—building brands. I spent my days putting out fires (but not in a fun way), dealing with HR, legal, and finance. The lawsuit we were dealing with at JWT was debilitating to the business, and I ultimately decided it was time to take control of my life. Life is just too short to spend your time doing things you don't love.

## What did you do to discover you had a new skill set you hadn't maximized?

I found that I'm very well suited for the entrepreneurial world. It requires using many different parts of your brain—one day, I'm focused more on analytics and finances; another day, I'm dealing with content creation. And while I did this in advertising, the speed we can operate now has been fantastic. I have discovered that starting a business later in life makes it much easier to make decisions—so essential to get faster traction. My most significant barrier has been time management, just figuring out how to juggle and prioritize everything. I'm a bit more organized with looking at both short and long-term goals.

## How are things going now?

It's tough to launch any business during a pandemic! But we've been lucky that people want clean beauty solutions and self-care. We have been able to get into some stellar salons like Spoke & Weal (they have eight locations nationwide), DreamDry, and BLVD. We've also partnered with other indie brands and believe that we can be stronger together. We've done giveaways, gift with purchase exchanges, blogs, live streams and have worked with great brands like Serucell, Isle de Nature, Romer Skincare, The Sexiest Beauty, Marea Wellness, Aila, Veronique Gabai, Ramen Hero, and Misaky Tokyo.

## Is there someone you are grateful to who helped you along the way?

I'm really fortunate that my co-founder, James, is an amazing human and great partner. So many people don't have that kind of relationship with their co-founder. It's such a critical relationship that can dramatically impact the business (good or bad). I knew we were going to get along when I first met him. He came over for dinner with his husband, Masa, and they loved my dogs (and my dogs liked them—which is critical!)

## Share an interesting or exciting moment that happened since committing to your second chapter.

I've had some brutal ageism situations. I knew that being an older founder may not be as "popular" as being a founder in my 20's, but it really hit me when my husband was on the phone with an investor. He was an early investor in Living Proof and didn't know I was listening on the call. He asked my husband about the team, and when Bill started describing me, the investor interrupted and asked, "How old is she?" Bill said 51 and was met with an immediate response of "It will never work. She won't have the energy." I was definitely taken aback. Anyone who knows me knows that I don't have a "lack of energy" problem, so I decided to forgo looking for outside investment money for now. We are totally self-funded.

## Have you ever struggled with believing in yourself? If so, how did you overcome that limiting belief?

This was never really a concern. I've done so much work for other people building brands that I knew I could do it for myself. But, of course, launching a business is super hard, and there are days when I wake up and think I'm crazy for doing this. So, my struggle is finding time for myself and throttling back on the work—I have a hard time with that.

**Typically, I encourage my clients to ask for support from those who believe in their vision before they embark on a new chapter. How did you create your support system?**

I'm a big believer in building a network of peers, advisors, mentors, supporters, and friends who can help you on the journey, so some of my most valuable insights have come from other founders who are in a similar position to me. And some of my best learning has been from younger people who specialize in SEO or TikTok, for example.

**Starting a new chapter requires leaving your comfort zone behind. How did you do that?**

I don't like to be on camera; that's definitely out of my comfort zone. But now, I find that people want to know who is behind the brand. So, I'm slowly getting more used to doing vlogs, live streams, and on-camera interviews. I'm not sure I'll ever really be truly comfortable, but I just don't look at the videos afterward. That way, I can pretend they don't exist!

**What are five things you wish someone had told you before you started leading your business, and why?**

It's 24/7. I knew that being an entrepreneur was an around-the-clock job, but dealing with a customer question at midnight or delivering products on the weekend is pretty much the standard.

Don't try to master everything. Like many people, I want to know enough to be dangerous. But it's so important to get expert help when you need it for things that you just don't have the depth of knowledge about. I have assistance with SEO, Facebook ads, CRM, and finance, and it's invaluable.

Cash flow management is complex. When you're a small business, there are a lot of demands on your cash. Given that we are self-funded and want to invest in our next product innovation, it's tricky to manage the cash flow to get ahead, and it is a daily job. For example, we needed to figure out how to fund our large-size refillable bottles (and essential innovation that aligns with our brand values) and ended up getting a QuickBooks loan, so sometimes you have to look at unconventional solutions.

There are just some things that can't be measured. Like influencer posts. Or podcast conversion. But you do them anyhow because it's about building the brand; just don't kill yourself trying to put an ROI on everything.

Press is hard. It takes a lot of time and energy to get PR traction, even if you have a team on board. We have also learned that during COVID-19, media priorities shifted, so you need to be committed to a long process.

## You are a person of significant influence. If you could inspire a movement that would bring the best outcome to the greatest number of people, what would that be?

Embracing clean beauty—there are a shocking number of harmful ingredients in most of our beauty products. And many of them are harmful to us and also to the environment.

## Dreams come true. If you could invite anyone in the world to dinner, who would that be?

I'd love to pick Gwyneth Paltrow's brain about goop.

## Where can we follow your work?

Website: lovemasami.com
Social:  Facebook / Instagram / Twitter / Pinterest
@lovemasamihair

# CHAPTER 27

# Ilyssa Panitz

ॐ ॐ

*If you want to remake yourself and renovate your career,*
*you should prepare for long hours on the phone and tons of*
*follow-up emails to really convey your message and why you*
*and the potential client share similar goals.*

Ilyssa Panitz is a divorce journalist and columnist. Ilyssa writes a daily column on Medium's *Authority Magazine* called "5 Things You Need to Know How to Survive and Thrive During & After A Divorce." Ilyssa also serves as the content and editorial producer for The National Association of Divorce Professionals and is the co-host of "All Things Divorce" on Clubhouse every Wednesday and Sunday evenings. Before shifting her focus to the subject of divorce in September 2020, Ilyssa spent over 20 years interviewing prominent names in Hollywood and producing photo shoots in their beautiful homes.

## Tell us a bit about your upbringing.

I spent my childhood on the stage. I would dream of being on Broadway, TV, or in the movies. As a kid, I devoted my Saturday afternoons to attending a theater workshop called, Showtime before being accepted at The American Academy of Dramatic Arts in Manhattan. Then in the summers, eight weeks at French Woods, a performing arts sleepaway camp. When my mom told me I could not pursue acting/singing as a career, I said, "What do you want me to do with my life? She said, "Figure it out!" I knew I had the gift of gab and could strike up a conversation with anyone. I also loved to write, talk on the phone, and thrive on a challenge. I just was clueless about what to do with those qualities.

When I was trying to piece this all together during college, I took a journalism class (because the line to sign up was short). The teacher was the local anchor for NBC, who told me I was a natural. She got me an internship at her station, and from the second I walked into the newsroom, I knew I found my calling!

### What is your life lesson quote? Can you share its relevance in your life?

My favorite quote is actually a chant from Ellen DeGeneres' character Dory in the movie *Finding Nemo*. It goes, "Just keep swimming. Just keep swimming." It resonates with me because, like the film, life is full of obstacles and challenges. So, take a cue from Dory; no matter what gets thrown in your way, you have to keep pushing and moving forward. You can't stop and give up because something is blocking your path. Instead, navigate and then march forward or, in Dory's case, swim through it all!

### You have been blessed with success. What are three qualities you possess that helped you achieve your goals?

Never give up!

Never lose your focus!

Always know who you are and what you are made of!

Whenever I need a reminder of this, I play Kelly Clarkson's song, "Stronger." It has become my mantra.

**Tell us about your career experience before your second chapter.**

Before pivoting my focus to covering the subject of divorce, I was a celebrity/entertainment reporter and producer. I was the girl on every red carpet at TV and film premieres. I spent most of my workday conducting one-on-one interviews with the A-listers and traveled to their homes for exclusive photo shoots.

**Your second chapter's transition was remarkable. What was the trigger that made you decide you needed to make a change in your life?**

The idea stemmed from an interview with Marie Osmond (my childhood idol) on January 3, 2017, at the NASDAQ in New York City. I asked the megastar how she had the strength to overcome so much heartache in her life because, sadly, she had experienced so much sadness. Marie put her hand over mine and said, "Ilyssa, sometimes life is not meant to be fair, but it is what you do with it that makes you who you are!" Out of all the hundreds or maybe thousands of interviews I have done, I never forgot those very words, and they stay with me to this day. Fast forward to August/September 2020, when I was in a personal transition and trying to find new meaning and purpose in my career. I woke up at two AM from a sound sleep because I heard Marie saying those words repeatedly.

**How did you reinvent yourself in your second chapter?**

I have always been a newshound and addicted to the media industry. One day I was flipping through all the networks and noticed a pattern. So many political, entertainment, sports, medical and weather correspondents but not one channel had a divorce correspondent. I thought of this because, on a personal note, I was going through my own divorce and desperate for information on this complicated matter. Here I heard facts on all of these other topics, but where was the one I wanted? Nowhere! So, poof, the idea was born that I would reinvent myself and interview every expert in the field of divorce and deliver information to the public. As journalists, we have a voice that can be broadcast on the airwaves, and we are in a position to help communicate the knowledge people are seeking. I made it my mission to be that person when it came to the matter of divorce.

## What did you do to discover you had a new skill set you hadn't maximized?

I always knew I was tough because I am a born and bred New Yorker (LOL). However, as I immersed myself in this new beat, I realized I am titanium, and nothing can break me! No matter how many times I got knocked down, I kept getting up because I was determined to do something when going through a divorce.

When I listen to these professionals talk about all aspects of divorce, it makes me realize how much I have overcome and how it gave me the power to use my experiences to raise awareness and help others. So many people going through a divorce have contacted me, and it pains me to listen to what they are dealing with. They are confused and feeling hopeless, which is natural when you are thrown into the chaos, your life has been turned entirely upside down, and your heart is shattered into a million pieces. What is worse, while they are trying to understand the legal system, everyone is telling them, "The sun will shine" or "There is a light at the end of the tunnel," and they are thinking, "WTF, I am drowning over here." That is where I come in!

My philosophy has always been when someone says good news, bad news, you start with the bad to end on a high note. I now devote my life to teaching my readers/listeners everything about divorce and reassuring them why they will survive and thrive once divorce is behind them. Since I moved my focus, the response has been amazing. Every day divorce pros call me and look to join forces, plus people going through this transition tell me how they find comfort from my columns.

## How are things going now?

I am growing and expanding, and I have never felt so inspired. Since I launched this new initiative a few months ago, I now work with the National Association of Divorce Professionals, co-host a twice-weekly discussion on Clubhouse called "All Things Divorce," and write a column for Authority Magazine called, "5 Things You Need to Know to Survive and Thrive During and After a Divorce." What is even more surprising? I have the press calling *me* for interviews.

## Is there someone you are grateful to who helped you along the way?

My parents Arline and Steven Panitz. I am not going to lie; there were times I felt sad, lost, and just needed a good cry. But, never, ever did they stop believing in me and instill in my head over and over that now I must believe in myself. They also reminded me of when I was a flighty teenager who only cared about my friends and the phone and what I have achieved once I found my calling as a journalist in college. Their support, guidance, and strength continue to lift me up, and it is why I am where I am today.

## Share an exciting moment that happened since committing to your second chapter.

The reactions and comments I receive from my columns have been overwhelming, but there was one that brought me to tears. It was from a woman going through a difficult divorce. She wrote me how my articles have been an enormous source of support and encouragement to her. Not only did she thank me for writing them, but she said, "She waits for them to post every day!"

**Have you ever struggled with believing in yourself? If so, how did you overcome that limiting belief?**

Umm, yeah! Whenever you embark on a do-over, you are always filled with self-doubt. Plus, I was changing direction in my personal and professional lives simultaneously so, the "struggle to believe in yourself" hit me from all directions. But, like I said before, I am forever grateful that my parents never let me fall, and if they saw I tripped, they were there to catch me and remind me of why I can succeed.

**Typically, I encourage my clients to ask for support from those who believe in their vision before they embark on a new chapter. How did you create your support system?**

As I said earlier, I was craving information on divorce. But, unfortunately, just Googling stuff was exhausting. When you are overwhelmed because divorces are incredibly time-consuming, and trying to sustain a job, take care of a family, and provide some sense of normalcy, you turn to places where it is easy to get the facts, and for me, that was television. But as I channel surfed, nowhere did I see a divorce correspondent on any network or their programming. So, I decided to take the lead and start something new.

**Starting a new chapter requires leaving your comfort zone behind. How did you do that?**

You want to talk about Hollywood and celebrities; I am your girl but talk about divorce—are you kidding me? This is such a complicated maze with layers and layers of convoluted legal terms, laws, not to mention all the players involved plus the numbers and the financials; my head swam at the thought of tackling it. I looked at myself in the mirror and said, "Are you crazy, girl?" But then my inner voice said, "This is your mission, and you are the perfect person to do this. People need you; children need you; the world needs you, and you can make a difference!" After that, I have never looked back. Every day I am excited to find a new angle, hop on the phone with someone, write a story, and take this subject to the next level!

## What are five things you wish someone had told you before you started leading your endeavor?

You may have to take a financial step backward to make a giant leap forward.

If you want to remake yourself and renovate your career, you should prepare for long hours on the phone and tons of follow-up emails to really convey your message and why you and the potential client share similar goals.

Remember, there will be good days and bad days. What I mean is there will be days when you close deals and other days when you can't get past first base. But, it is okay and part of the process. Remember Dory's philosophy, "Just keep swimming!"

You are stepping out of a familiar zone and into unchartered territory. You may make mistakes and not have the answers you did before. So did other innovators, and it helped make them successful.

The tax benefits. If you are running your business from your home, you may be able to write things off.

## You are a person of significant influence. If you could inspire a movement that would bring the best outcome to the greatest number of people, what would that be?

That divorce does not have to be doom and gloom. I always say if you play the word association game and say the word "ice cream," people's faces light up, and they say words like delicious and recite their favorite flavor. If you say the word "divorce," everyone's face turns to a frown, and they think, how awful and sad. I want everyone to shift that mindset and instill that it is not all bad. There are endless possibilities and many positives that lie ahead, like feeling happy again, meeting someone better suited for you, carving out "you" time, reconnecting with people you lost contact with, and becoming the CEO of your own finances. Basically, taking charge of your life.

**Dreams come true. If you could invite anyone in the world to dinner, who would that be?**

Reese Witherspoon. I admire everything about Reese, and I am in awe of her brilliance and talent. What's more, is this Oscar winner went through a public divorce with two minor children and came out swinging. She is a movie mogul, top business leader, devoted mom, remarried to a wonderful guy, and respected by everyone in her industry. If Reese reads this, tell her I would love to collaborate with her!

**Where can we follow your work?**

Social: Facebook, Twitter, Instagram, LinkedIn @Ilyssa Panitz.

# CHAPTER 28

# Simone Noordegraaf

ॐ ॐ

*Listen to the voices inside you carefully to ensure your choice is fully authentic—understand, recognize, and welcome both your fears and your excitement so that your voice becomes clearer and clearer.*

Simone Noordegraaf partnered with the Institute for Professional Excellence in Coaching (iPEC) as CEO of her company, BeTouched Coaching BV, or iPEC Europe, in 2018. In just two and a half years, Simone has been instrumental in tripling the number of European and APAC students in iPEC's Coach Training Program. In addition, iPEC has expanded into new locations overseas to expand on its mission: "Raising the consciousness of the world, one person at a time." Before joining iPEC, Simone held senior executive positions in some of the most significant global companies in the world (e.g., Royal Dutch Shell, EY, Royal Philips, and AkzoNobel).

## Share with us a bit about your upbringing.

I started my career as a chartered accountant (comparable to CPA in the United States). It was an education I chose because my father did not want to pay for my advanced education, so I found a way to work and study simultaneously. He wasn't a bad person, but he was anxious about life's securities, and, looking back, that fear has driven me too for a long time in my own life. Our parents' experiences drive our choices in life until we become fully aware of the connections. I am not an exception.

I chose Finance and did pretty well. I ended up in the most senior leadership teams of large listed multinationals, led global teams of more than 4,000 people, and substantial transformation efforts. Yet, I felt unfulfilled and lacked a sense of belonging.

I trained to become a coach in 2011 with The Institute for Professional Excellence in Coaching (iPEC). Before then, I had experienced executive coaching with two marvelous individuals. They made a real difference in how I saw myself, also concerning others. All three experiences taught me how my mindsets, filters, and attitudes influenced what was possible and/or held me back to achieve my full potential. In addition, the same is true for the people (including leaders) around me.

After more than 30 years in a corporate career, I finally found the strength and courage to leave that career behind and start my own company, and bring iPEC's certified coach training to the world outside of North America. I became an advocate for conscious leadership to combat the emotional poverty in our workplaces. That role now changed into a global leadership role in the global company that iPEC changed into. During that journey, I learned many lessons of value to me and, no doubt, to others.

## What is your life lesson quote? Can you share its relevance in your life?

I don't really have a favorite quote. Depending on where I am on my journey, my quote changes, which makes perfect sense because life is a flow, and while one quote may make complete sense at some point in my life, getting attached to it may hold me back during the next period. Helpful quotes are part of my favorites until they have served their purpose, and letting them go is as much part of my growth journey as hanging on to them.

I regularly return to a quote: "We have thoughts, feelings, and emotions, but we are not our thoughts, feelings, or emotions." I identified myself with labels for much of my life—whether a label of being sensible, intelligent, sensitive, or otherwise—the label would define me as one thing. As a result, it would exclude the opposite. I have come to the realization that humans are not simply one thing. When we believe we are, we limit ourselves more than we can see or care to admit.

It's relevant to think about this in light of this interview too. As long as I identified myself as an Auditor or a Finance Professional, the label would hold me back from making a bold choice. When I believe my thoughts or feelings are absolute, I limit myself. When I realize that there is someone or something underneath those thoughts or feelings that are universal and versatile, nothing can genuinely hold me back.

I love the thoughts and feelings that make up my internal universe. Knowing that we have thoughts, feelings, and emotions and can change them when ready is a human superpower. Whenever you are prepared to embrace that superpower, it can be taught and learned.

## You have been blessed with success. What are three qualities you possess that helped you achieve your goals?

Curiosity. I have always been impossibly curious about what life offers, feeling that there is more to know about life than meets the eye. I have not been disappointed. Where I look, there are lessons, and most of those lessons lead to the expansion of possibilities. The boundaries of potential for myself and others are elusive, and the more I look, the more they can be moved. Curiosity extends much beyond the larger questions of life too. I love a good Sunday where I can nerd around in a system, finding a new way to look at data. If I had all the time in the world, I would learn more and probably change careers more often.

Truth-telling. This can be an immensely challenging quality for both myself and others. Many people prefer a solid rationalization above the truth because the truth will initially hurt. We miss so much of our potential because we prefer to tell ourselves why we are right instead of seeing where we are avoiding potential and possibility. The truth can be painful, and the one telling you the truth may be perceived as an enemy or an aggressor. In fact, the complete opposite may be true. Truth-telling is often an act of love. Humans are energy circuits, and our circuits have resistors built in to keep us safe from energetic surges that could hurt the entire system. Our bad experiences teach us to "never go there again."

When someone feels remote, distant, or resistant, I sense those resistors in the system and ask about them. I may reach beyond someone's comfort zone at times, and as a result, magic happens when a resistor is recognized and released. To learn more about how to articulate my truth helpfully is by doing it, taking feedback, and building the strength in our relationship so that we may be caring and daring together. How can we build strong relationships if we are unable or unwilling to speak the truth to each other? As I learn and practice being both caring and daring with myself and others, there is more acceptance when I share my observation, and, fortunately, more magic happens.

Acceptance. For much of my life, I fought the status quo and wanted it to be different. I am (and may always want to be) a change agent. I love change. Through much of life's lessons, though, I have learned to love change while accepting the present. There may be possibilities to make things better, but it does not make the existing state "bad." These two thoughts can be held in the same space.

**Tell us about your career experience before your second chapter.**

At 18 years old, I was an assistant auditor 3b at Ernst & Young; my career started the lowest entry job the audit firm had to offer. Since my dad did not want to pay for university, I found this position to study and work at the same time. So, I literally started at the bottom. I always like to mention the 3b part. On the one hand, I find it immensely funny to give someone a job title with a 3b in it because it makes me think of R2D2 in *Star Wars*. But, on the other hand, I like to also think it serves as a helpful example that life is full of possibilities. There is a path from such a humble entry position to the board room, even if it is not immediately visible.

It took quite a while for my inner world to catch up with the progression of my career. I always seek the boundaries of what is possible and found it challenging to comprehend that pushed boundaries were not met with push back, instead of more space to grow. So, for a long time, I kept identifying myself by that 18-year-old assistant auditor 3b. The consequence of that was that I suffered from a healthy level of imposter syndrome, needing to prove myself to others all the time.

My choice of career was influenced by the choice my parents made to become entrepreneurs out of necessity. There is beauty in understanding one's lifeline, understanding how the choices of our parents and grandparents influence our choices from an early age. My mother, the butcher's daughter, who was taken out of school to help in the shop, married my father at a relatively late age. It is possible that they would never have married but for my father's accident in which he lost his leg. That accident changed the course of their lives and probably mine too.

My father loved his life and possibly himself a lot when he started working in his twenties. My mom tells me the story of how he would walk past her house, looking slick in his suit and hat in the very early sixties. She clearly noticed him, but not necessarily in a way that would suggest they were to be married. And yet, faith decided differently.

The same night they met in a cafe for the first time, my father's dramatic accident happened when he was driving home on his scooter. During his recovery, my father asked for my mother to come and visit him. Their relationship blossomed. Life had changed quite dramatically, though, because a disability was a reason to dismiss someone at that time, and my father lost his job. Imagine how that must have felt . . . you lose a leg, which in itself is pretty traumatic, and on top of that, you lose a job you absolutely love as well.

There was a time of recovery, a new relationship, and the search for a new occupation. My grandfather thought he knew the answer and advised his son to buy a store and become an entrepreneur. The business turned out quite well in the booming sixties and seventies, but the unprocessed trauma and the experience of a life that has happened (instead of chosen) weighed heavily on my father. He made his decisions to ensure his three daughters would have more choice in their lives—not necessarily realizing it was his choice he was imposing on his girls rather than our own. Beautiful motivation to keep his girls safe, however, not always with the intended outcome of happiness.

By the time the eighties came around, the business was not as successful as it once was. More importantly, my father's physical and mental health and my parent's marital struggles had become a part of our daily lives. My father had become unable to work and started to become concerned about future financial security.

All of this led to my choice to become an accountant. I had this sense of wanting to study psychology, but it was not very well developed yet. My father's search for financial security and his desire for his daughters to choose what he considered "sensible" choices drove me to consider studying economy or law—the hard stuff, rather than the soft stuff of life. Since I was the third one of the three girls, he was not very inclined to contribute to my further education, so I found another way. I chose a career where I could work and study at the same time and became an auditor.

I must tell you that it was an ordeal at times to work at an audit firm. Some afternoons stretched out in front of me as if they would never end, checking off folders of invoices, comparing them with the entries in the general ledger with a green pen. It was mind-numbing, and some days, I would cry of unhappiness or have to fight off sleep. Being a "sensible" girl, though, I stayed the course.

Eventually, as I started to lead teams, things became more interesting. The experience of promotion from within the team to a leadership role was a challenge I still remember to this day. How people responded to me from one day to the next as my position changed was immensely interesting. In general, I found the development of myself and the people around me a source of joy and fascination. Leadership, as clumsy as I went about it, was something that gave my days color and spark.

For years, I stayed in Finance. I knew I was rather good at it, even though it remained boring to me. Auditing made me look through the rear windshield of other companies. Nothing that I did was of my own doing or creation. I was simply looking at other people's work in different companies, judging what they did as "right" or "wrong," and suggesting improvements for their world. So, when I moved into financial controlling positions, it helped me shift my attention from the back seat to the rearview mirror in the car's front seat. I could stop looking at the work of other companies and started to work more proactively at the processes and financials of the company I was part of.

That was an interesting and satisfying step. I see accounting and controlling today as value contributors, registering and analyzing the outcomes of all other activities in the company. They can be incredible partners to the business! I can't help but see the limitations of how financials are educated, though, with a great focus on risk avoidance and management. Much more is possible within the finance profession when the finance function chooses to focus on growth and sees risks as a possibility.

## How did you reinvent yourself in your second chapter?

If I think about the many times I have reinvented myself, my head sometimes spins. I started off as an assistant-auditor, became a CFO, conducted business in more than 100 countries, and lived in three. After that, I ran my own licensed international startup and moved on to become a Chief Business Development Officer of iPEC Coaching, the premier coaching school in the world. Each one of these steps required both big and small reinventions, breaking through my own boundaries more than once.

For most people looking at my career, the synopsis of the reinvention would be from Finance into Business Development and Sales. There are no two professions that are further apart, and that leap was years in the making.

I needed an external chance to experience and demonstrate what was possible. In traditional companies, the labels and functional designations are often constricting. Most leaders will struggle to see the potential of a global Chief Business Development Officer in the local assistant auditor 3b. And as a result, managers will often struggle to take a perceived risk, giving you the chance to try your hand at something radically new. Sadly, that becomes even harder if you have demonstrated your skill in a function. The label sticks. Although I did find reinventions within Finance, I needed to create my own chances as an entrepreneur to completely break out of my back-office box.

More importantly, though, I needed an internal chance too. We believe most of the labels we are tagged with and internalize them. They become so natural and are confirmed throughout our lives. Breaking away from those labels requires much inner work and awareness. I had many conversations with myself and my many fears. I adopted a new adage for personal development: "your history does not define your future." In a future where we will be required to reinvent ourselves many times during a lifetime, we will be better off if we choose to believe in our ability to change and adapt to new careers.

## Your second chapter's transition was remarkable. What was the trigger that made you decide you needed to make a change in your life?

I love the question because it is so difficult to answer.

My journey of reinvention was about getting to know myself—understanding my filters and conditioning, which were driving me in one specific direction, repeating patterns—so I could disarm them and free myself from the unconscious choices I was making. I learned about trusting life and my own abilities. In essence, I learned about loving more and fearing less.

As I was coaching prospective clients, I noticed that our loved ones often try to talk us out of our transformational ideas. Did you ever notice that? Finding the courage to make a dramatic change in life is already daunting enough. Yet, we have that courage in us. Most of the time, when we are drawn to follow that feeling and engage with the people we love, they will be the ones to ask us a million questions and enlarge any fear we already had to begin with.

Your loved ones don't do that because they are bad people, of course. They love you, and their highest aim is probably to keep you safe. It may even be a little bigger than that—they love the image they have of you and dread seeing that change. Occasionally, your courageous choice may even trigger an introspection for the other that they may need to make a change too, and your choice will make them uncomfortable in their own inertia. We don't always know what goes on in their minds unless they are conscious of themselves and tell us. I understand that the pull into safety is a strong one, both for ourselves and others.

One significant trigger that drove me to change was the unconsciousness that happens in large organizations. I just did not want it anymore. I read once in the book, *Sapiens* that people are wired to work in groups of a maximum of 150 and that people start to separate themselves if the group becomes more extensive. Politics is a side-effect of people trying to manipulate their environment to feel safe. I don't really like the word politics because it is too generic, implying ill will. That is rarely the case, though it is unconscious behavior to create personal safety most of the time.

It is draining, though, to live and work in environments where people work in unawareness. Learning how to coach helped me tremendously dig deeper under stakeholders' resistance to help make decisions that are good for the whole organization and individuals in it. And yet, it is difficult to consistently do this within an organization with a high percentage of unaware leaders who will be using their best tools to lead, yet at times create separation and force rather than oneness and personal power to do that.

The second trigger is that I became more confident to simply follow the breadcrumbs of my joy. Finding new things to love is easier if you feel safe enough to do that. Doing what you love seems to innately make a person successful. I have been leading, training, and coaching so many people throughout my career, and all that holds them back to live their best lives is resistance and their powers to buy into and rationalize that resistance. It's a fascinating, self-fulfilling, and invisible prison.

This last trigger, a positive one, is still there and guiding me into the refinement of operating at my greatest potential. It has become my close friend and is reflected in my most intimate relationships with the people who love me enough to remind me that I am pushing up against the wrong obstacles or coasting in my comfort zone.

### What did you do to discover you had a new skill set you hadn't maximized?

The first capability I had to discover was my strategic mind. Climbing the ladder from one of the lower ranks, you actually are hired for a lot of the "doing." My mind, my belief in myself, had not caught up to the fact that I might have more in me. I felt exposed as I grew into more prominent roles and struggled for a while to find my footing, especially in an organization with very little sensitivity. Achievement through force was considered a badge of honor. I tried to cope by "doing" more, which had worked for me in the past. But, it simply was not enough. I found myself close to burnout as I was sitting on the floor crying, and my husband was telling me that he did not "think I was a lot of fun this way." He was right.

Have you ever heard about the "Hero's Journey"? All stories follow a similar pattern, and the hero has to go into the abyss to return with new wisdom and insight. I can only say that every abyss did that for me in its own unique way. This one showed me that I had much more in me than I had initially thought. A coach I worked with helped me see that I was more strategic, creative, and sensing than many others who chose finance as their profession. I had never understood why it was so hard to explain myself to my peers and finance leaders until I understood how I differed from them. Learning that helped me embrace my newfound strengths in strategy and intuition and better communicate with people whose brains work differently from mine.

Moving into Business Development became a necessity after leaving my large multinational positions. There was no other option than to dive right into Admissions conversations to build my business, and, as I did that, I learned that my whole perception and judgment I had around sales was wrong. Walking with the image of the encyclopedia salesperson, who quickly pushes their foot in the door as the potential unexpecting client is disturbed in the middle of their day, my sense of sales was distorted. I found my first steps into the field terrifying, and yet, as I leaned in, I met the most amazing people with the most amazing stories. They already knew what they wanted and gave me the option to help them dream bolder and objectively consider the obstacles.

I had learned to coach years before and was now realizing that selling is coaching. If you do much beyond that, you are actually not serving your customer. In the well-informed world we live in, many buyers already know their desired state. They need someone to talk to, truly understand how the product or service fits with what they want, and more importantly, understand how to overcome the obstacles to that desired state. Most people have an innate ability to know what they want. However, they are holding themselves back to follow their joy because of their own fears and the fears of their loved ones. Understanding that made all the difference!

## How are things going with this new initiative?

I am now in a role where I do nearly everything differently from how I started my career. I develop strategies, lead people, and focus mainly on developing new offerings and growing our business in a mission-driven company. I get to do what I love by building this new movement, working with people that I genuinely enjoy and care about, and working in an environment where I am accepted for who I am.

At the end of the day, most professions and careers are not that different. It depends on the perspective one chooses. You can always find the differences if you look hard enough at the caricatures of each profession. Finance is a back-office function, primarily busy with keeping scores. Business Development is all about scoring rather than keeping score. Nothing is less accurate if you change perspective and look at a company more holistically. The car is driving and gaining speed, and we drive the car together. We need the gas and brakes, the dashboard and mirrors, the engine and tubes, for the whole thing to work. In addition, everything is a process running horizontally through the organization if you look at a company through the lens of the customer.

I do want to emphasize the importance of being accepted for who I am. In all of my roles in large organizations, I have never felt so accepted. I am intelligent, emotional, and passionate. I like to ask tough questions and challenge someone if I think I am getting a superficial answer. Superficial answers have never helped us move beyond our wildest dreams. I question myself just as freely as others. I guess that has made me odd in senior roles in large corporations and forced me to also suppress parts of who I am with varying levels of success. I find myself in an environment not threatened by who I am, both at home and at work. It is the most liberating experience! Being who you are, knowing that someone will hear your emotion, and asking a question about it rather than judging it is refreshing! I wish that for anyone.

I am still untangling years of conditioning from my corporate world, so I regularly tighten up, bracing for a response. Every time the answer is different than my conditioning leads me to believe, I feel a surge of happiness and appreciation to my environment for genuinely seeing and hearing me beyond my words.

## Is there someone you are grateful to who helped you along the way?

Everyone who was ever on my road has helped me to get to where I am today. I most appreciate the people who had faith in me when I made my biggest turns. I remember those conversations vividly, especially when they came from someone or at a time that surprised me.

When Philips split into a Healthcare and a Lighting business, my position was split as well. All this was happening right around when I lost my husband and found the company not particularly sensitive to my grief. In the midst of all of this, without a clear path forward in the company's separation, I decided to pursue an exit plan.

Where I anticipated pushback and complexities, I found understanding and a reasonable conversation from the leaders I engaged with. Or when I decided to leave my corporate position to pursue my new career as the international license holder for iPEC, and I sat down with two people I trusted, their excitement and unwavering support in my new path was refreshing and reaffirming. None of them talked about the risks, possible failures, or what might get in my way. Instead, they provided me reassurance and confirmation, seeing me in all my possibilities rather than their fears or concerns. They were able to advise me from my vantage point, rather than how they wanted to see me or what it would say about them when making a different choice.

## Share an exciting moment that happened since committing to your second chapter.

Tough one! I feel I am still in the middle of the transition, making it hard to zoom out and pick a story.

The most exciting story that I can think of is the story of my developing trust. If I had known everything that happened in the past three years, I probably would not have chosen this path. But, I guess that it is better not to know sometimes.

I had just decided to quit my job at a multinational company, where I worked for two years. I was unhappy. Good, and yet, unaware people can be really clumsy, and when the stress runs high, the clumsiness can wear on everyone in a system. I needed a break from large and unaware systems. So, I decided to leave and become an independent executive coach. Before I had the time to hand in my letter, the CEO of iPEC, Joan, called me to tell me that iPEC was ready to go global and whether I was still interested in partnering. Of course, my (near-immediate) answer was yes.

You should know that I had been flirting with iPEC for more than six years by that time, looking for opportunities to work together in different forms. Going through iPEC's certified coach training program in 2011 was immensely meaningful. I wanted to offer that experience to more people in the world. Until that decision to resign, all options to collaborate failed. Interestingly, in the fall of 2017, the pieces fell together.

The years after that have been intense. I learned to form new partnerships and new companies, master international growth, enter new markets, develop marketing and sales skills, and much more. I learned to see someone's potential separate from today, becoming more realistic about how much ground there was to cover between now and possibility. We alternated failing and succeeding so that we could accelerate our learning. As a result, I felt the fear and the freedom in equal measure most of the time.

Interestingly enough, the iPEC CEO and I ran our separate companies without unnecessary boundaries and limitations. Where possible, we operated as one. We were weaving the fabric of a global company even when we were still in separate entities and groups. Seeing my views of how we could work as one reflected in my partner was a revelation. Seeing how some lawyers might try to instill the fear of separation in us was utterly eye-opening as well. My ability to trust and believe in the magic happening right in front of us was challenging. Experiencing a business relationship devoid of "us" versus "them" was a dream come true.

In life, I had made big steps in trusting and releasing my judgments, and yet, I found that I had lots of room to grow under this speed and stress. I am amazed by the gift that trust had brought me when I finally dared to lean in this past year.

We brought our companies together into one global group in the middle of a pandemic during an unprecedented year, challenging our entire company to be completely agile.

If I had known everything upfront, I probably would have never been able to say "yes" with as much conviction as I did. And yet, saying "yes" was the most significant gift I could have ever given myself because I know how to trust at a much deeper level and know myself loved exactly how I am.

**Have you ever struggled with believing in yourself? If so, how did you overcome that limiting belief?**

To the surprise of many, I always struggled to believe in myself, and to some extent, I still do. Right now, I find those moments mainly at night when I lie awake at the witching hours, in this space between waking and sleeping. My reasoning is that I have processed a lot of those limiting beliefs, but the deepest fears show up when I am least conscious. So now, I am training my awareness to see if I can get to a deeper level of consciousness and bring part of me on a journey of possibility and love rather than risk and fear.

**Typically, I encourage my clients to ask for support from those who believe in their vision before they embark on a new chapter. How did you create your support system?**

Great question! I think there are three big secrets to this.

Trust you! You are your own support system, first and foremost. Getting to know yourself and your triggers, shadows, and emotions are essential to freedom of choice. I have learned to use my emotions like a compass. When I feel an emotion, it's time to sit down and see what is out of alignment. I don't take the emotion as an absolute because I may be angry at someone or something, but that is not at the heart of the emotion. Usually, there is some value that is being challenged or a few being triggered—spending time with my emotions helps me understand what is going on at a deeper level than my drama.

Build your secure bases consistently and deliberately. Know people whose perspective is invaluable and their level of trust is high. Share yourself, connect, explore. In addition to people, consider your spaces, rituals, and everything else that gives you support and a base to soar from with courage.

Share yourself shamelessly. This is one of the most demanding and most rewarding things you can do to overcome obstacles and resistance within yourself. You are perfect just as you are, and most of the issues you carry shame about are shared with others. Once you start to share yourself, you become a mirror to others and their feelings of shame. What you hide consciously or unconsciously from the world and others becomes a barrier or a resistance in the relationship. If you can face these barriers and befriend them, energy flows within you and your relationships with others.

## Starting a new chapter requires leaving your comfort zone behind. How did you do that?

How interesting is it if your mind is open enough to consider so many changes and different careers in different jobs?

I remember leaving my job at Ernst & Young in 1997 after 12.5 years. I cried—really hard—when I carried my little box out of that big office into the wide world and felt so uncertain whether I would be able to perform outside of the environment that had been my safe haven and comfort zone for all those years.

Less than 24 hours later, all was forgotten, and I was completely clear of what I could accomplish in a new role and capacity. This remains true to this day. I always feel the pull to stay within the familiar, constantly reminded by my loved ones that I take a risk and always find that I would not do it any other way after taking the plunge. For a long time, I was waiting for my fear to disappear before making a change. You can prepare all you want. But, the fearful thoughts will not disappear until you actually take the plunge.

## What are five things you wish someone had told you before you started leading your organization, and why?

Listen to the voices inside you carefully to ensure your choice is fully authentic—understand, recognize, and welcome both your fears and your excitement so that your voice becomes clearer and clearer.

Listen to the voices around you carefully and see the love of the person telling you not to do it—understand, recognize, and welcome their fears too. What are they trying to say? What is love, and what is their fear? What shall I bring along, and what shall I leave behind?

My father, who I considered larger than life for a long time, counseled me against quitting my Ernst & Young job to go to Shell. He wanted me to be safe and thought I was throwing my career away by leaving. It scared me to hear that, and I did not want to listen to it, really. Whenever people around me tell me not to do something, I take it seriously and sometimes too seriously. So, it takes a bit of time and contemplation to fully consider their reasons for telling me not to go or do something. And yet, as he was counseling me, I still had the vivid image in my mind of the partners who walked the EY corridors for 40 years before they could go and enjoy their pension. I dreaded to be in the same role in the same company for so long and thought about the possibilities in the world that I wanted to experience. If I would choose to stay in my comfort zone and avoid all risks to keep what I had, how could I keep growing and experiencing what life has to offer me? I wanted to remain relevant and fresh with broad horizons and sweeping ideas.

Try it—you will be richer for the experience! You cannot make a mistake—telling me would not have done the trick. Most of the things I need to learn I don't "just" learn through my ears and in my head. The most meaningful things I have learned in life are experiencing new situations, countries, capabilities, and more. Even when I did not enjoy the new environment much, I learned from what I did not love and how I responded to it. I remember when I stood in an airport with my life packed into a sea container and my husband with me thinking, "Why am I making my life so complicated?" Those were the moments I would have turned around if I wasn't already so profoundly committed—they made my life richer, though, in many different ways.

Find and appreciate your secure bases in life. Even when everything is uprooted, we crave our safe-havens. A secure base is a person, place, ritual, or practice which provides you a safe place in life from where you can take a chance, transform, and experiment. Learning about secure bases was crucial for me to anchor myself somewhere and find the safety that I could not always find inside me yet.

Who is on your advisory board? What are the habits that are an anchor in your day and offer you comfort that is pure and your own? How are you honoring those secure bases rather than take them for granted in life, even when your relationship with that secure base is at times a little bumpy?

I married Joeri a year and a half ago after losing my first husband, Niek, to early-onset Alzheimer's disease. Both Joeri and Niek are my secure bases. I know to my core that my life and experience with Niek allow me to build a life with Joeri. They are two profoundly different human beings and both amazing in their own unique way. Niek's illness and our struggle through discovery, understanding, and acceptance of the disease and even of each other in our individual and joint struggles were something I needed to see the beauty, strength, and courage in Joeri. Our lives together are never perfect, and yet, they are perfect in that imperfection. Knowing Joeri as someone who will always stand beside me, however strong-willed and persistent as we both are, allows me to soar into whatever direction I may choose. I know he will perhaps disagree with me, but he will never stop loving me. I can't say with certainty that I would have been able to see and understand this had I not had Niek as my teacher and secure base in the 25 years before.

Nothing is ever binary; life is about so much more than ones and zeroes—there is no such thing as right and wrong, only shades of grey. I am not sure where I developed my strong judgments early in life, but I most definitely did. Life was easier if I could label things or box them into a category or a "right" or "wrong" box. Over time, I learned how much of that is an illusion that I created to make sense of life and create safety and some kind of order. But what it does, in fact, is create separation. Once something is categorized, it limits our ability to engage with an object, person, or place. Nothing is simply one thing. Turn it upside down, and your whole perception changes with it.

I enjoy watching Netflix or Prime series more than movies because I have a huge admiration for the people who write and deepen their characters. Nobody is flat, only good or only bad. Nobody is static either; we constantly evolve. When I stop looking,

I miss their evolution. The really great writers of series, especially those that span multiple seasons with high quality, understand this. They manipulate my heartstrings softly and gently until I see the humanity in the villain, what caused them to become who they are. The opposite is true too. What happens to the hero when he gains the power to manipulate the audience or the other characters? What if we embrace the fact that we are all the hero and the villain — we are never just one or the other. Maybe we don't even need to be.

**You are a person of significant influence. If you could inspire a movement that would bring the best outcome to the greatest number of people, what would that be?**

That is the easiest question on the whole list! That movement would be about conscious leadership and governance. We all go to work and adjust ourselves to what we expect professionals to be. All focused on the doing, unconscious about the impact we have on each other, many people feel less satisfied with their working life than they could be. In the process, we rush to an outcome and avoid having the conversation under the conversation, connecting around an actual purpose (instead of the words), and creating meaningful connections and results. We may need to slow down to speed up in meaningful ways, staring our fears in the eyes to build deep and trusting relationships.

I wish everyone to be aware of who they are and make choices about how they show up and feel aligned with something bigger than they are. I love the idea of large teams forging ahead, knowing and understanding how thoughts and beliefs trigger feelings which, in turn, trigger our actions. Unfortunately, our workplaces' unawareness and emotional poverty sub-optimize the use of all of our resources. I am committed to making a difference in that space.

**Dreams come true. If you could invite anyone in the world to dinner, who would that be?**

One of the things iPEC Coaching is well known for is our Energy Leadership™ model. For me, it was a game-changer to start living my life in love rather than in fear. It allowed me to become aware of my conditioning and choose more freely and consciously rather than what had been modeled to me in the past. Most recently, I was listening to the audible biographies of Matthew McConaughey and Barack Obama. It struck me how graciously they describe their lives and the choices they make—the awareness they bring to the situations they found themselves. McConaughey called it "greenlight" in his book, and every time he said it, I heard the smile in his voice. Obama describes his "greenlight" moments under pressure so eloquently too. I am pretty sure they kicked the garbage can every once in a while, too, feeling the low energy of victimhood or anger when their life felt heavy under responsibility or clumsy choices.

I am curious about those low points in their lives, too, and their methods to shift from their lows to more constructive energy levels, simply because that is what leaders do. Both of them developed their strategies to keep experiencing their personal power of choice. I'm not sure whether they ever met each other, but I would love to have dinner with them and ask how they might share the power of choice with the people who don't always feel they have that power in the palm of their hands.

**Where can we follow your work?**

Website: ipeccoaching.com.
Social:   LinkedIn

# CHAPTER 29

# Sheila Jackson

ॐ❧

*I have been told by many people that I write well. However, I didn't really have the luxury of exploring that skill set until I founded emergewell + co and found myself creating quite a bit of original content for our platform. Writing can be cumbersome and challenging for many people, but I've come to understand that when you are creating content for something you believe in, researched, and experienced at the cellular level, it flows onto the paper in a seemingly effortless way.*

As the Founder of emergewell + co, Sheila Jackson is building a platform that unites modern medical science with one of the world's oldest holistic whole-body healing systems. Focused on the deeper investigative work that many women have not experienced within the standard American medical system, Sheila is shining a light on the unseen elements of autoimmune disease and addressing the contributory factors that diminish female healthiness (energy), productive capacity (effort), and vivaciousness (enthusiasm). Before founding emergewell + co, Sheila held leadership positions in logistics, construction, and healthcare. Attending college classes at night, she studied business administration at Tarrant County College while working her way up the ranks from a 20-year-old single mother administration assistant to a national practice management consultant with 1–800-DENTIST. She is the Founder and CEO of award-winning multi-million-dollar companies JA Jackson Construction and Principle Logistics Group.

## Share with us a bit about your upbringing.

As a young girl growing up in Northern California, my life seemed to flow in a narrative—only child, only granddaughter, and the only niece; I spent most of my time with the adults in my Italian family. My best friend was Billy Jo. She and I would walk to school together. School and chores always came first in our home, so I could go outside and play when my "work" was done. Most often, I could be found building habitats for tree frogs and lizards. I've always had a deep love and connection with animals and back then believed I was somehow creating a safe space for the little critters when I'd build a natural enclosure using broken flower pots, stones, sticks, vines, and plants.

Weekends were spent with my grandparents, Virginia and Vatuch—his birth name changed to William when he was processed through the immigration station on Ellis Island. Summertime was my favorite; I'd spend it in Hollister, California, with my Aunt Lynn and a quarter horse named Louie. We'd take long rides through the mountains, and I'd participate in the summer rodeo. That is until I was eight years old, and my dad's career moved us away from them all.

From this point, my childhood had many stops and starts. Leaving California and landing in Chicago was cold, and I'm not just referring to the weather. The girls weren't kind, my dad was always traveling, and my mom was noticeably unhappy. I became more introverted. That lasted for two and half years before we would move to Texas, where my dad would leave us for good. Maybe if they had yelled, threw things, and stayed away from one another for hours or days, I would have known something was wrong. My mom was coming apart. She tried to hide her grief, but her deep sadness had a heartbeat all its own—one that reverberated through me too.

My mother looked like a blue-eyed Mary Tyler Moore, and my dad could easily have been a body double for Al Pacino, looking like he might have just walked off the set of *The Godfather*. Finally, after 20 years, my dad, "No longer wanting the responsibility of the life he had created with her," walked away. Leaving her alone to do the dirty work, she broke the silence and told me.

It was not known, seen, or heard in our home until that point if something were ever wrong. So, from the outside looking in, my childhood was orderly, untroubled, "perfect"—until it wasn't.

At 13, I learned I'd have to be strong on my own.

## What is your life lesson quote? Can you share its relevance in your life?

"You can't go back and change the beginning, but you can change where you are and change the ending."—C. S. Lewis.

The best way to describe how this is relevant in my own life is when I've failed forward. By that, I mean that I've had an innate sense to look ahead more than look back and understand that I am (to no small degree) responsible for the circumstances and the outcomes in my own life. This life lesson quote has been a lifeline, keeping me grounded when my reality is not to my liking, or I find myself in a position I'd not planned to be in—I can change.

A profoundly personal example is when I'd not planned or ever given a thought to becoming a mother at 20 years old. Still, at 19, I was pregnant. I certainly did not go into it knowing what I was doing. However, I was old enough to have gotten myself into that position. I embraced my reality and chose to raise my now

31-year-old son. This was an experience that proved to be the most precious relationship of my lifetime — motherhood. He cracked my heart wide open. I also learned about my limitations as a single woman and parent and that doing my best by him meant I'd not get myself into that position of solo parenting again. As corny as it might sound, believing that I can change the ending gives me a sense of confidence and peace that no matter the lemons life leaves me with, there is always a way to make lemonade.

### You have been blessed with success. What are three qualities you possess that helped you achieve your goals?

The three qualities I possess that helped me accomplish so much in my life are kindness, action, and truth.

Entrepreneurship isn't very natural. It confronts and even defies many of our most basic human instincts, our desire for security and comfort, the fear that comes with risk-taking, and the human tendency to want to go with the flow, not make waves, and fit in. But, wanting to grow and be chosen by those with experience, that's how our entrepreneurial wagons got hitched. But, of course, I'm talking about a joint-venture partnership with a wealthy Texas businessman.

He was a client first before I accepted his offer to partner. I entrusted him with the best interest of the brokerage and consulting firm that I'd spent seven years building, nurturing, and growing in an entirely unfamiliar industry to me but not to him. He (and his family) had a 100-year history in the business of transportation and logistics. As foreign as the territory felt, my boutique business grew into a vital, multi-million-dollar company. Unaware of it then, my achievements in industry and my desire to grow and scale the business made me his target.

It's easy to be kind when everything is going your way. But what about when your whole existence is being threatened personally, professionally, and financially by your "partner"? There's this moment that is burned into my memory when Big Tex and I sat still, silent, in the grand office space he had built for himself in his newly constructed 20,000+ square foot house on the hill. Intent on being heard, he looked me in the eyes, breaking the silence; he said, "Sheila, as long as I've known you, you have always done the right things for the right reasons." I sensed that this unsolicited message came from a place of guilt.

While he and I both knew the relationship was heading in a direction that would most likely require high-powered attorneys, he'd just been given less than six months to live. It's the time when he acknowledged something that, up to that point, I'd not heard from him — the truth. He had been deceptive, breached his duties as my business partner, and leveraged his role and authority, playing big-money games and putting everything I'd worked for personally and professionally at risk for his own personal profit. He knew he was leaving me with a million-dollar fight with his estate and the bank where he'd sat on the board of directors. I knew he was facing an even bigger battle, coming to terms with the truth that the fortune he had just recently received could not save his life. I softened. I forgave him.

After his passing, it took another three years of fighting for the truth, but to this day, I believe with all my heart the reason I lost the battle with him but won the war is that under all the pressure and posturing that goes on with litigation, my personal posture remained one of kindness, action, and truth.

## Tell us about your career experience before your second chapter.

Before my second chapter, I have what some might call diverse career experience. I've spent 31 years in leadership roles within three industries: healthcare, logistics, and construction.

My passion for helping people was illuminated at the beginning of my career when I spent three years as a patient services coordinator for a large, multi-location chiropractic clinic in Texas.

In 1992 I wanted a change. I'd had my fill of medical insurance and ambulance-chasing attorneys dictating patient care protocols.

So, I became curious about what it would be like to work in the dental field. Back then, we still used the yellow pages. I started with the A's, and I called out. I don't recall exactly what I said on the phone back then, but I got the attention of Dr. Alexander. I was told he wasn't hiring, but something I said caught his attention, and we met in his office one afternoon. At the end of that conversation, he said, "I don't have a position open, but I'll create one if you come to work for me."

I spent the next twelve years growing the business with him while remaining an integral part of the collaborative care team that led patients to better health through education and improved oral care. I instituted practice protocols that increased new patient case acceptance by 37% and word of mouth referrals by 11%. In addition, I established a 10% reduction in hours worked per employee that improved employee morale while increasing practice productivity and profitability. These results caught an executive's attention with the national marketing and consulting group 1-800-DENTIST, based in Los Angeles, CA. That was a high for me because I loved what I was doing, and at the same time, I was feeling ready for more. After some courting and contract consulting work they hired me to do (a part-time working relationship that was out in the open with Dr. Alexander, too), they extended an offer to join the consulting group as a full-time national practice management consultant.

Advancing into that role, I got to advise and coach hundreds of practitioners and staff by building profitable practices while teaching the team to recognize and overcome the fears that often stop people from getting the care they most need and want.

In 2005 a merger between 1-800-DENTIST and a global consulting firm offered a more prominent role and considerably more travel. Unfortunately, traveling more was not aligned with my number one priority, parenting, so I embarked on an entrepreneurial endeavor that kept me home.

Between 2005 and 2017, I founded and grew two multi-million-dollar businesses in completely unrelated industries, transportation logistics, and construction. So, let's say I learned quite a bit that I hadn't known, including how underrepresented women are in these two industries and that female-owned businesses get far less funding from the banks than male-owned companies do.

In 2017, at the height of my best fiscal year, two things happened — I was navigating a nasty breakup with a former business partner's estate. Then I experienced a medical crisis called acute adrenal insufficiency, also known as Addison's disease.

## How did you reinvent yourself in your second chapter?

It's not one thing that I did. I know today that it rarely ever is. Reinventing myself began because I knew too much to keep traveling the path I had been on. My body broke. My entrepreneurial spirit had also taken a massive hit. I just kept going. By that, I mean I took the next step and did something I'd never done; I began reprioritizing everything in my life to heal. I embarked on a three-year wellness change journey, where I found and studied functional medicine.

Putting my body first, reversing my autoimmune condition, and choosing to close a company that had been profitable (but deafeningly stressful), became my priorities. However, along my journey to healing my body, and with the guidance of some unique relationships, I saw the gap, an underserved population of high-functioning females who aren't getting their healthcare needs met.

It took some soul searching on my part. But, ultimately, I could not turn my back on the truth that human health is suffering to such a vast degree. So, I decided to become the practitioner and reinvest my reinvented self to help other high-functioning females reverse chronic stress-related health conditions like autoimmune disease and rebuild life the way they most want to live.

**Your second chapter's transition was remarkable. What was the trigger that made you decide you needed a make a change in your life?**

It was the beginning of 2018 when I found functional medicine. I learned just how fortunate I was that a high mortality event like the acute adrenal crisis I'd experienced in October 2017 did not become the moment I'd take my final exhale. Instead, it was the distress message my body sent that led me to make a huge transition.

**What did you do to discover you had a new skill set you hadn't maximized?**

I have been told by many people that I write well. However, I didn't really have the luxury of exploring that skillset until I founded emergewell + co and found myself creating quite a bit of original content for our platform. Writing can be cumbersome and challenging for many people, but I've come to understand that when you are creating content for something you believe in, researched, and experienced at the cellular level, it flows onto the paper in a seemingly effortless way.

I would say that I found my way through persistence in the practice of writing daily.

Writing began as part of my own private healing process. In the beginning, it was everything but picture-perfect. In truth, there were hours spent writing where I was a real mess. I've joked that one day I might be brave enough to reveal just how messy I and it was. My thought in exposing some of my earlier writing has little to do with me and more to make visible the writing path I took to turn something turbulent and complex into something purposeful, helpful, and healing. You see, emergewell +co didn't begin with a business in mind. It started as my mantra; healing my body was my target, my indicator of success, you might say.

At the same time, I traversed the new terrain of autoimmunity;

I was also entering into another new environment—litigation. The legal battle with my former business partner's estate had begun. In many ways, I felt like a raw nerve. That doesn't lend itself well to healing. My mantra again was to emerge well. In this case, it was to emerge well financially from a business relationship that had already cost me significantly.

For a time, the only place I felt safe to share my innermost thoughts and feelings was writing on a blank white sheet of 8 ½ x 11 copy paper. The paper itself presented me with an opportunity to overcome a barrier—perfectionism.

My entire life, I've been complimented for my writing. Not the creative kind of writing. Rather the neat, rounded, balanced, "perfect" appearance of my handwriting. This time I pressed my perfectionism buttons, "writing outside any lines," to seek meaning beneath what was going on in my body and business at the same time. My writing has improved and evolved as I've continued to press past the edge of perfectionism. As I allowed my writing to be a bit edgy and not so perfect, writing became the thing I didn't want to put down. The writing was revealing some of my blind spots and barriers.

As I've chosen to go forward in the emerging field of Functional Medicine and Functional Diagnostic Nutrition, as a practitioner who has now spent hundreds of hours working with various people, all of these encounters have definitely enriched my writing. I also have a great team that reviews my work and gives me candid feedback I can trust. Additionally, I'm a huge fan and couldn't live without Grammarly—just saying.

## How are things going now?

One of my favorite quotes is from Pablo Picasso—"The meaning of life is to find your gift. The purpose of life is to give it away."

When you discover your true purpose and passion in life (personally, physically, and professionally), the universe opens doors. It connects you with the right people and resources to realize your greatest dreams. The path will not always be linear or straightforward (believe me, I have a gold medal in pivoting at critical junctures in starting and scaling a business), but you can navigate those challenges knowing that you are working from a place of purpose and destiny.

Creating emergewell + co has been a visceral experience. In truth, it has already been the most satisfying entrepreneurial journey I've taken. We are less than two years old, and already we have created a vibrant community of women we affectionately refer to as our eco-tribe. Women who want to take charge of their own healthcare journey after the conventional, Standard American Model (SAM) has failed to treat them successfully. In January of this year, we launched a monthly online educational series called Tea and Talk Tuesday, focusing on a particular topic related to the onset, progression, and reversal of autoimmune conditions.

We are meeting our monthly targeted number of new emergewell + co clients who have signed up for our signature nourishing YOU™ program. Plus, I am working on a manuscript for my first book, *Solving the Trauma Puzzle: Heal Your Body. Free Your Mind. Unleash Your Higher Self.* It will launch in early 2022. I am also looking forward to the day, hopefully in the not-too-distant future, where we can gather in person again to restore our human connection with one another.

## Is there someone who you are grateful to who helped you along the way?

My husband, Joe. We met one another thirteen years ago. Having been married before, both of us were clear on what unhealthy personal relationships can look like. Outside of the love a mother has for her child, I had never really experienced what intimate, safe, sound, resilient love could feel like coming from another adult. I'd mostly been the one giving to others in a relationship, perhaps to fill the emptiness humming in the background I never wanted to acknowledge after my father left.

Doing life with Joe, I have someone who always has my back, who listens, who will tell me what I need to hear, not just what I want to hear, who is an amazing father and dad to his three kids as well to my son, Bo. Someone who always keeps his word.

It's easy for anyone to do good once in a while. It's something else entirely to do life alongside an excellent human all of the time. A man who sees an uprooted tree in the road's median drives home to gets his tools and returns to replant and stake the tree. That tree still stands today big and robust. He is one of the most intelligent engineering and construction minds I have ever known, he is pretty nice to look at, and he is the proud and loving co-parent to our six dogs; yes, you heard that right. He is my rock, my partner, my everything. I think you get the picture.

## Share an exciting moment that happened since committing to your second chapter.

The most exciting and satisfying thing that has happened to me since beginning this second chapter of my life is that I have reversed my own autoimmune condition. Adrenal insufficiency also called Addison's disease, nearly killed me three and half years ago. It's been quite a journey! I have achieved this reversal by shifting from the outdated practices and often incomplete protocols of conventional medicine and using the 5 Rs of Functional Medicine 1) Remove 2) Replace 3) Repair 4) Re-inoculate 5) Rebalance. Today I use the same 5 R approach to healing at emergewell + co within a framework that addresses the needs of the whole body through 1) Food and Nutrition; 2) Rest and Sleep; 3) Exercise and Movement, 4) Stress Reduction and Supplementation and 5) Helping Relationships.

## Have you ever struggled with believing in yourself? If so, how did you overcome that limiting belief?

Sure. I'm human, and I think we all experience some inner struggle or insecurities. I struggled with a couple of limiting beliefs that so many women (and girls) do.

Perfectionism, which I shared, was really in my face when I began writing. The other is what Oprah calls "the disease to please." I've learned some hard lessons expending too much of my time, energy, and financial resources with people and things that did not align well with the core of who I am. I won't say it didn't serve me well because, in truth, it is that hard stuff, even the high mortality health crisis in 2017 and learning that I have an autoimmune condition where I've met myself. Seeking to be better (in this case, heal), I've discovered blind spots, unresolved trauma, and reprioritized where I placed my energy, effort, and financial recourses. Healing has led to my growth as a human and businesswoman.

Shutting down a toxic (yet profitable) business in logistics was hard. Still, it ultimately gave me the margin I needed in my own life to turn toward building a legacy business in the wellness space that serves women's unmet healthcare needs. Unfortunately, women have been let down time and time again by a conventional, Western medicine mindset and model.

Failing to be treated successfully, and by that, I mean offered something beyond prescriptive symptom care, I became intimately aware of how underserved women's healing needs in healthcare still are today. My journey revealed the actual gap.

Today, I am using all my business acumen and past success to focus on something I am 100% passionate about. Something that I've seen makes a huge difference in women's lives, the men that love them, and the children they raise. Every day, I invite and encourage women to befriend their bodies first, make peace with past events, and quit the habitual lifestyle patterns negatively influencing how we eat, love, work, and manifest in the world.

**Typically, I encourage my clients to ask for support from those who believe in their vision before they embark on a new chapter. How did you create your support system?**

Number one, I wanted and received the buy-in from my husband. His support and understanding of this new direction were vital since it would impact both of us. He and I agreed that shutting down the logistics company (despite the financial risk) was a no-brainer. The partnership and the chaos associated with that business were in no small way contributing to my body's physical decline. No promise of financial gain nor the risk of losing money is worth staying in a toxic environment with toxic people. But, unfortunately, that's what it had become. Once I became clear on this, my perfectionism and people's pleasing tendency were no longer obstructing my view of what is most important—living.

It's essential to know and name what matters most in one's own life at the end of the day. For me, being trapped inside a body that doesn't function well, in pain, ill, symptomatic, and medicated (prescribed and/or self-medicated) has never been my idea of living well. I still have mountains to climb, literally and figuratively. All the money in the world means nothing without one's ability to function at their highest. I got to see that up-close and personal with Big Tex.

No question, supportive relationships are vital. My husband, our kids, and our dogs, those relationships behind the one I am having, are primary. There was a time I wouldn't have said that publicly for fear of judgment and feelings of shame. There's a good reason when the plane is going down; the pilot instructs the parents to put the oxygen mask on themselves first—just saying.

Second, I've built long-standing relationships with a high-powered team of advisors and mentors for more than a decade. I've built my own collaborative care team. These relationships go beyond the physical realm of healers and health practitioners. Whether it is a doctor, CPA, financial advisor, attorney, or mentor, these are the people that over the years have proven time and time again to be highly skilled in their respective fields, good listeners, candid communicators, and trustworthy. I've also learned to walk away from those who aren't sooner than later.

Third, I reached out to women that I knew would be team players, understood, and share the vision I hold for emergewell + co. I had to find the right sisterhood to go on this journey with me. And thankfully, I found them. But, as we scale the business, it will remain vitally important to continue to find the right people who embody what we are about — healing.

### Starting a new chapter requires leaving your comfort zone behind. How did you do that?

I think that's my superpower; I've spent most of my personal and professional life outside my comfort zone. As a kid, being outside my comfort zone was thrust upon me when my dad's ambition moved us away from family and friends — our foundation. Then he left. The thread of dysfunction that followed with my mom questioning if she even wanted to go on with her life, plus the distress and discomfort, certainly wasn't mine by any choice. So, as a young solo parent and professional woman, I had to traverse a new territory — I was the provider.

Entrepreneurship, well, that's all about knowing how to do well outside your comfort zone. It's the only way one does well and survives for any time in the entrepreneurial world. Kelly Clarkson sang it best in her song, "Stronger" — "What doesn't kill you makes you stronger."

As for the comfort zone, I believe it can also be one of the most dangerous zones. Constant comfort doesn't challenge us or invite the discovery of our highest human potential. I feel like my life experience has prepared me to be well and resilient all at the same time.

**What are five things you wish someone had told you before you started leading your company, and why?**

Protect your energy and your effort. Stephen Covey knew what he was talking about when he said, "Fast is Slow. Slow is Fast."

Find your sisterhood. We will be weird, different, unique to someone—that is the beauty of being human. Not everyone is going to like or get what you are doing. So, climb your own mountain and see who shows up to help and scale it with you.

Build a collaborative care team. Find trustworthy practitioners, advisors, and mentors. For example, don't ask a broke CPA (even if she is the nicest woman in the world, your aunt, or your sister's best friend) to help you handle your financial affairs. Um hello.

Put up and hold healthy boundaries between yourself and other people. This is a learned skill that happens over time. A collaborative care team will help strengthen your confidence with this, and in time the experience will nurture a higher intuitive capacity. Befriend your body first. Take care of yourself first and foremost to help others thrive.

Being vulnerable is difficult but the best way to connect with your authentic audience.

**You are a person of significant influence. If you could inspire a movement that would bring the best outcome to the greatest number of people, what would that be?**

We are blessed to live in this time. Our Standard American Medical (SAM) model works wonders for acute conditions and traumatic injuries. However, it fails to treat people successfully when it comes to the growing number of chronic health conditions negatively impacting people's ability to think, feel, and function at their highest. And, in one way or another, we are all paying for it. Americans' chronic health problems and disease not only come at the expense of the individual's well-being and quality of life but constitute a massive burden on the US economy.

The movement I believe that brings the most amount of good to people disrupts the dysfunction of this system, reverses the conditions, and empowers people to heal. Until this happens, feeling better and functioning at our highest human potential is little more than an excellent idea. That's what we're doing at emergewell + co, disrupting the dysfunction, reversing chronic conditions, and empowering people to heal so that they become the highest functioning humans they know.

## Dreams come true. If you could invite anyone in the world to dinner, who would that be?

One of my favorite things is to eat breakfast for lunch — to brunch with a girlfriend and talk about life and love. Elizabeth Gilbert, journalist, and author, that's who I would love to have breakfast for lunch with.

Being a new writer, I admire her work. She's a successful multi-genre author, so that's a given. But really, it has much more to do with her spirit. She personifies what I think of as a girl's best friend — kind, trustworthy, and candid. That's the beauty of the second chapter — understanding the power and influence of the company we keep. Today, I only eat breakfast for lunch with my best girlfriends.

## Where can we follow your work?

Website: emergewellco.com
Social media: @emergewellco

# CHAPTER 30

# Marjorie Zandi

❧ ❧

*As I explored the startup universe—looking at it through
the lens of an angel investor—I knew I could walk into
many companies, help the founder or founders and their
team. Then, as a board member or advisor, I could put
them on a growth, scale, and go-to-market trajectory. But,
most importantly, I was excited to realize I could invest
as an angel in bright, innovative startups that had the
potential to positively impact the world. So, now I invest
money and time in teams and missions that I believe in
and actively seek out female and people of color founders
and entrepreneurs worldwide who have a deep passion
and drive to succeed.*

Marjorie Radlo-Zandi is a seasoned angel investor, board member, mentor, and consultant based in Boston. She invests in early-stage tech, life science, veterinary, food, and food tech companies. Fifty percent of her investments are in women-led businesses, and fifty percent are led by people of color. For more than 20 years, Marjorie led a company that reached across 100 countries, positively impacting the lives of millions by protecting and enhancing the global food supply.

She later sold it to a two billion dollar publicly-held firm and now primarily focuses her time on consulting, mentoring, and impact investing in companies that make a difference in areas she cares deeply about.

## Share with us a bit about your upbringing.

Entrepreneurship is in my blood—I come from a family of entrepreneurs. My family, starting with my great grandfather and great grandmother, were entrepreneurs. He had a grain merchant business in Saint Petersburg, Russia, and she had a coffee brokerage business on the lower east side of Manhattan. As you can imagine, this was the impetus for generations of entrepreneurs in the family. When I was nineteen, I established the first sailing program in my college town. From there—whether in New York City, Silicon Valley, or Boston—I've been responsible for growing and expanding new technologies to be used throughout the world.

## What is your life lesson quote? Can you share its relevance in your life?

> "I've learned that people will forget what you said, people will forget what you did, but people will never forget how you made them feel." —Maya Angelou.

Whether building a business, leading an organization, or in one's personal life, how you make people feel is key to building and sustaining relationships that lead to fulfillment. Trust is the backbone of any relationship. Make sure that at the end of any conversation, everyone leaves feeling good. This is key, regardless of where you live or do business. The cautionary tale is accurate in that it takes years and often decades to build deep relationships, only to be broken in a flash if you don't take care.

**How would your best friend describe you?**

Someone with extraordinary EQ, globally aware, independent, highly determined, and compassionate.

**You have been blessed with success. What are three qualities you possess that helped you achieve your goals?**

Emotional intelligence or EQ, tenacity, and independence. I'm blessed with a high amount of EQ that enables me to empathize with others, communicate effectively to my target audience, and lead compassionately with a clear vision. In addition, I'm tenacious with persistent determination to commit to things and achieve goals. And I'm internally driven and independent. This dual-driven/independent trait enables me to welcome input from others while ultimately making my own decisions.

**Tell us about your career experience before your second chapter.**

Although I was entrepreneurially driven, instead of starting a business after my MBA, I chose to work in Silicon Valley tech firms to give me the kinds of skills needed to bring about business growth. After eight years in Silicon Valley, I joined an early-stage food diagnostic business that needed to scale. I was part of the founding team that led the expansion to over 100 countries using angel funds and sold it to a two-billion-dollar player. After leading the sale, I ran this company for many years as a business unit of a public company. During the time I became a successful corporate executive, my entrepreneurial passions bubbled just below the surface.

**How did you reinvent yourself in your second chapter?**

Some years after the sale, I yearned to be in an entrepreneurial environment again. I happened to mention it to my friend John, who was a member of Launchpad Venture Group, the largest angel investment organization of its kind in the Northeast and the third-largest in the US. He invited me to a meeting. It was a perfect fit. I've now been a member of Launchpad Ventures for five years and a member of Branch Venture Group for three years.

As I explored the startup universe—looking at it through the lens of an angel investor—I knew I could walk into many companies, help the founder or founders and their team. Then, as a board member or advisor, I could put them on a growth, scale, and go-to-market trajectory. But, most importantly, I was excited to realize I could invest as an angel in bright, innovative startups that had the potential to positively impact the world.

So, now I invest money and time in teams and missions that I believe in and actively seek out female and people of color founders and entrepreneurs worldwide who have a deep passion and drive to succeed.

### Your second chapter's transition was remarkable. What was the trigger that made you decide you needed to make a change in your life?

A few years after the sale of the food safety tech company I had led, grown, and scaled to the public company, I realized I'd become restless and yearned to be back in an entrepreneurial environment.

You know how they say when the student is ready, the teacher appears? I happened to chat with my colleague and friend Dr. Dorothy Phillips, who had worked at Waters, the public firm that acquired the company I led.

Dorothy had recently been honored as the first African American to graduate from Vanderbilt University with a lifetime achievement award and two fellowships in her name. Growing up in the segregated south, Dorothy always thought outside the box. After earning her Ph.D. and a successful career at Waters, she joined the board of the American Chemical Society—this was her second act.

Speaking as a trusted friend, Dorothy stressed how important it was to plan for one's next act and encouraged me to discover what that could be. That conversation turned out to be the jolt that booted me out of my restlessness. My friend, John, whom I mentioned earlier and was the person who introduced me to the world of active involvement in early-stage companies, blew my mind open when he talked about consulting, mentoring, and angel investing, and that I could participate in each of these areas.

## What did you do to discover you had a new skill set you hadn't maximized?

I uncovered two skill sets—mentoring and early-stage company evaluation in multiple industries. While leading VICAM, the food diagnostic business unit of Waters, I mentored my team to achieve their personal goals along with the company's overall goals. Now I intentionally mentor and consult early-stage company founders and their teams—all in different industries—to shoot for the stars while ensuring they keep their eyes firmly on building and scaling the business.

At Waters, I evaluated companies in our industry that the corporation potentially could acquire. After joining angel groups Launchpad and Branch, I quickly realized I had the skills to assess a broad range of early-stage companies across many industries. But now, the stakes are much higher because my decisions impact the personal financial interests of others in my angel investment group and my investments in these young companies. Another way I manifest my skill sets: I join the company board as a director or advisor to keep my eyes on how a founder and team are progressing and offer targeted suggestions for them to consider.

## How are things going now?

I'm intensely focused on finding, vetting, investing in new ventures in the US and globally and sitting on the board or taking on an advisory role. I'm publishing my ideas and writing a book about leadership in early-stage companies, and spreading the word about diversity—that funding needs to go to female founders and ventures founded by people of color. I seek out startups with products and services for impact.

## Is there someone you are grateful to who helped you along the way?

I was fortunate to learn from many talented leaders. The best was Bart, who taught me about strategy and how to build a worldwide business. This wonderful person faced the challenges of being Black in a primarily white male Silicon Valley culture that was—and still is—not very welcoming to people of color or women. Yet, despite the barriers Bart faced, he gave his time generously to me and to others.

## Share an exciting moment that happened since committing to your second chapter.

Now that I was out of the corporate structure and on my new journey, it became clear to me pretty quickly that I would invest for impact with both my head and heart.

Torigen Pharmaceuticals was the trigger. This startup uses a dog's own tumor cells to create personalized immunotherapy. It's highly effective, kind to animals, easy to administer, and costs a fraction of traditional chemotherapy and radiation. When I invested in Torigen, my standard poodle Sabrina was already ill with cancer, and unfortunately, too late for Torigen's treatments. Had I known about this company when Sabrina was initially diagnosed, she would likely be alive today. It gives me great satisfaction that my investment will help the company treat many dogs stricken with cancer. In addition, this company's female founder/CEO was recently named in the "30 under 30" in Science 2020 by *Forbes Magazine*.

As a first-time angel investor, I needed to get up to speed in investing. I was deeply knowledgeable about the industries I had worked in and needed to learn to trust that I could apply that knowledge to evaluating early-stage companies across many industries. Being exposed to numerous startups, scouting for these companies, and hearing their pitches, plus my time as an angel investor, learning from my angel colleagues, and participating in education programs at Launchpad Venture Group, made me a better and more confident investor.

**Typically, I encourage my clients to ask for support from those who believe in their vision before they embark on a new chapter. How did you create your support system?**

Just as I was beginning my transition from corporate to solo, a friend of mine returned from a conference in California raving about Roberta Guise, an extraordinary British-born woman she met there. Roberta is an accredited delegate and speaker representing San Francisco at the UN Commission on the Status of Women and has a global perspective from living on three continents. When I reached out to Roberta, she graciously gave me essential advice on developing my brand to be a messenger for how I want to do good in the world. She's helped me succeed with this transition, and I'm forever grateful!

**Starting a new chapter requires leaving your comfort zone behind. How did you do that?**

Fortunately, Launchpad Venture Group, the angel group I belong to, has many educational programs for new angel investors. I've attended many of them to build up my knowledge of investing and develop a deeper understanding of AI, Edtech, Cleantech, SaaS, and Life Sciences, plus business valuation and other relevant topics in investing.

## What are five things you wish someone had told you before you started leading your endeavor?

Lead by asking questions vs. statements. Sandra Kassing, a global talent development leader I had the privilege to work with, passed on this key piece of advice many years ago, "As a leader, continually ask your team targeted questions." Instead of suggesting, for example, how something could be improved, ask questions that help them come to a solution through their own thought process. Her wisdom helped me engage my team as an entrepreneur and guides how I help early-stage company leaders with their development.

Those challenging personalities won't last long. Challenging personalities will eventually leave an organization. So, when hiring, look for the "red flags" of disruption. Some examples: evasive answers during the interview; they don't make eye contact; excessive focus on "me" vs. team accomplishments; and reluctance to give their past manager and direct report references.

Looking back over my career, I've known disruptors. In each case, the challenging personality was asked to leave. That's because disruptors upend team morale, hamper innovation and take up too much oxygen. Tap into your experience and wisdom, and you'll realize the "shelf-life" of a disruptor is short-lived.

How can you as a leader filter out these challenging personalities? First, enact a 90-day probation period. If a disruptor made their way into the company, they could easily pursue other endeavors during their probation. If you're not in a decision-making capacity, know that this person's tenure likely won't last.

You are never too experienced to stop learning. The best leaders continually learn, ask questions, and remain humble. You can achieve some of your best learning through others' experiences and practicing curiosity. Cherish people who share their insights with you, and never be afraid to ask why.

Seeking support is a sign of strength, not weakness. Strong leaders know that asking for support is a sign of strength. When leaders can't admit they need help to improve, that lack of humility and vulnerability becomes an obstacle that hinders the organization and its own success. Acknowledge when you need assistance, and seek it out. For example, at the company I led, I needed to project our potential revenues and market size over the next seven years. I was fairly confident about years 1–3 and needed assistance going out further. Around the same time, I read an article that quoted an industry expert. His comments about market size resonated, so I reached out to the expert. We ended up hiring him to conduct research for us, and I could fill in the missing projections. Recognizing where I needed help and being willing to act boldly made a significant difference to the accuracy of our forecasts.

Turning over the keys to your business is life-changing. The transition from an entrepreneurial, creative, fast-moving private business setting to the reserved, quarterly earnings-focused public company was like a mental earthquake that shook up what I knew about leading a business. I wasn't primed or ready for how different things would be when I turned over the keys of privately-owned VICAM to publicly-held Waters. For example, public firms are subject to rigorous governance and oversight of their finances. On the other hand, small, nimble private companies focus on growth, scale, go-to-market strategies, and in the case of my company, healthy financial returns and return on social impact.

We need both types of companies—private and public—in our wonderfully diverse and exciting economy. And if you're an entrepreneur planning to sell your company to a well-heeled public firm, be prepared to immerse yourself in a new vocabulary, financial strategy, and culture for your company to be successful under the new public company umbrella. Big firms like Apple, Google, and Facebook regularly buy successful startups. In many instances, the founders stay on for a couple of years to lead the transition, then leave. A primary reason for leaving: they yearn to be entrepreneurs again.

Despite the radically different business environment at Waters, I loved my role and the company's team I led and stayed on after the sale because I also deeply revered the product—food safety diagnostics—and the difference it made in people's lives globally. But, eventually, my entrepreneurial spirit broke loose, and I left, pivoting to my current role as an angel investor, mentor, board director, and advisor to early-stage companies.

**You are a person of significant influence. If you could inspire a movement that would bring the best outcome to the greatest number of people, what would that be?**

I am committed to inspiring and helping build diverse entrepreneurship in communities and countries challenged by gender and racial inequities, chronic poverty, and conflict. Whether in the US or globally, entrepreneurs facing poverty and discrimination frequently lack the capital, network, and expertise to start enterprises. Therefore, I encourage funders to mentor and consider investing in diverse founders with promising ideas for substantial social or environmental impact and sound financial return.

**How would you like to be remembered?**

By leading, mentoring, and funding, I enable diverse entrepreneurs worldwide to bring to market products and technologies that impact and make people healthier and more prosperous.

I want to be known as a compassionate person who encourages empathy, respect, trust, and reciprocity and helps others understand that what they do is much bigger than themselves.

**Where can we follow your work?**

Website: jazzas.com
Social: LinkedIn @marjorieradlozandi

# Book Authors Quotes List

꙳꙳

1. "The love in your heart wasn't put there to stay; love isn't love until you give it away." — Oscar Hammerstein, Vickie Aigner

2. "Being selective — doing less — is the path of the productive. Focus on the important few and ignore the rest." — Tim Ferris, Leena Alsulaiman

3. "Making fear my friend." — Lewis Pugh, Nancy Volpe Beringer

4. "Worry is like a rocking chair, it will give you something to do, but won't get you anywhere." — Glenn Turner, Cynthia Besteman

5. *"Leap and the net will appear"- Julia Cameron, Rachel Binder*

6. "The two most important days in your life are the day you are born and the day you find out why." — Mark Twain, Michelle Tunno Buelow

7. "There is no limit to the amount of good you can do if you don't care who gets the credit." — Ronald Reagan, Beth Campbell

8. "Leap, and the net will appear." — Julia Cameron, Monti Carlo

9. "Life's a marathon not a sprint." — Phillip C. McGraw, Melissa Clayton

10. "If you believe it, you can achieve it."—Napoleon Hill, Lindsay Droz

11. "You create your thoughts, your thoughts create your intentions, and your intentions create your reality."—Wayne Dyer, Kristi Lord

12. "It's not the age, it's the stage."—William Shakespeare, Michelle Edgar

13. "How you do some things is how you do all things."—Martha Beck, Rick Elmore

14. *"The work you do while you procrastinate is probably the work you should be doing for the rest of your life."*—Jessica Hische, Ruth Elnekave

15. "You can't go back and change the beginning, but you can start where you are and change the ending."—C. S. Lewis, Lisa Gair

16. "You don't get to the Promised Land without going through the Wilderness. You don't get there without crossing over hills and mountains, but if you keep on keeping on, you can't help but reach it."—Martin Luther King Jr., Sassy Gran

17. "Fortune favors the brave."—Terence, Kristy Woodson Harvey

18. *"She believed she could do it, so she did!"*—R.S. Grey, Carole Hopson

19. *"Passion illuminates the path experience has yet to walk."*—*Ralph Waldo Emerson, Belinda Fraley Huesman*

20. "Know when 'good enough' is good enough."—Donald Winnicott, Chad Hutson

21. "You can't go back and change the beginning, but you can change where you are and change the ending."—C.S. Lewis, Sheila Jackson

22. "Style is a way to say who you are without having to speak."
—Rachel Zoe, Traci Jeske

23. "If you're not the lead horse, the scenery never changes."
—Lewis Grizzard, Mindy Keegan

24. "The difficulty of a task is irrelevant if it's vital to your success."—Mayur Bardolia, Ed Latimore

25. "We have thoughts, feelings and emotions, but we are not our thoughts, feelings or emotions."—Eckrart Tolle, Simone Noordegraaf

26. "Just keep swimming. Just keep swimming."—Dory in Finding Nemo, Ilyssa Panitz

27. "Beware; for i am fearless. And therefore powerful."—Mary Shelly, Lynn Power

28. "Tell the story of the mountains you've climbed. Your words could become a part of someone else's survival guide."
—Morgan Harper Nichols, Lindsay Yaw Rogers

29. "Success is going from failure to failure with no loss of enthusiasm."—Winston Churchill, Janet Wischnia

30. *"I've learned that people will forget what you said, people will forget what you did, but people will never forget how you made them feel."—Maya Angelou, Marjorie Radlo-Zandi*